HISTORY'S GREATEST WARRIORS

WARRIORS

– Volume II –

JOHNATHAN KINGSBURY

RodgerLaz Publishing S.E.N.C.
www.Rodgerlaz.com

Ordering Information:
Quantity sales. Special discounts are available on quantity purchases by corporations, associations, and others. For details, contact the publisher at the address above.
Orders by U.S. trade bookstores and wholesalers. Please contact the publisher at the address above or by email: slazaroff@rodgerlaz.com

Printed in Canada

Publisher's Cataloging-in-Publication data
Johnathan Kingsbury.
History's Greatest Warriors Vol. II/ Johnathan Kingsbury.
p. cm.
ISBN 978-1-7752922-4-1
1. The main category of the book —History —Other category. 2. Warriors.

First Edition

14 13 12 11 10 / 10 9 8 7 6 5 4 3 2 1

DEDICATION

Interesting Lives

Some people out there think history is *boring*.

I took a lot of time putting all this together, and after I got started, it became a regular routine of writing and rewriting and then going back and doing it all again. I was probably going to go on living that way, but one morning a friend of mine came to visit and asked about the large stack of notebooks on my desk, thumbing through them and reading a few pages. I can't resist satisfying someone's honest curiosity, so I sat him down and told him about the lives of Spartacus, Attila the Hun and the many battles of Julius Caesar. Interested, he remarked that whenever (if ever) I finished my compilation it was going to be several thousand pages long, and that made me realise that I needed a different format in which to tell my stories, so back I went to rewriting again. When the dust settled, I had too many subjects to put all in one book, so I randomly chose just some of them and created History's Greatest Warriors Volume I with the intention of producing Volume II as soon as I could. And here it is.

This has been a labour of love, and I am grateful to my friends and family for not taking it personally when I have ignored them for months and seemed to disappear for long periods; this is what I was working on. When something that you are passionate about takes hold of your imagination, it can transport you to other places and times, and as I worked through the chronicles of the warriors I have come to know here, I became wonderfully immersed in their personal stories and how history has come to remember them and not others.

To those close to me, and to all the people who want interesting lives – this is dedicated to you.

CONTENT

"Even the finest sword plunged into salt water will eventually rust."

— Sun Tzu

INTRODUCTION

This is the second of my "History's Greatest Warriors" books, and I hope you enjoy it. When I sat down to create Volume One, it was going to be a standalone collection of the stories of my favourite warriors until my enthusiasm got in the way. I have a massive library of military history, and as I combed through it looking for interesting material, I found that many more additional warriors kept finding their way into my notes until I realised two books made more sense than one.

I am an amateur historian, a generalist, and in particular a military enthusiast. My parents are both off-the-boat Scottish immigrants, and as a young boy, I was given a set of plastic toy soldiers by my father who spent many hours helping me paint them as he regaled me with stories of war, glory and conquest. I suppose now that it gave him a sense of detached pride in the military history of Britain and maybe made him a little less homesick. For me, our time together formed my most powerful memories of bonding with my dad and gave me a lifelong interest in historical warfare. It has grown into a passion that I like to share.

This is not an academic work, but rather my effort to put forward some of history's most interesting military characters in a way that a casual reader might find interesting and informative, even if they've never heard of them before. This is a tour, not a deep dive. Some of my readers who enjoyed History's Greatest Warriors Volume 1 gave me high praise when they told me that some of my chapters interested them enough that they went on to do further reading on my subjects. That's ultimately what I'm aiming to do – share a little of the passion I have for some of military history's most interesting figures and encourage others to do a little digging into the past themselves.

The little boy I was grew up in a world without the Internet, without cell phones and can you believe it – only a handful of TV channels. I amassed hundreds, then thousands of toy soldiers in my collection and fought then refought epic miniature battles in every room of my parent's house, and then into their back garden. For many years after I had moved out, my father would call me to report that he had found and mangled some lost plastic platoon with the lawnmower again. I believe to this day there are still more to be found out there. During all of those wonderful hours of childhood play, I created entire battles, campaigns and wars in my imagination, rich and with back-stories. I invented my own drama of the battlefield, gave my little warriors personalities, motivations and loyalties. I could become emotionally invested in their combats, and this made me curious and interested in the life tapestries of their historical, real counterparts. It is from this foundation that my exploration of History's Greatest Warriors comes. Thank you for sharing it with me.

SPARTACUS

"The Rebel Gladiator"

We all know how it feels to be in the wrong place at the wrong time, isn't that true? For the people of Thrace, the wrong place was their entire national homeland, and the wrong time was spanned roughly the first 300 hundred or so years after the birth of Christ. As part of the Romans' regular slave route, the Thracians are described as "the biggest nation in the world, next to the Indians"[1] which meant that "the demographic density of potential persons in Thrace that could be sold into slavery... produced a constant stream of commodified humanity"[2]. With the Thracians "willing to sell their children for slave export" it's little wonder that like many others, Spartacus found himself sold into slavery in the greatest city in ancient times - Rome. As slaves go, he was probably fortunate in some respects, having reached adulthood by the time he was enslaved. In

---

[1] Herodotus, *The Histories*. Translated by A.D. Godley. Harvard University Press, Cambridge, 1920. Book V, Chapter 3, Section
http://www.perseus.tufts.edu/hopper/text?doc=Perseus%3Atext%3A1999.01.0126%3Abook%3D5%3Achapter%3D3%3Asection%3D1

[2] David M. Lewis, 2018, *Greek Slave Systems in their Eastern Mediterranean Context, c.800-146 BC*. Oxford University Press. Chapter 1.

fact, some sources suggest he had already served some time fighting for the Roman army[3] before he was sold into bondage.

According to the Greek biographer Plutarch, when Spartacus first arrived in Rome with his wife, both ready to be sold into slavery, "a serpent was seen coiled about his face as he slept". His wife was "a prophetess, and subject to visitations of the Dionysian frenzy" and perceived it to be a "sign of a great and formidable power" that would enable him to achieve great things in the future[4]. As recounted in some of our previous chapters, such dreams and vision interpretations were far from unusual in ancient times; Alexander the Great and Scipio Africanis both were purportedly born after snakes had visited their mothers and restored their fertility. Great things were still a long way off, however, and after being sold into bondage, Spartacus was to become a gladiator trained at the famous fighting school in Capua, run by the notorious Lentulus Batiatus[5].

While there is little documentary evidence relating to Batiatus, Plutarch is singularly dismissive of the man others referred to as the "'butcher-master' of Capua"[6] stating that

---

[3] Appian, *The Histories*. Loeb Classical Library, 1913. Book 1, pp.217.

[4] Plutarch, *The Parallel Lives*, Vol. 3. Loeb Classical Library, 1916. "The Life of Crassus", pp.338.

[5] Plutarch, *The Parallel Lives*, Vol. 3. "The Life of Crassus", pp.337.

[6] Cyrenus Osbourne Ward, 1888, *The Ancient Lowly: A History of the Working People from the Earliest Known Period to the Adoption of Christianity by Constantine*. Charles H. Kerr & Company Co-operative, Chicago, pp.252.

Spartacus and his fellow gladiators were "[t]hrough no misconduct of theirs, but owing to the injustice of their owner... kept in close confinement and reserved for gladiatorial combats"[7]. In a discussion of the history of ideas on BBC Radio 4, Professor of Classics at the University of Cambridge, Mary Beard, suggests that "going to be a gladiator for no good reason but simply the cruelty of your owner would have had some impact on his [Spartacus'] plans for revolt"[8]. Prior to his famous rebellion, Spartacus started performing and fighting professionally as a murmmillo gladiator, donning "a brimmed helmet with an angular crest in the shape of a fish" while fighting bare-chested from behind a tall, oblong shield. As one of the heavyweight gladiators, murmmillo usually fought against the thraex who "used a small rectangular shield and curved (thrusting) sword or scimitar"[9].

Born in 111 BC, by the time Spartacus was aged 38 he'd had enough of his gladiatorial lifestyle which was at odds with his "humane and generous" nature and yearned for nothing more than the opportunity "to reach home and spend in quiet the remainder of his eventful life"[10]. At least, that's one interpretation of what motivated Spartacus to begin the slave revolt that turned him into a legendary hero that fundamentally terrified the Roman slaveholding households. Others argue that his motives were less about

---

[7] Plutarch, *The Parallel Lives*, Vol. 3. "The Life of Crassus", pp.337.

[8] https://www.bbc.co.uk/programmes/b03wq2p3

[9] Donald G. Kyle, 2015, *Sport and Spectacle in the Ancient World*, John Wiley & Sons, UK, pp.299

[10] Cyrenus Osbourne Ward, 1888, *The Ancient Lowly*, pp.250.

going home than they were about revenge and looting. After all, if his main aim was to escape and return home, one wonders why Spartacus took so many men with him. Dr. Maria White, Professor of Latin at the University College London, posits that "when he escaped, he didn't try to escape on his own... if you want to go home, you would try and escape on your own at the dead of night... and you would probably cross Italy west to east rather than all the way up north and south, hundreds of miles, with ... a hundred thousand followers". Bearing that in mind, let's return to Capua and that fateful day in 73 BC which was to mark one of the most embarrassing periods of Roman history.

We will never know what really happened to start the slave rebellion or the number of fellow gladiators who supported Spartacus' escape and joined him in his breakout that day. Plutarch suggests that at least two hundred men initially planned to flee Capua, but only 78 actually made it, seizing "cleavers and spits from some kitchen"[11] which they used to overcome the guards prior to "arming themselves with clubs and daggers that they took from people on the roads"[12]. Having made their escape, the renegade gladiators headed to Mount Vesuvius seeking refuge and hiding places in the lush vegetation and high ground. Although the Romans sent the military out after the fugitives, initially these were "forces picked up in haste and at random", which merely fuelled Spartacus's fire. These poorly-prepared troops sent to take out the runaway slaves were actually

[11] Plutarch, *The Parallel Lives*, Vol. 3. "The Life of Crassus", pp.337.

[12] Appian, *The Histories*. Loeb Classical Library, 1913. Book 1, pp.217.

SPARTACUS

heavily armed, which meant that when Spartacus and his
expert fighters easily defeated them, they secured some of
the best military equipment available for their own use,
"getting hold of many arms of real warfare ... [and] casting
away their gladiatorial weapons as dishonourable and
barbarous".[13]

The Romans quickly realised that the situation was
rather more serious than they had initially appreciated and
decided to increase the stakes, sending 3,000 men under the
command of the arrogant politician, Publius Claudius
Pulcher.[14] A competent if not inspiring military leader,
Pulcher went right to work and laid siege to the gladiators,
blocking the only narrow path that allowed access to their
mountaintop refuge. He reasoned that with only one way
off Mount Vesuvius, he could easily bottle up the gladiators
and starve them out; he positioned his troops in defensive
blocking positions and made camp to wait for Spartacus to
come down and surrender. Innovative and aggressive, the
Thracian leader decided on a novel plan. Harvesting the
strongest branches of the vine that grew wild over Mt.
Vesuvius, they were "woven into strong ladders" that
reached over the cliff-face and dropped down to the plain
below, behind the Roman defences. Using these ladders, he
and his men descended, leaving one man behind to guard
their weapons and armour and subsequently throw them
down to the men below once they were ready. According to
Plutarch's version of the story, the Romans were completely
unaware of the danger massing all around them and

[13] Plutarch, *The Parallel Lives*, Vol. 3. "The Life of Crassus", pp.339.

[14] Plutarch, *The Parallel Lives*, Vol. 3. "The Life of Crassus", pp.338.

"therefore their enemy surrounded them, threw them into consternation by the suddenness of the attack, put them to flight, and took their camp"[15].

This was the first of several victories Spartacus won against the Roman army, and after each triumph over the military the greater his legend grew. Plutarch was very much an admirer of the Thracian, and created a stirring account of his rebellion, accomplishments and fighting prowess that formed the "basis for the myth of Spartacus as the noble barbarian warrior"[16]; other contemporary sources are less complimentary about the slave revolt. The Roman historian and poet Florus was so appalled by Spartacus' uprising that he wrote "One can tolerate, indeed, even the disgrace of war against slaves... But I know not what name to give to the war which was stirred up at the instigation of Spartacus; for the common soldiers being slaves and their leaders being gladiators ... added insult to the injury which they inflicted upon Rome"[17]. The one aspect of the conflict that seemed to particularly offend Florus was that free men joined with the gladiators willingly, taking on the role of lowly infantry soldiers to serve their gladiator masters – to him this was a complete inversion of the so-called "natural" hierarchy of the Roman Empire.

---

[15] Plutarch, *The Parallel Lives*, Vol. 3. "The Life of Crassus", pp.339.

[16] Boris Badenov, 2010, "'As Many Enemies as There Are Slaves': Spartacus and the Politics of Servile Rebellion in the Late Republic", https://libcom.org/history/many-enemies-there-are-slaves%E2%80%99-spartacus-politics-servile-rebellion-late-republic

[17] Lucius Annaeus Florus, *The Epitome of Roman History*, Loeb Classical Library, 1929. Book 2, Chapter 8, pp.242.

By accounts, Spartacus was both an inspiring leader and a generous one, dividing "the profits of his raiding into equal shares" for his supporters. The prospect of loot was probably the largest attractor of new recruit manpower, including so-called free men. Compared to the life of slaves, free citizens could enjoy a modicum of luxury or at the very least, weren't subjected to the cruelty that the slaves endured on a daily basis. As Seneca the Younger recalled, for household slaves in Rome "Any murmur is checked by a rod; not even involuntary sounds - a cough, a sneeze, a choke - are exempted from the lash. If a word breaks the silence, the penalty is severe"[18]. The poor, lower-class citizens could arguably be less well-off than the slaves were, considering that most lived in cramped, unhygienic conditions, citizens of the lower classes lived on a diet of wheat and lived in "cramped, kitchen-less rooms" largely without any running water or heat[19]. To many the prospect of joining Spartacus and his slave renegades seemed an attractive option, if for nothing else than to gain some loot and the possibility of improving their lives.

With his numbers growing by the day and his confidence boosted by his defeat of Claudius, Spartacus was in a strong position when he faced the next Roman generals sent against him, an army under Publius Varinus supported by another force under Lucius Cossinius. Spartacus clearly respected Cossinius, and Plutarch reports that he "narrowly

[18] Seneca the Younger, cited in Joshua J. Mark, 2016, "The Spartacus Revolt", *Ancient History Encyclopedia*.
https://www.ancient.eu/article/871/the-spartacus-revolt/

[19] Joan D. Barghusen, *Daily Life in Ancient and Modern Rome*. Runestone Press, Minneapolis, pp.21-24.

watched the movements" of the Roman commander "and came near seizing him as he was bathing near Salinae"[20]. Spartacus almost captured Varinus too, but had to be content with just taking "the very horse he rode"[21]. For a time, the slave army was able to either evade or defeat local Roman garrisons and forces, but Spartacus knew that it was just a matter of time before the Roman war machine really would be set against him, and no composite mob of untrained slaves and gladiators could ever stand against a proper field army led by a competent commander. In a move that many historians find perplexing and difficult to explain, Spartacus began to lead his supporters up through Italy to the north; in Plutarch's analysis of the situation, he posits that Spartacus' motivation was that they could cross the Alps and "go to their respective homes"[22]. He may have certainly started out with these intentions, but despite his capacity for leadership Spartacus never achieved complete authority and control over his followers, and soon there were groups of them wandering off in search of loot or revenge on wealthy, slave-holding landowners. Plutarch declared that the slaves "were now strong in numbers and full of confidence, and would not listen to him, but went ravaging over Italy"[23].

Professor Theresa Urbainczyk of the University of Dublin remarks that it's surprising that this huge force of

[20] Plutarch, *The Parallel Lives*, Vol. 3. "The Life of Crassus", pp.341.

[21] Plutarch, *The Parallel Lives*, Vol. 3. "The Life of Crassus", pp.341.

[22] Plutarch, *The Parallel Lives*, Vol. 3. "The Life of Crassus", pp.341.

[23] Plutarch, *The Parallel Lives*, Vol. 3. "The Life of Crassus", pp.341.

tens of thousands of fugitives marched up and down the length of Italy unchallenged. She theorised that organising enough food and supplies for such a large force would have been challenging and therefore a nomadic approach best suited their needs; this would also put them in a better position to gather more supporters as they travelled[24]. After winning easy victories and widespread fame, the real challenge facing a triumphant Spartacus and his men was – what next? At one point, it appeared that Spartacus was looking for a passage to Sicily, perhaps inspired by the success of the slave revolts that had previously taken place on that island. Marching with a force numbering something in the region of 70,000 fully armed followers, the threat posed to the Roman empire went from "indignity and disgrace" to "fear and peril" under the Thracian gladiator. Eventually, Spartacus was able to focus the attention of his men on one goal in particular for practical as well as symbolic reasons – the capture of Rome itself. As they marched closer to the capital city, they were intercepted by the latest in a series of Roman formations sent to stop them, this time not far from the great city walls. Predictably, the morale of the slaves was as high as it had ever been, knowing that their ultimate goal was tantalising close, and they smashed the soldiers in front of them in "another great battle, and there was, too, another great defeat for the Romans"[25].

---

[24] https://www.bbc.co.uk/programmes/b03wq2p3

[25] Plutarch, *The Parallel Lives*, Vol. 3. "The Life of Crassus", pp.342.

The Romans were infuriated by this latest defeat and responded with the strongest military force they could muster, and sensing a turning of the tide, Spartacus turned his supporters towards the Alps to seek higher ground. Before they could get there, they were met by yet another blocking Roman army, led by the latest commander looking for glory by putting down the "rebellious rabble". This force too was essentially destroyed, and was defeated so conclusively that the Roman general "escaped himself with difficulty"[26]. For the Romans, it was time to bring in the big guns, and they finally decided to summon one of their best commanders in the person of Marcus Licinius Crassus. A capable and ruthless military leader, Crassus welcomed the opportunity to add another victory to his fighting record but was cautious when assessing the size and scope of the rebel forces. Spartacus was leading "between 70,000 and 120,000", and Crassus pronounced such numbers would prove difficult to overcome[27] and decided to delay attacking until the moment and situation was most favourable. Unfortunately, Crassus' second in command was less adept; Lucius Mummius believed that the best strategy was bold action, and proved less than reliable when he completely disregarded Crassus's ordered "to follow the enemy, but not to join the battle or even to skirmish with them"; Mummius launched an attack at the first opportunity and was promptly defeated with many men killed and others fleeing for their lives[28]. Cowardice by legionary soldiers on this scale was assured the harshest of punishments.

---

[26] Plutarch, *The Parallel Lives*, Vol. 3. "The Life of Crassus", pp.342.

[27] Mark Cartwright, 2013, "Marcus Licinius Crassus", *Ancient History Encyclopedia,* https://www.ancient.eu/Marcus_Licinius_Crassus

[28] Plutarch, *The Parallel Lives*, Vol. 3. "The Life of Crassus", pp.343.

Crassus was incensed and "gave Mummius himself a rough reception" while reserving the worst of this anger for the soldiers that ran from the fight with the slaves. He ordered that the units concerned be decimated. This ancient military punishment involved assembling his men into groups of ten, and each soldier would draw lots. One man in the group of ten would randomly be selected to be beaten to death by the other nine, brandishing wooden rods to club him with. It was a brutal, horrific penalty to be paid for running from the enemy, but Crassus wanted the point made that there would be no more retreating from Spartacus[29]. With his soldiers disciplined and clear that running was not an option, Crassus set out to pursue the slave army and seek a decisive confrontation to settle the rebellion once and for all. Spartacus and his supporters were now heading south, seeking the Italian coast in the hope of reaching Sicily by boat and rekindling the "servile war there, which had not long been extinguished"[30]. They appealed to the Sicilians to send transport ships, but this never materialised, and the slave army was left without any means of leaving the country, as Roman forces continued to close and surround them. Turning away from the sea, Spartacus continued south until he established his camp in the very toe of Italy. Crassus was delighted, as he could now move to cut off the rebels from the rest of the country, and responded to Spartacus's decision by building a huge wall across the isthmus, "at once keeping his soldiers from idleness, and his enemies from provisions"[31]. Now effectively trapped, Spartacus wasn't about to give up and waited until a winter

---

[29] Plutarch, *The Parallel Lives*, Vol. 3. "The Life of Crassus", pp.343.

[30] Plutarch, *The Parallel Lives*, Vol. 3. "The Life of Crassus", pp.343.

[31] Plutarch, *The Parallel Lives*, Vol. 3. "The Life of Crassus", pp.345.

storm blew in.   Taking advantage of the inclement weather and low visibility, he and his men "filled up a small portion of the ditch with earth and timber... and threw the third part of his force across"[32].   Concerned "lest some impulse to march upon Rome should seize Spartacus"[33], Crassus was anxious to quash the rebellion once and for all, and hedged his bets by sending for the support of two other Roman armies under their generals "Lucullus from Thrace and Pompey from Spain"[34].

Vanity and political advantage were very much at the front of his thinking, so as his supporting forces drew closer Crassus reconsidered his plans, fearing that "success would be ascribed to the one who came up with assistance, and not to himself" and subsequently decided to accelerate the situation by attacking an exposed portion of Spartacus's rebel army that had become separated from the main group and its leader.   Crassus virtually wiped out the rebels, although their bravery and courage were recorded as exemplary, with "only two who were wounded in the back. The rest all died standing in the ranks and fighting the Romans"[35].   Spartacus was left with no choice but to turn and face the Romans. Accounts of the subsequent battle vary considerably, with Appian applauding the Romans and reporting barbaric deeds performed by Spartacus, including that he crucified a Roman prisoner "in the space between the

---

[32] Plutarch, *The Parallel Lives*, Vol. 3. "The Life of Crassus", pp.345.

[33] Plutarch, *The Parallel Lives*, Vol. 3. "The Life of Crassus", pp.345.

[34] Plutarch, *The Parallel Lives*, Vol. 3. "The Life of Crassus", pp.345.

[35] Plutarch, *The Parallel Lives*, Vol. 3. "The Life of Crassus", pp.348.

two armies to show his own men what fate awaited them if they did not conquer"[36]. During the "long and bloody battle", Spartacus "was wounded in the thigh with a spear and sank upon his knee" and soon he and his fellow fugitives were over-powered and defeated, with Florus reporting "Spartacus himself fell, as became a general, fighting most bravely in the front rank"[37]. The rebellion was over, and the survivors were crucified along the road into Rome as a warning to all that passed along the route to the city.

Defeat was inevitable, given the totality of Roman military might against him, but Spartacus could count a total of nine victories against the greatest army in the world at the time – an unprecedented success that has cemented the Thracian gladiator as a mythical hero of the common men for future generations. Two thousand years after he died, notable men have continued to point to him as a historical hero. Karl Marx lauded him as a symbol of "the West's conflict with totalitarianism" and exalts the man as the epitome of the class struggle that has shaped history since the beginning of human civilisation. In a speech he gave to the British government a couple of weeks prior to the end of the Falklands War, President Ronald Reagan refers to Spartacus as one of those historical heroes "who sacrificed and struggled for freedom", making the gladiator rebel probably the only thing Reagan and Marx could ever agree on. "A great general... of noble character", for Marx, Spartacus was "a 'real representative' of the proletariat of

---

[36] Appian, *The Histories*. Loeb Classical Library, 1913. Book 1, pp.222.

[37] Lucius Annaeus Florus, *The Epitome of Roman History*, pp.245.

ancient times"[38]. A slave, a rebel and a general, the humble man from Thrace carved a place for himself in history that the world will likely never forget.

[38] Karl Marx, 1861, "Letter from Marx to Engels in Manchester", *Gesamtausgabe*, International Publishers, 1942.
https://www.marxists.org/archive/marx/works/1861/letters/61_02_27-abs.htm

LOZEN

"The Apache Warrior Woman"

There aren't many modern-day warriors that I consider including in my list as one of history's most renowned fighters and military tacticians, but Lozen definitely makes the grade. Born somewhere in the 1840s, Lozen was an Apache woman belonging to the Warm Springs Tribe of the Chihenne Chiricahua and was sister to the famous Apache chief, Victorio.

Her people were known as the Red Paint People, because of the ochre they used in their burial ceremonies[39], and the young girl Lozen spent much of her childhood gathering food like nuts, seeds and roots and the culturally significant agave cactus. By the age of seven, she began learning to ride horses and immediately proved her abilities as an equestrian, soon able to leap onto her mount from the ground and control it using only her knees and a rough rope halter. For the Apaches of the 1840s, it was essential that every member of their tribe was fit and able regardless of

[39] https://en.wikipedia.org/wiki/Red_Paint_People

15

gender, so Lozen and her girlhood friends would run to the top of the sacred mountain near Ojo Caliente on a daily basis to boost their strength, endurance, and fitness[40].

As she entered puberty, Lozen underwent the Sunrise Ceremony which recreates the Apache Legend of the White Painted Woman. According to the story, White Painted Woman went on a walk as she aged and headed east until she met up with her younger self. The two selves merged, making her young again and enabling her to continue the circle of life[41]. The Sunrise Ceremony is a complex, multi-day event that takes place in the summer after the girl's first menstruation and marks the passage to womanhood. Over four days and nights of songs, prayers and dances, the girls were said to be fused with the power of the White Painted Woman and receive blessings and gifts from the tribe. Lozen's Sunrise Ceremony was unusual, and her experience at this crucial time would change her destiny forever.

It is said that during Lozen's Sunrise Ceremony, a stranger arrived from the east. Known as Grey Ghost, he rode alone and was a mysterious figure, rarely approached. The young 16-year-old fell in love with the enigmatic stranger, but he soon disappeared, leaving her to a life of unrequited love. Though many suitors made her offerings of horses and other precious goods, Lozen's heart would always

---

[40] Peter Aleshire, 2001. *Warrior Woman: the story of Lozen, Apache warrior and shaman.* St. Martin's Press, New York, pp.22.

[41] http://traditionalnativehealing.com/apache-sunrise-ceremony

belong to the Grey Ghost[42] and none other. As a result, Lozen never married but received a potent power from her Sunrise Ceremony – a keen ability to always discern the location of any enemy. This talent would prove fundamental to her warrior legacy and made her a keen asset to her powerful brother, Chief Victorio. According to her nephew James Kaywaykla, Lozen would demonstrate her ability by standing alone with her arms outstretched and chant, and when her power manifested and began to work she would feel her hands tingle; her palms would change colour, and she would be able to detect the direction of the enemy[43].

Much of what we know about Lozen's life has been shaped by Eve Ball's account, as narrated by one of the few Apache survivors of the Battle of Hembrillo, James Kaywaykla. As the son of Lozen's sister Gouyen, Kaywaykla gives one of the only first-hand accounts of Lozen's life, with her being more notable by her absence rather than her achievements in many of the other texts dealing with this period[44]. The fact that Kaywaykla actually met and knew Lozen lends tremendous weight to his recollections and is generally considered to be accurate. According to Kaywaykla, other members of the tribe were reluctant to speak of Lozen, fearful that she would be criticised or ridiculed which the Warm Springs Apaches wouldn't

---

[42] Sherry Robinson, *Apache Voices: Their Stories of Survival as Told to Eve Ball*. University of New Mexico Press, Albuquerque, pp.6

[43] Sherry Robinson, *Apache Voices: Their Stories of Survival as Told to Eve Ball*. University of New Mexico Press, Albuquerque, pp.6

[44] Eve Ball, 1970. *In the Days of Victorio: Recollections of a Warm Springs Apache*, pp.4.

tolerate. To them, Lozen was a holy woman with the power of healing as well as that of locating the enemy[45]. For most Apaches, details of Lozen's life were not meant to be shared with anyone not a member of the tribe.

Although at least 20 years younger than her brother Victorio, it is believed that Lozen was equally adept at riding, hunting and fighting. Kaywaykla recalls "she had more ability in planning military strategy than did Victorio"[46]. While all the women in the Warm Springs tribe were required to learn how to ride, shoot and evade potential enemies, Lozen demonstrated talents for warfare that made her stand out. She rapidly became accepted as a tribal lieutenant to her brother due to her physical abilities and her spiritual power. It was also said that she was known for her honesty and integrity amongst her tribe. Victorio described Lozen as his own right hand the shield of her people, saying he depended on her just as much as he did Nana, chief of the Chihenne band of Chirichua Apaches[47]. This was high praise indeed.

Live as a Warm Springs Apache was consistent struggle and turmoil; Kaywaykla is quoted as saying it was only when he reached the age of 10 years old that he began to realise that people could die of other reasons, not just

---

[45] Ibid.

[46] Ibid.

[47] Ibid, pp.7.

violence[48]. Pressed on every side by the Mexicans, the Americans and rival tribes like the Navajo, the Warm Springs Apaches were accustomed to lives of endless combat territorial disputes. The Apache Wars began when Lozen was only a child, but after her Sunrise Ceremony, she was permitted to accompany her brother into battle against the US Army and other enemies of the Apache people.

Many of the conflicts originated from a constant need to raid for horses and other supplies on the Apache side, and the desire for gold and copper resources sought by the Americans. Along with some of the warriors' wives, Lozen often accompanied the men of her tribe as they raided their rivals and quickly became appreciated as one of the most talented horse thieves they had. To the Apache, the name Lozen means "dexterous horse thief"[49] and is indicative of the importance of this skill, irrespective of her other abilities and prowess as a healer. Most of the raids the Apache conducted were largely non-violent, but they wouldn't stay that way as they became more desperate for resources. Chief Victorio realised that his tribe's situation was going to become steadily worse unless the Apache could settle and reoccupy tribal lands at Ojo Caliente, ending the escalation of violence. Repeated appeals to the US government to facilitate this solution failed, and his calls for peaceful resolution were ignored. Historically Apache tribes had raided both enemies and one another for livestock and food, but the increasing strain that was placed on their traditional

---

[48] Donald E. Worcester, 1979. *The Apaches: Eagles of the Southwest*. University of Oklahoma Press, Norman, pp.219.

[49] Donald E. Worcester, 1979. *The Apaches: Eagles of the Southwest*, pp.53.

hunting grounds forced them to increase their raiding simply to stay alive[50]. The stage was set for a collision with the forces of the Americans.

The situation for the Warm Springs Apache became increasingly desperate until 1862 when they finally engaged with the US military in the Battle of Apache Pass. At least 500 Apache warriors under the leadership of Mangas Coloradas and Cochise ambushed 2,500 Union volunteers from the California Column as they marched through to capture Confederate Arizona. Exhausted and thirsty, the US forces were caught by surprise by sharp attacks launched by the Apaches from hiding places behind mesquite trees and boulders. Initially shaken and battered, the Union troops withdrew and regrouped, eventually gaining the high ground with their howitzers. Apache historical records tell us that both Victorio and Geronimo were present at the battle, which suggests strongly that Lozen was likely there with them and witnessed the slaughter of 63 Apache warriors[51] as they fought for their lands and freedom[52].

Less than a year later, Mangas Coloradas was killed, and the Chiricahua and Mibres tribal bands joined forces with the Chihenne, spending the next few years roaming and constantly raiding between Mexico and their homeland near Ojo Caliente. During this period, the Apaches secured some

---

[50] https://apps.dtic.mil/dtic/tr/fulltext/u2/a436261.pdf

[51] https://en.wikipedia.org/wiki/Battle_of_Apache_Pass

[52] http://newmexicohistory.org/people/the-story-of-lozen

semblance of victory and dominated the region. Their fast, hit-and-run raids and constant ambushes wore down prospectors, miners and the Union soldiers sent to protect them, and their ability to simply melt away into the landscape frustrated efforts to pursue and hunt them down[53]. For a time there was a lull in the fighting, but Lozen, Victorio and the other tribal leaders knew that this was a game that they could not win against the United States as soon as serious resources were sent against them. It was only a matter of time, and amongst themselves, they agreed that they would collectively accept any offer of peace that would allow them to remain in the Ojo Caliente area[54]. They had heard news of the Bosque Redondo reservation where over a thousand Navajo and Apache died of exposure, sickness and starvation and were determined not to submit to such an end[55].

Victorio himself attempted to negotiate directly with the Superintendent of Indian Affairs Michael Steck, who promised he would do everything in his power to secure them a treaty and give them a reservation near Ojo Caliente. The Apache surrendered their guns and themselves in order to avoid more bloody conflict, but Steck's promise was never fulfilled, and in 1872 the Warm Springs Apache were forcibly removed to Tularosa, some 300 miles south of their home[56]. Lumped together with enemy factions, conditions at the Mescalero Reservation were appalling in general but worse

---

[53] Peter Aleshire, 2001. *Warrior Woman*, pp.74.

[54] Ibid., pp.83.

[55] http://nmhistoricsites.org/bosque-redondo

[56] Sherry Robinson, *Apache Voices: Their Stories of Survival as Told to Eve Ball*, pp.7.

still for Lozen and her people who were allocated a location that had been abandoned as a result of the high risk of malaria[57]. Food and water were in extremely short supply, while summer temperatures soared. According to Kaywaykla, Chief Victorio and his followers assumed that as the White Eyes had put the Warm Springs Apache in this place where "insects with the long beaks... devoured the babies taken there", it must have been intentional – the White Eyes wanted them to die[58].

By 1879, Victorio had had enough and remembering his success at resisting the Bosque Redondo round-up, decided to take his tribe back to Ojo Caliente and reopen negotiations to allow his people to stay here. Victorio hoped he would be able to convince the US forces that it would be preferable to allow the Warm Springs tribe to inhabit their homelands than engage in a war that would cost hundreds of dollars... and lives[59]. He was mistaken about the US resolve.

Victorio, Lozen and around 300 other Apache fled from the San Carlos reservation on the 21st of August 1879. Victorio feared that he would be imprisoned for horse theft by a newly arrived territorial judge in town[60]. Ironically, he stole horses as he went and news travelled quickly of a new

[57] Debra J. Sheffer PhD, 2015. *The Buffalo Soldiers: Their Epic Story and Major Campaigns*. Praeger, California, pp.71

[58] Eve Ball, 1970. *In the Days of Victorio: Recollections of a Warm Springs Apache*, pp.32.

[59] Peter Aleshire, 2001. *Warrior Woman*, pp.104.

[60] Kendall D. Gott, *In Search of an Elusive Enemy*, pp.17.

Apache rebellion. Victorio's success was greatly exaggerated and although he encouraged a mass tribal uprising to join him, his total number of followers probably never exceeded 300 people. Victorio and his little rebel band survived by raiding and constant movement in the old style, managing to elude a detachment of the 9th cavalry who pursued them down to the banks of the Rio Grande River [61]. Knowing their enemies were in hot pursuit, Victorio sent Lozen ahead with the other women and children, while he and his men remained behind scouring the land for supplies and providing a rearguard for their people.

When Lozen and her party arrived at the river, they found it was a swirling, swollen torrent of rapidly moving water and both the Apaches and their horses baulked at the idea of crossing it. Uncertain where to go and trapped by the river, the group was leaderless until Lozen decided to set an example and pushed her powerful black horse through the crowd until she reached the water's edge. With her rifle held high above her head, Lozen urged her mount down and plunged into the flooded river, striking him on the shoulder with her right foot until "[H]e reared, then plunged into the torrent"[62]. The others hesitated and then followed behind her, and once they were all safely on the opposite bank Lozen instructed the women to seek shelter in the San Andreas mountains while she returned to her brother and his warriors.

---

[61] Ibid, pp.18.

[62] Peter Aleshire, 2001. *Warrior Woman*, pp.123.

This is just one example of Lozen's bravery, determination and ability on horseback. Like her fellow Apaches, she was capable of riding a horse quite literally to death. Once exhausted the horse would be slaughtered and eaten to give the Apaches the strength to continue on foot, and they were known to be able to cover up to 40 miles in under 10 hours, "moving as quickly as a horse could trot"[63]. These qualities of high mobility and resilience combined to make the Apaches an elusive enemy for the US and Mexican forces tasked with stopping them. Having arrived in Mexico, the Warm Springs Apache were no safer on the southern side of the Rio Grande than they had been on the north and a militia force was soon established by the Mexican authorities to try and deal with the Apache rebels. Luzon and her people began to be pursued by armed forces from all sides.

For several months the Warm Springs band hopped in and out of Mexico, avoiding large groups of soldiers by following Lozen's intuition and trusting in her Power to evade the enemy forces. In the summer of 1880, the Warm Springs Apache were travelling back towards Mexico via West Texas when one of the women in the party went into labour. In her capacity as both warrior and healer, Lozen left the main group of her people to assist and protect the woman as she gave birth. Hiding from pursuing enemy cavalry, Lozen helped deliver the baby before embarking on a dangerous journey through hostile territory to return the woman and her newborn infant to their family and the relative safety of the Mescalero reservation.

[63] Ibid, pp.125.

Immediately following the birth, the Mescalero woman and Lozen were all but trapped by the patrolling cavalry with no water and little food. In an effort to secure their survival, Lozen is reported to have single-handedly killed a Longhorn cow using only her knife as a weapon. The Longhorn cattle are large, impressive beasts with horns that extend over 1.8m from tip to tip. Few Apache warriors would have attempted to kill such an animal alone and armed only with a small blade, but Lozen succeeded and secured food so that they could have enough to eat. Desperate for water, they were unable to travel any great distance until Lozen spotted a group of Mexicans camped on the south side of the Rio Grande River. She decided that she needed to steal a horse.

To prepare, Lozen cut a length of hide from the longhorn she'd killed and made a rough bridle from it, leaving it to dry in the daytime sun. As night fell, she stripped naked and slipped into the fast, cold current of the Rio Grande and swam silently across the water, oriented on the warm glow of the Mexican campfires on the far bank. Wet, shivering, and alone, Lozen crept into the camp and through the sleeping group of men until she reached their horses, standing hobbled just a few feet away. Silently, she approached the horse she had selected and removed his restraints, leaping onto his back as he snorted and reared. Alerted and awake, the Mexicans assumed that they were under attack and started shooting at her as she plunged the horse into the river. No bullet found her, and by the time the men could organise themselves into a pursuit, Lozen had reached the far bank of the river and safety[64].

Lozen helped the woman and newborn child onto the horse, and they started on their perilous journey back to the reservation. The most direct routes were too risky, as vigilant US troops were stationed at every waterhole along the way. Instead, the two women and infant were forced to take a long and meandering course which meant it took several weeks for them to reach the comparative protection of the reservation lands. Despite all the hardships of the open trail, Lozen delivered her charges safely back to her people and was lauded for accomplishing what few others could or would have done. It was said that she combined the best qualities of woman and warrior both, able to protect the mother and child while being able to supervise the birth – a task that would have been impossible for a man as it was believed to "weaken and debilitate a man"[65].

Unfortunately, there was little for Lozen to celebrate after she arrived at the Mescalero reservation. While she had been embarking on her own dangerous mission, her brother Victorio and his fellow warriors had been running for lives. The soldiers that Lozen had seen around guarding the waterholes were members of the 10th Cavalry under the command of Colonel Benjamin Grierson. A grim and

[64] Ed. Theda Purdue, 2001. *Sifters: Native American Women's Lives*. Oxford University Press, New York, pp.101-102.

[65] Jessica Dawn Parker, *The Apache Peoples: A History of All Bands and Tribes Through the 1880s*. McFarlane & Company Inc., North Carolina, pp.117

determined Indian fighter, the US commander had adopted a defensive strategy to combat the Apache style of hit, run and manoeuvre warfare that made Victorio's men so formidable. In an attempt to block all access to water and ammunition, Grierson placed his troops in strategic defensive positions and waited. In the event that the Apaches couldn't be defeated in a set-piece battle, they would at least be prevented from securing new supplies[66].

In response, Victorio also changed his strategy and adopted a new plan. Leaving behind the security and familiarity of the mountains, he led his men to a small desert plain where a nearby lake provided water and game enough to support his forces while he evaluated his next move. He named the place Tres Castillos, in reference to three distinctive rock pile formations on the land. Briefly, the Apache raiders enjoyed a brief respite while the combined American and Mexican forces searched northern Mexico without finding a trace of them. The short lull in the fighting did not last, and on September 29th 1880 their hiding place was discovered. Led by Tarahumari Indian scouts, a large Mexican infantry force under the command of Colonel Joaquin Terrazas came across a muddied waterhole where there was ample evidence of a recently-butchered cow. Convinced that he had found the trail of the elusive Victorio, Terrazas decided to send his allied US forces back across the border on the basis that "it would be objectionable on the part of his government for American

---

[66] https://en.wikipedia.org/wiki/Battle_of_Tres_Castillos

troops to advance farther into the interior"[67]. The Mexicans would take on the Apaches by themselves.

Without Lozen's ability to sense an enemy, Victorio was caught by surprise when the Mexican soldiers advanced on Tres Castillos, charging towards them at close range. Victorio ordered 30 of his men forward to meet the attack, but after killing one of the enemy scouts they gave ground rapidly and retreated when the large size of Terrazas's force became apparent, and they could see what they were facing. Outnumbered and outgunned, the Apaches withdrew to what they thought was safety – the rocks that gave Tres Castillos its name. These defensive positions were soon surrounded by the superior numbers of Mexicans, and Victorio was soon trapped with no escape route except to flee out into the open desert where it was certain that his men would be cut down by a hail of Mexican bullets[68].

Surrender was not an attractive option, so the trapped Apache warriors fought on through the remainder of the day and all the next night. The outcome of the one-sided struggle was never in doubt and by 10 am the next morning, 62 warriors were dead, Victorio among them. Lozen learned of the battle just as she arrived at Mescalero and was also told of the rumours surrounding her brother's death. Some said that Victorio killed himself with his own knife, other

[67] C.L. Sonnichsen, 1958. *The Mescalero Apaches.* University of Oklahoma Press, Norman. pp.210.

[68] Kendall D. Gott, *In Search of an Elusive Enemy: The Victorio Campaign.* Combat Studies Institute Press, Fort Leavenworth, Kansas, pp.41.

stories abounded that he was executed by the victorious
Mexican soldiers; there was no way to know what his true
fate was other than he was most certainly dead. To Lozen, it
mattered little whether he died at his own hand or that of
another – almost all her band were gone. As James
Kaywaykla said, "I am the only survivor of my people, of
those who remember Victorio"[69]. Many believe that had
Lozen been present with her brother and his warriors that
night, the outcome of the battle might have been very
different. As it was, Victorio was gone.

Lozen promptly left the reservation to go in search of
what remained of her people. Around the same time, the
Mescalero-Chiricahua leader Geronimo and 70 other
Chiricahua fighters escaped from their reservation at San
Carlos, and like Lozen headed for the Sierra Madre
mountains where the remaining Apache chiefs and their
bands were hiding[70]. Unlike the ground around Tres
Castillos, these mountains provided the Apaches with an
impenetrable natural fortress, enabling them to conduct a
number of dangerous raids from the safety of their rocky
stronghold. Although under the leadership of Chief Naiche
of the Chokonen tribe, it was the warrior Geronimo that
ultimately gained the respect of the band of 600 or so
survivors[71]. A natural leader of men, Geronimo quickly
became known as a talented and resilient military tactician,

---

[69] Sherry Robinson, *Apache Voices: Their Stories of Survival as Told to Eve Ball*, pp.17.

[70] Ed. Theda Purdue, 2001. *Sifters: Native American Women's Lives*, pp.103.

[71] Peter Aleshire, 2001. *Warrior Woman: the story of Lozen, Apache warrior and shaman*, pp.210.

and it was he that the Apache looked to for any chance of victory over their enemies.

Although the Apaches could survive on the game they hunted and the food they both grew and gathered, they had become used to the resources they could steal through raiding. Even though Kaywaykla recalls "on the mountainside [there was] lots of fruit and honey", the Apaches needed a constant supply of ammunition, weapons and were driven by Geronimo's "insatiable hatred for Mexicans"[72]. While Lozen didn't share his bloodlust, she did join Geronimo on many of these raids, and it was said that her powers as a shaman contributed to many of the Apaches' early successful raids from the mountains. Most of Geronimo's attacks were motivated for supplies, but a great deal of them were launched out of a desire for revenge. James Kaywaykla recalls seeing a war dance take place prior to an important raid, the aim of which was purely to avenge the death of an Apache warrior killed in a previous attack.

In 1882, Geronimo led sixty warriors on an audacious trip back to San Carlos where they killed a police officer and persuaded hundreds of Chiricahuas to leave the reservation and join him as raiders in the mountains. The attack provoked the US army into aggressive action, and US General George Cook was sent against them at the head of a substantial force of cavalry and infantry. Lozen's talent for detecting her enemies kept the Apaches one step ahead of

---

[72] Ibid, pp.213.

the government soldiers, but Crook's men seemed to be everywhere and always in greater numbers than the Apaches were. On the run for months, Geronimo's people were constantly hounded by US cavalry and were prevented from settling or securing food and water on a consistent basis. Eventually, the Apaches simply couldn't run anymore. According to Apache accounts, the eventual surrender of Geronimo and his remaining rebels was orchestrated by Lozen herself and another woman warrior, Dahteste. Lozen's powers of divination had revealed to her that continued fighting would mean the annihilation of her people, so she persuaded the other Apache leaders that seeking an end to the conflict and a peaceful return to the government reservations was their only option for survival.

At first, this seemed successful and approximately 300 Chiricahuas settled at a reservation known as Turkey Creek, some 300 miles away from Ojo Caliente. Kaywaykla remembers this as a happy, peaceful time during which they successfully grew crops and enjoyed relative comfort.

Tensions and rumour on the reservation soon destroyed this sense of safety, especially when word spread that captured Native American leaders were being imprisoned at Alcatraz by the US government. Geronimo feared he would be the next to face arrest and exile, and so coordinated another escape. In May 1885 he and Lozen led 140 others back to the Sierra Madres Mountains with General Crook and his troops in hot pursuit. As the soldiers chased down the warriors, many of the women and children were inevitably captured and forcibly returned to the confines of the government reservation. This continued for almost a full year, until an unnamed Apache woman (most probably Lozen) approached the Americans with a proposition for peace and an end to the conflict, advising that they were ready to renegotiate[73]. In March 1886 a deal was made. The Apaches, keen to "restore the ties of kin and community" agreed that the renegades would surrender and submit to two years' imprisonment. Upon their release, they would be allowed to return to Turkey Creek and live there peaceably and face no further charges or persecution. This was a reasonable solution, but the terms were overruled by Crook's superior, and the General resigned from his command in protest. A large troop of 5,000 US soldiers were tasked to pursue and eliminate the remaining 36 Apaches hiding in the mountains. Even with these outrageous odds, the US troops failed to secure a convincing victory and negotiations reopened. In the end, the last Apache rebels conceded to the inevitable and on September 3rd 1886 the renegades "laid down their arms for the last time"[74].

Lozen and the remaining survivors were herded onto a train and taken to two military camps in Florida. There, the battle for survival continued as the Apaches began to die from the ravages of tuberculosis, malaria and smallpox. Evidence suggests that by "1890, 119 of the 498 Chiricahuas... had died"[75]. When the Chiricahuas finally secured some semblance of freedom in 1913, Lozen was no

---

[73] Ed. Theda Purdue, 2001. *Sifters: Native American Women's Lives*, pp.104.

[74] Ibid, pp.105.

[75] Ibid, pp.106.

longer around to celebrate. Having been transferred as a prisoner of war to Mount Vernon in Alabama, Lozen died quietly of tuberculosis 1889 leaving behind her legacy to inspire her people. Buried in an unmarked grave with as many as 50 other dead, Lozen was not forgotten and continued to be remembered and celebrated. Dahteste, another noted female Apache warrior, spent the "rest of her life honouring Lozen, the Apache Warrior, Seer, and Shaman"[76].

In 1913, the Chiricahuas were finally given the choice of returning to New Mexico. Dahteste was among those who chose to settle on the Mescalero reservation. She remarried and raised a family, but she was said to have mourned Lozen's death in a deeply spiritual way as long as she lived. An important Apache leader in her own right, she honoured and shared the legacy of Lozen with the subsequent generations of her people so that this Apache Warrior, Seer, and Shaman would never be forgotten and continues to be remembered in the stories of her tribe right down to today.

---

[76] https://www.facebook.com/HistoricalTrauma/posts/the-story-of-lozen-apache-woman-warrior-and-healer/695920117138256/

HANNIBAL BARCA

"Scourge of Rome"

As soon as he was born, Hannibal Barca seemed to realise his destiny was to become one of the world's greatest military strategists, and for generations, after he was dead and gone, Roman mothers would scare their children with tales of how Hannibal was coming to get them if they weren't good. As a child, he pleaded with his father the great Hamilcar Barca to be allowed to join him on his military expeditions so that he could help defeat the enemies of his people. Born in Carthage (modern-day Tunisia in North Africa), Hannibal left his homeland at the tender age of nine to be with his father and headed to Spain with the army where Hamilcar would spend the next nine years subjugating the country to Carthaginian rule, "during which he reduced many Iberian tribes to obedience either by force of arms or by diplomacy"[77]. According to the Roman historian Titus Livius Patavinus, prior to departing for Spain Hannibal's father made him swear "that as soon as he possibly could, he would show himself the enemy of Rome"[78]. Another

---

[77] Polybius, *The Histories*, Loeb Classical Library, 1922. Book II, p.243.

[78] Titus Livius Patavinus, *History of Rome*. Trans. Rev. Canon Roberts. J.M. Dent & Sons Ltd., London, 1905. Book 21, pp.2.

account suggests that the nine-year-old said "I swear as soon as age will permit, I will use fire and steel to arrest the destiny of Rome"[79]. This may have been a big proclamation from such a young boy, but as events would prove he was singularly equal to the task he has set himself and devoted his entire life to proving it.

Hannibal's father was an able and famous Carthaginian military leader in his own right, and the Barca clan were one of the leading families in Carthage. Prior to his departure for Spain, Hamilcar had been instrumental, if not successful in the First Punic War between his own people and Rome. Eventually defeated and forced to resort to guerrilla warfare tactics, Hamilcar "felt as if his family's character had been smeared. This resentment simmered in his heart and that of his sons for years"[80]. According to the historian Livy, "he was meditating a far greater war than any he was actually engaged in", setting a precedent for Hannibal's epic journey into Italy some years later and lighting a fire in his son's heart that would burn against the Romans for as long as he drew breath. Unfortunately, Hamilcar's desire to hurt the ambitions of Rome ended abruptly when the people of Iberia rose in rebellion and turned on him, endangering both his sons at the same time. Diodorus wrote that both Hannibal and his brother "clung to him and desired to share his death" but that Hamilcar

---

[79] Clifford W. Mills, 2008, *Hannibal.* InfoBase Publishing, New York, pp.36.

[80] Michael Shammas, *An Indomitable Will: Hannibal Barca and the Start of a World War,* http://lacunajournal.blogspot.com/2012/10/an-indomitable-will.html

"drove them off with whips" and soon after safeguarding his sons and his army, bravely faced his own defeat alone[81].

Young as he was at the time, Hannibal had already had been exposed to extensive military training and had received a comprehensive education, studying Greek philosophy, mathematics and science[82]. Although only 18 years old, Hannibal was well equipped to offer support to his brother-in-law Hasdrubal the Fair when he ascended as the military leader of Carthage and took "supreme power for eight years"[83]. Upon Hasdrubal's death in 221 BC, Hannibal was the most obvious choice as successor, but not everyone was convinced that the 26-year-old was ready for command. Hanno, "the leader of the opposite party" was reluctant to give his support to Hannibal's claim, saying "I, for my part, consider that this youth ought to be kept at home and taught to live in obedience to the laws and the magistrates on an equality with his fellow-citizens"[84]. According to Livy however, "Hanno's proposal received but slight support". Physically, Hannibal's strong resemblance to his father stood him in good stead, and the veterans in the Carthaginian army "saw the same determined expression the same piercing eyes, the same cast of features", convincing them that "they saw Hamilcar restored to them as he was in his youth"[85].

---

[81] Diodorus Siculus, *Library of History*. Loeb Classical Library, 1957. Book XXV, pp.19.

[82] Clifford W. Mills, 2008, *Hannibal*.pp.36.

[83] Titus Livius Patavinus, *History of Rome*. Book 21, pp.2.
[84] Titus Livius Patavinus, *History of Rome*. Book 21, pp.3.

[85] Titus Livius Patavinus, *History of Rome*. Book 21, pp.4.

Livy goes on to describe Hannibal as a natural leader who was both fearless and self-possessed. By all outward appearances a humble man, Hannibal dressed as his soldiers did and ate what and where they did, sleeping amongst them and avoiding anything that would distinguish him as coming from one of Carthage's most powerful and wealthy families[86]. Personally courageous and skilled in combat, Hannibal was usually the first man to draw his sword and the last man to leave the battlefield. Great men usually attract great criticism and Livy notes "these great merits were matched by great vices - inhuman cruelty, a perfidy worse than Punic, an utter absence of truthfulness, reverence, fear of the gods, respect for oaths, sense of religion". His fellow Carthaginian Hanno may have been right when he suggested that Hannibal must first learn obedience before he learnt the art of commanding an army, but the pace of history swept along too rapidly to make time for regrets - Hannibal was in command, and his sights were set squarely on the destruction of Rome[87].

Following their defeat in the First Punic War, Carthage had signed the Treaty of Lutatius in order to secure peace. The terms of the treaty were harsh and crippled them financially, forcing them to give up territories in Sicily and cede them to the Romans. Neither side thought the uneasy people would last long, and the Carthaginians were "eager to be avenged" for their defeat in Sicily "while the Romans...

---

[86] Clifford W. Mills, 2008, *Hannibal.*pp.36.

[87] Titus Livius Patavinus, *History of Rome.* Book 21, pp.4.

mistrusted them profoundly"[88]. As Polybius asserts, it was "evident to all... that it would not be long before war broke out" and with the passionate and patriotic Hannibal leading the mercenary Carthaginian army, the conflict was bound to be both long and bloody. It can be said that Hannibal's single-minded obsession with destroying Roman power mandated that a new war would begin as soon as he could arrange it and almost as soon as he was proclaimed commander-in-chief and war leader of Carthage he set out to kick the Roman hornet's nest. Manufacturing an excuse to attack the Saguntines, he was well aware that any aggression by Carthage would be viewed as a violation of the terms of their peace treaty and "would inevitably set the arms of Rome in motion"[89]. Hannibal was strategic in his provocations though, first attacking and raiding other cities and territories around Saguntum, which dominated eastern Spain. By the time he arrived with his forces and laid siege to Saguntum itself, Hannibal and his army were in a strong position. The supplies and loot that they had collected had ensured a comfortable winter in New Carthage while his string of victories had secured for Hannibal "the allegiance of his own people and of the allied contingents"[90]. Following the humiliating defeat in the First Punic War, Carthage was eager to recover her lost territories and prestige.

---

[88] Polybius, *The Histories*, Book II, pp.332.

[89] Titus Livius Patavinus, *History of Rome*. Book 21, pp.5.

[90] Titus Livius Patavinus, *History of Rome*. Book 21, pp.5.

Hannibal's offensive moved swiftly on Saguntum, pre-empting any Roman response and he was hopeful that he could secure the town before the Saguntines' plea for help could generate Roman forces that would outnumber the Carthaginians. Initially, the siege went to plan but when Hannibal himself was struck and "fell with a severe wound in his thigh from a javelin", his army lost all momentum and simply held their positions while his wound healed[91]. When the fighting resumed it was "fiercer than ever" and although the Carthaginians outnumbered the Saguntine defenders as "the hotter and closer the fighting became the greater grew the number of wounded"[92]. Carthage was committed to a battle that could only end one way – war with Rome. Back home, Hannibal's devoted critic Hanno argued that the attack on Saguntum was just as much an attack on Carthage, saying "it is Carthage whose walls he is shaking with his battering rams. ...the war which was begun with Saguntum will have to be carried on with Rome"[93]. Saguntum was duly captured, and while the Roman military started mobilising their forces for war, Hannibal began planning his next steps. After having "reduced all the tribes in Spain", Hannibal suggested to his men that they had little choice but to either disband their armies or "transfer our wars to other lands", a notion that would be the first step in his epic journey across the Alps[94].

---

[91] Titus Livius Patavinus, *History of Rome*. Book 21, pp.7-8.

[92] Titus Livius Patavinus, *History of Rome*. Book 21, pp.7-8.

[93] Titus Livius Patavinus, *History of Rome*. Book 21, pp.10.

[94] Titus Livius Patavinus, *History of Rome*. Book 21, pp.21.

Like many of the warriors we've met during the course of this book, prior to departing on his invasion of Italy itself Hannibal reportedly saw a strange vision in which "a youth of god-like appearance" appeared before him, saying "he had been sent by the gods" to guide Hannibal safely through to Italy. The apparition instructed Hannibal to stay close and follow, and not take his eyes off him. Although initially, Hannibal followed these instructions, eventually curiosity overcame him, and he turned to look behind where he saw "a serpent of vast and marvellous bulk" being followed by a threatening thunderstorm. Asking his guide what this was, he was told "it was the devastation of Italy" and that he must journey on, leaving his destiny hidden.[95]

News of Hannibal's preparations to cross the Alps and invade Italy inevitably reached the ears of the Romans and not long after Hannibal had crossed the Rhone River at the foot of the great mountains, the Roman commander Scipio Africanus arrived with his army. Himself a gifted commander and military strategist, Africanus was ready to fight but found no opponent. Unfortunately for him, Hannibal had already long departed and with a significant head start on them, the Romans had little chance of catching him before he began his ascent into the mountains.

The story of Hannibal and his march across the Alps has survived through the ages as a legendary feat, even if how he did it and what route he took remains largely a

[95] Titus Livius Patavinus, *History of Rome*. Book 21, pp.22.

mystery. Circumnavigating the daunting mountain range with "fifty thousand foot and about nine thousand horse" and up to 40 elephants[96] is almost incomprehensible even by today's modern militaries, but he was able to do it while keeping his forces intact and largely alive to emerge in Italy. Through his exceptional leadership and brutal enforcement of discipline, Hannibal led his forces across exceedingly difficult terrain and beat back repeated attacks by mountain tribes resisting the transit of his army. At one point, his entire force was in peril with the hidden tribesmen "hurling stones" from their higher ground until "Hannibal was compelled to pass with night with half his force… separated from his horses and pack-train"[97]. Despite the challenges of weather, mountains and men, the Carthaginian crossed the Alps in 15 days, according to Polybius[98]. Although most of Hannibal's famous war elephants survived the perilous journey, they ended up playing only a nominal part in the subsequent battles he fought, proving their worth only at the end of 218 BC in the Battle of Trebbia, during which the majority were killed.[99]

The precise route taken by Hannibal has been the subject of intense debate since the time of Livy and Polybius, although recent discoveries suggest he crossed the border into Italy at Col de Traversette. Quite why he would have chosen such a notoriously difficult crossing remains

[96] Polybius, *The Histories*, Book III, pp.85.

[97] Polybius, *The Histories*, Book III, pp.129.

[98] Polybius, *The Histories*, Book III, pp.136.

[99] Jon Guttman, 2016, *Carthaginian War Elephant*, http://www.historynet.com/carthaginian-war-elephant.htm

something of a mystery, although some suggest that pressure from the "major military force" of the Gauls may have forced him "to take this more difficult and unexpected route to avoid a devastating ambush"[100]. In any case, Hannibal successfully accomplished the challenging task of traversing the mountain passes and arrived in Italy ready and eager to fulfil his destiny as Rome's nemesis. According to Polybius, having descended from the snowy mountain tops, Hannibal's men "had become in their external appearance and general condition more like beasts than men" so they took the opportunity to rest and regroup[101] before they resumed their invasion southward. Plans to recover from their journey ultimate had to be cut short when news arrived that Africanus "had already crossed the Po and was quite near at hand"[102]. Impressed and surprised at the Roman speed, Hannibal spoke to his men to prepare them for battle and reminding them that flight was not an option, isolated as they were deep in Roman territory. Pointing out that the enemy was close to home, he assured them that it wouldn't take too much to send the Romans fleeing for their families, as they were "sure of finding safety in flight" and suggesting that the courage of the Carthaginians would be far greater as "the courage of those who despair of safety will carry all before it"[103].

---

[100] Leon Watson, 2016, "Has Hannibal's route across the Alps been uncovered? Scientists use 2,000-year-old trail of dung to track legendary general". *The Telegraph*, 5th April 2016.
https://www.telegraph.co.uk/news/2016/04/05/has-hannibals-route-across-the-alps-been-uncovered-scientists-us/

[101] Polybius, *The Histories*, Book III, pp.144.

[102] Polybius, *The Histories*, Book III, pp.146.

[103] Polybius, *The Histories*, Book III, pp.154-5.

Meanwhile, on the other side of the Po plain, Africanus addressed the Roman army in a similar fashion, assuring his troops of victory and reassuring them that while Hannibal had successfully invaded Italy, he had "lost most of his army and the rest are weak and useless owing to hardship"[104]. Certainly they had been worn down it was said, and would be no match for the fresh Roman troops. However, before the two armies were to clash there were seriously bad omens. First, a wolf then a swarm of bees made it into the Roman camp, where they caused much consternation amongst the superstitious soldiers. Rumours soon circulated that they were cursed and as they marched forward to face Hannibal and his troops they were disorganised and fearful. Initial clashes did not go well for the Romans. According to Livy, "the result made it quite clear that the Carthaginian was superior in his cavalry", encouraging the Romans to seek another battlefield other than the plains of Po.[105]

With the Celtic tribes firmly on the side of the Carthaginians, the Roman plans were further disrupted, this time by their allies from Gaul who performed a "murderous outbreak" on the Roman camp near Placentia and "deserted to Hannibal"[106]. Soon after, the two armies met in the first major set piece of the Second Punic War – the Battle of Trebbia, where Hannibal's elephants finally had a taste of victory. The Roman cavalry, tired from marching and heavily outnumbered were soon thrown into chaos by the

[104] Polybius, *The Histories*, Book III, pp.157.

[105] Titus Livius Patavinus, *History of Rome*. Book 21, pp.47.

[106] Titus Livius Patavinus, *History of Rome*. Book 21, pp.48.

Carthaginian war elephants; their strange smell and appearance terrified the Roman horses, making them difficult to control and creating extensive chaos and panic.[107] The Romans counterattacked but were defeated when Hannibal choose his moment and sent his best troops storming into the centre of the fight, inflicting "an immense loss on the enemy". With victory beyond them, the surviving Romans fled back to their fortified camp at Placentia with the Carthaginians close on their heels. "The Carthaginians stopped their pursuit at the banks of the Trebia and returned to their camp so benumbed with cold that they hardly felt any joy in their victory"[108].

Hannibal successfully won this first battle, but the war itself raged on for 17 years, with the Romans begrudgingly realising that in order to win, they needed to avoid a direct confrontation. As a military strategist, Hannibal was just too dangerous to fight head-on, so rather than risk another disastrous battle, the Romans bided their time, following the Carthaginian army closely with their own forces were waiting for the Carthaginians to exhaust their supplies and become vulnerable. The Roman dictator Fabius Maximus advocated this strategy (aptly called the "Fabian" strategy) as he conducted the war against Hannibal and his army. "Rather than fight, Fabius shadowed Hannibal's army and avoided battle... manoeuvring the Roman army in hilly terrain, so as to nullify Hannibal's decisive superiority in cavalry"[109]. In

---

[107] Titus Livius Patavinus, *History of Rome*. Book 21, pp.55.

[108] Titus Livius Patavinus, *History of Rome*. Book 21, pp.56.

[109] Michiko Phifer, 2012, *A Handbook of Military Strategy and Tactics*. Vij Multimedia, New Delhi. pp.119.

the end, Hannibal was defeated not by a more effective fighting force but by time. As his army wandered around Italy, running short of supplies and reinforcements word reached him that a Roman army had landed in Africa and was marching on Carthage itself. He was recalled back to defend his capital and had to leave Rome behind. The Fabian strategy had proved effective, despite the protestations of some Romans that it was a "cowardly approach"[110].

The Second Punic War really came to a close when Scipio Africanus and Hannibal Barca faced one another one last time at the Battle of Zama. Both were certain that this would be the definitive and decisive battle, but Hannibal was less confident of victory than Africanus. Two legendary generals faced each other and "as the proverb says, 'A brave man meets another braver yet,'" with the Romans winning a hard-fought victory. Soundly defeated, the Carthaginians had little option but to accept the Roman terms for treaty which Hannibal ultimately supported, saying "It seems to me astounding and quite incomprehensible, that any man who is a citizen of Carthage ... does not bless the stars that now that he is at the mercy of the Romans he has obtained such lenient terms"[111]. Although the words must have stuck in his throat, Hannibal had enough admiration for Africanus to graciously accept his generous surrender conditions. Despite his defeat, Hannibal remained an important figure in Carthaginian society and was elevated to high office, proving himself just as effective as a statesman as he had been as a

---

[110] Michiko Phifer, 2012, *A Handbook of Military Strategy and Tactics*, pp.120.

[111] Polybius, *The Histories*, Book XV, pp.507.

soldier.[112]   Unfortunately, his political rivals remained as unconquered threats, and as Carthage began to rebuild its treasury and political power following its defeat, his enemies conspired to bring him down. Whispers and rumours found willing listeners in Rome, and it was soon said that Hannibal was playing a double game, pretending to abide by the peace terms while secretly negotiating with the Syrians to make an alliance and forge a coalition which would once again challenge Roman supremacy.[113]

Hannibal realised that he was universally hated by the Romans, and with his enemies at home fearing his influence and wanting him removed he knew that it was just a matter of time before he would be arrested and probably quietly executed. Not waiting for the Romans to arrive, Hannibal fled Carthage with his family and left Africa altogether, "the country for whose misfortunes he had felt much more pity than for his own"[114]. Reluctant to give up military life, Hannibal operated as a mercenary general for a time, engaging in several battles in the pay of foreign kings, most markedly against Rome's ally King Eumenes II. The Romans decided that he needed to be eliminated and began to hunt him down. Finally cornered and about to be caught, according to some reports Hannibal decided to "dispatch himself by poison"[115] rather than surrender and be taken by his lifelong enemy. The Greek writer Pausanias gives a

[112] Jacob Abbott, Hannibal pp.245.

[113] Jacob Abbott, Hannibal pp.248.

[114] Titus Livius Patavinus, *History of Rome*. Book 33, pp.55.

[115] Corneli Nepos, *A New English Version of the lives of Cornelius Nepos*. Barcelona, 1828, pp.226.

different account of his death, suggesting that in an effort to flee the Romans, Hannibal leapt on his horse, cutting his finger on his sword in the process. "When he had proceeded only a few days his wound caused a fever, and he died on the third day"[116]. Hannibal would never live to return to Carthage, dying in Libyssa in modern-day Turkey.

Although he didn't die a hero, he died a legend and Hannibal's legacy has lived on thousands of years after his death. He is remembered for his incredible logistical and command abilities, as well as his strategic and tactical brilliance on the battlefield. He is best recalled as Rome's greatest adversary and threat, a man who marched elephants through impassable mountains and slaughtered tens of thousands of Roman soldiers on battlefields all over the ancient world. As one historian so appropriately said - "As a soldier... Hannibal stands alone and unequalled."[117]

[116] Pausanias, *Description of Greece*. "Arcadia", Chapter 11, pp.11.
http://www.perseus.tufts.edu/hopper/text?doc=Perseus:text:1999.0 1.0160:book=8:chapter=11&highlight=hannibal

[117] Theodore Ayrault Dodge, 1896, *Hannibal: a history of the art of war among the Carthaginians and Romans down to the battle of Pydna, 168 B.C., with a detailed account of the Second Punic War*. Houghton, Boston, pp.652.

PYRRHUS OF EPIRUS

"The Man Who Would be King"

Like the great Hannibal, the man who would become known to the world as Pyrrhus spent little time enjoying any child frivolity and had to grow up quickly as events grand and historic swept him away in their currents and he was crowned a king at the tender age of 12. Born four years after the death of Alexander the Great in 323 BC, Pyrrhus was the son of Aeacides, who succeeded Alexander as the King of Epirus. The kingdom of Epirus was on the outer fringes of Greek territory but still regarded as "un-Greek and barbarous"[118] by its critics that lived closer to where all the real culture was thought to reside – the city of Athens. When Pyrrhus was just two years old, his father was driven out of power in Epirus by rebellious Molossian factions determined to wipe out the royal family. According to the historian Plutarch, while King Aeacides' allies and friends were being caught and executed, the child Pyrrhus was

---

[118] Graham Wiley, "Pyrrhus Πολεμιστής". *Latomus*. April-June 1999, pp.300.

"stolen away"[119] by loyal servants of his father. According to his version of events, the group of fugitives was slowed down by the presence of the young prince, and the need to bring along both servants and "women for the nursing of the child"[120]. Fearing imminent capture by the rebel forces, the allies of the ousted king handed Pyrrhus over to three "sturdy and trusty young men, with orders to fly with all their might and make for Megara, a Macedonian town; while they themselves, partly by entreaties and partly by fighting, stayed the course of the pursuers until late in the evening"[121].

Unfortunately, heavy rains had swollen the stream that ran alongside the edge of Megara, giving it a "forbidding and savage look" and although Pyrrhus' three custodians knew that safety lay on the other side "its current was greatly swollen and violent from rains that had fallen, and the darkness made everything more formidable"[122]. Carrying the precious cargo of the baby Pyrrhus and the women charged with caring for him, the men realised they could not cross the engorged river unaided and called out to the Macedonians on the far bank of the river for help. Their voices couldn't carry over the raging torrent of water, and neither group could understand what the other was saying. Eventually, one of Pyrrhus's protectors thought of an

---

[119] Plutarch, *Plutarch's Lives*. Translated by Bernadotte Perrin. Harvard University Press, London, 1920. Chapter 2, section 1.
http://www.perseus.tufts.edu/hopper/text?doc=Perseus%3Atext%3A2008.01.0060%3Achapter%3D2%3Asection%3D1

[120] Plutarch, *Plutarch's Lives*. Chapter 2, section 1.

[121] Plutarch, *Plutarch's Lives*. Chapter 2, section 2.

[122] Plutarch, *Plutarch's Lives*. Chapter 2, section 3.

alternative method of communication and "stripped off a piece of bark from a tree and wrote thereon with a buckle-pin a message telling their need and the fortune of the child; then he wrapped the bark about a stone, which he used to give force to his cast, and threw it to the other side"[123].

The Macedonians read the message and acted quickly, cutting down trees and lashing them together to create a makeshift raft. The first to the other side was a man named Achilles who "took Pyrrhus in his arms" and carried him to safety. Once across the river, the fugitives sought out the assistance of "Glaucias, the king of the Illyrians". Glaucias was sympathetic, but ultimately reluctant to get involved and intervene in what he assessed as a lost cause for the deposed King Aeacides. Cassander, the new ruler of Epirus, might make a powerful enemy and as listened to the appeal of the refugees he "held his peace a long time as he took counsel with himself"[124]. As the Macedonian king mulled things over, the infant Pyrrhus wriggled free of his guardian, crawled over to him and used his robe to pull himself unsteadily onto his feet. This moved Glaucias "first to laughter, then to pity". Young Pyrrhus didn't implore the king, who Plutarch notes was, by this time, "weeping like a formal suppliant" but stood with his arms around "an altar of the gods" in a stance that Glaucias perceived as "a sign from heaven"[125]. The matter was decided, and Pyrrhus was accepted into Glaucias's home and family.

---

[123] Plutarch, *Plutarch's Lives*. Chapter 2, section 5.

[124] Plutarch, *Plutarch's Lives*. Chapter 3, section 1.

[125] Plutarch, *Plutarch's Lives*. Chapter 3, section 3.

Upon learning later that the dispossessed prince was living safely under the protection of the Macedonians, Cassander "demanded his surrender", offering two hundred talents in exchange for the boy, but "Glaucias would not give him up". As he grew, the king kept Pyrrhus close to him until at the age of twelve, at which time he "conducted him back into Epirus with an armed force and set him upon the throne there"[126], restoring him to his royal birthright. According to Plutarch, what Pyrrhus lacked in "the majesty of kingly power", he made up for with his countenance of terror[127]. Physically, he was said to be particularly ugly. With few teeth in his mouth and his upper jaw being made almost entirely from one solid bone "on which the usual intervals between the teeth were indicated by slight depressions", Pyrrhus was far from the handsome, gallant hero one might have imagined. He did, however, have a strange talent for healing people suffering from what Plutarch described as "splenetic habit" which appears to have been a generally bad-tempered disposition. Pyrrhus's knack for curing this problem involved the sacrifice of a white cockerel, after which Pyrrhus would instruct the patient to lay flat on his back while he "would press gently with his right foot against the spleen". Apparently, Pyrrhus himself was so convinced that he had a magical healing power that there was no one was "as obscure or poor as not to get this healing service from him if he asked it"[128]. Perhaps this was a form of self-promotion for the public, the better to validate Pyrrhus'

---

[126] Plutarch, *Plutarch's Lives*. Chapter 3, section 3.

[127] Plutarch, *Plutarch's Lives*. Chapter 3, section 4.

[128] Plutarch, *Plutarch's Lives*. Chapter 3, section 4.

"divine empowerment from heaven for his authoritative role on earth"[129].

Returned to his father's throne to rule, Pyrrhus was not to sit on it long and soon his authority to rule the kingdom was challenged; at the age of 17 Pyrrhus had been evicted by Neoptolemus, "a rival member of the royal family"[130] and deposed. Thus "stripped of his realm", Pyrrhus joined forces with his brother-in-law Demetrius Poliorcetes, son of Antigonus who had fought for Alexander the Great. Alongside his father, Demetrius went into battle against Pyrrhus' old archenemy Cassander and the ruler of the Egyptians, Ptolemy Soter. It was during this conflict that we learn of the first documented military experience for Pyrrhus when he participated in the Battle of Ipsus when the two rival armies clashed. Things didn't end well for his alliance, and although his side was defeated Plutarch declares the young man "made a brilliant display of valour" and "though Demetrius lost the day, Pyrrhus did not abandon him but kept guard over his cities in Greece which were entrusted to him"[131].

Pyrrhus survived the turmoil of his kingdom and would go on to become a celebrated general by the time he was 40, although exactly how he established this distinctive

---

[129] Wendy Cotter, 1999, *Miracles in Greco-Roman Antiquity: A Sourcebook for the Study of New Testament Miracle Stories*. Routledge, London, pp.39.

[130] Plutarch, *The Age of Alexander*, "Introduction to Pyrrhus", https://erenow.com/ancient/the-age-of-alexander/12.html

[131] Plutarch, *Plutarch's Lives*. Chapter 4, section 3.

fame is largely unclear. As historian Graham Wiley points out, "[t]he only major battle in which he is recorded as taking part was Ipsus" at which he held a minor command position, suggesting that he was already accustomed to a fairly senior level of military command.[132] Wiley postulates that Pyrrhus may have fought in tribal wars in both Epirus and Illyria, gaining both experience and local fame. In any case, Pyrrhus fought valiantly for Demetrius and "when Demetrius made peace with Ptolemy, sailed to Egypt as a hostage for him"[133]. History tells us that Pyrrhus volunteered himself as a hostage; while going into captivity with a foreign enemy wouldn't appeal to most, the circumstances worked out well for Pyrrhus who developed a close relationship with his former enemy Ptolemy, giving him "proof of his prowess and endurance"[134]. Some dispute the fact that Pyrrhus volunteered himself as a hostage, suggesting rather that Ptolemy hand-picked him after seeing him fight at the Battle of Ipsus.[135]

Plutarch sounds less than complimentary when he describes Pyrrhus as being "adept at turning to his own advantage the favour of his superiors", hinting that perhaps Pyrrhus was less than gallant in the amount of attention and

---

[132] Graham Wiley, "Pyrrhus Πολεμιστής". *Latomus*. April-June 1999, pp.301.

[133] Plutarch, *Plutarch's Lives*. Chapter 4, section 3.

[134] Plutarch, *Plutarch's Lives*. Chapter 4, section 4.

[135] Jonathan Recaldin, 2010. *Pyrrhus of Epirus: Statesman or Soldier?: An analysis of Pyrrhus' political and military traits during the Hellenistic Era.* https://www.academia.edu/1558273/Pyrrhus_of_Epirus_Statesman_or_Soldier_An_analysis_of_Pyrrhus_political_and_military_traits_during_the_Hellenistic_Era?auto=download, pp.17.

"especial court" he paid to Ptolemy's influential wife, Berenicé. Perhaps he was particularly charming, or simply persuasive. In any case, Pyrrhus was able to secure himself an important and influential wife when "he was selected from among many young princes as a husband for Antigone, one of the daughters of Berenicé whom she had by Philip1 before her marriage with Ptolemy"[136]. He married well, but ultimately this might have really been just political and social climbing. Plutarch certainly is unkind in his assessment of the man's character, and he isn't the only historian to have painted Pyrrhus' character in less than complimentary brush strokes. In his biography of Pyrrhus, noted scholar Jacob Abbott describes him as a volatile man, "governed by a sort of blind and instinctive impulse" that meant he engaged in battle enthusiastically but "without regard to any ultimate end"[137].

While Pyrrhus may have been impulsive without any power or influence, Ptolemy took a strong liking to his former enemy and formed a close personal alliance with the former king. Eventually, he changed his mind and actually supported the restoration of Pyrrhus to his throne, as if they had never been on opposite sides previously. It has been suggested that Ptolemy liked the idea of helping Pyrrhus take power in Epirus again, as "it no doubt suited him to see a vigorous rival, friendly to himself, established on the western

---

[136] Plutarch, *Plutarch's Lives*. Chapter 4, section 4.

[137] Jacob Abbott, 1901. *The Life of Pyrrhus*, Harper & Brothers, New York and London, pp.235.

flank of Macedonia to worry Cassander's successor"[138]. With Ptolemy's political and military support, Pyrrhus was supposed to share the Epirot throne with another - his rival, Neoptolemus. This shared power arrangement was not to last, and Pyrrhus soon began to hear rumours that Neoptolemus was plotting to kill him and become the sole ruler. Evidently a practical man and not content to bide his time, Pyrrhus acted and "on a day of sacrifice invited Neoptolemus to supper and killed him"[139]. Subsequently, Pyrrhus was able to extend his rule "to that of king, or hegemon, of a federation of all the Epirot tribes"[140]. Once the sole ruler of his people, his popularity increased in keeping with his "growing military reputation" and his soldiers honoured him with the title "the Eagle", to which Pyrrhus reportedly responded, "May I deserve the title while I am borne upon the wings of your arms."[141]

While this remark makes Pyrrhus appear to be a humble man indebted to his men's loyalty, his determination to invade the neighbouring region of Macedon indicates otherwise. Although the incursion was probably intended only as a "predatory incursion in the country for the purpose of plunder", the expedition gathered its own momentum and

---

[138] Nicholas Geoffrey Lemprière Hammond, Frank William Walbank, and Guy Thompson Griffith, 1988. *A History of Macedonia: 336-167 B.C.* Oxford University Press, New York, pp.213.

[139] Plutarch, *Plutarch's Lives.* Chapter 5, section 6.

[140] Graham Wiley, "Pyrrhus Πολεμιστής". *Latomus.* April-June 1999, pp.302.

[141] https://www.bartleby.com/344/330.html

soon assumed "the character of a regular invasion"[142]. When the fighting reached a virtual stalemate, Pyrrhus reluctantly agreed to make peace with the Macedonian leader Alexander, who was the son of his old enemy Cassander and Lysimachus, a successor to Alexander the Great. The three kings agreed to meet, sign a peace treaty and would mark the occasion with the sacrifice of "a bull, a boar and a ram". When the three animals were brought forward the ram "fell down dead", an event that one of Pyrrhus' priests explained was a sign "that Heaven thus betokened in advance the death of one of the three kings"[143]. Inspired, Pyrrhus later renounced the peace deal entirely and "became involved in five years' intermittent and somewhat pointless warfare"[144].

Pyrrhus' conflict with the Macedonians may well have continued had he not been offered another opportunity that appeared more appealing than continued fighting in what was becoming a losing position. A series of military defeats had pushed his forces out of Macedon entirely, and everything he had gained with his initial invasion was lost. In addition, the "great power of Lysimachus" was also growing and threatening to overthrow his leadership in Epirus[145]. He made a face-saving peace and decided to look elsewhere for an easier glory. Subsequently, when the inhabitants of Tarentum appealed to him to help them fight

---

[142] Jacob Abbott, 1901. *The Life of Pyrrhus*, pp.238-240

[143] Plutarch, *Plutarch's Lives*. Chapter 6, section 5.

[144] Graham Wiley, "Pyrrhus Πολεμιστής". *Latomus*. April-June 1999, pp.303.

[145] Geoffrey Neale Scott, 1930. *Epirus: A Study in Greek Constitutional Development*. Cambridge University Press, Cambridge, UK, pp.69.

off the Romans, Pyrrhus promptly "accepted the invitation, seeing an opening for empire-building in nearby Sicily"[146]. With his customary energy and rapidity, Pyrrhus had soon gathered a force of "twenty-five thousand foot, two thousand horse, and a troop of twenty-four elephants"[147]. Employing considerable stealth and efficient planning, Pyrrhus managed to successfully transport all these men and beasts into Italy "before the Romans knew of his approach"[148].

The Battle of Heraclea was the first real clash between Pyrrhus and Rome, and it was a nearly the end for the opportunistic Greek. At one point he was in real danger of being surrounded and killed by Roman soldiers, so Pyrrhus swapped his royal cloak "purple-dyed and shot with gold" with the plain coat and breastplate of his "most faithful of his companions and the bravest in battle, Megacles" in an effort to save his own life[149]. Eventually, the tide of battle turned, and the Romans were defeated, but not before large numbers of men were lost. Most historical sources estimate that Pyrrhus lost approximately 4,000 men in his first encounter with Rome[150], although Dionysius places it closer

---

[146] Graham Wiley, "Pyrrhus Πολεμιστής". *Latomus*. April-June 1999, pp.305.

[147] Jacob Abbott, 1901. *The Life of Pyrrhus*, pp.268.

[148] Pausanias, *The Description of Greece, Volume 1*. Translated by Thomas Taylor. Priestley & Weale, London, 1895, pp.30.

[149] Dionysius of Halicarnassus, *Roman Antiquities*. Book XIX, pp.361.

[150] H.H. Scullard, 1935. *A History of the Roman World 753 – 146 BC*, Routledge, USA. Chapter 5.

to a much more significant 13,000[151]. More significant to him personally were the irreplaceable men close to him that were killed, as Pyrrhus "lost the friends and generals whom he always used and trusted most", making the victory all the more empty. "Pyrrhus had a won a decisive victory, but not a war" and had little to show for his efforts, with no new allies or territories to call his own[152].

Pyrrhus' next battle with the Romans would prove even more costly. After securing victory at Heraclea, he headed north towards Rome hoping that "the allies of Rome would rally to his cause". These hopes were in vain, and he gathered no new support. Frustrated and with the good campaigning weather ending he halted his advance some 40 miles from Rome and headed back to Tarentum, releasing his army to their winter quarters some 300 km north[153]. Realising that Roman tenacity and manpower reserves might be much deeper than he had anticipated, Pyrrhus entered into tentative peace negotiations with the Roman Senate but had little success. Some suggest that Pyrrhus lacked the sophistication to negotiate with "political adults", framing his conciliatory efforts as though he was "dealing with a hostile tribal chief"[154]. Reportedly Pyrrhus' private conversations with the Roman statesman Fabricius Luscinus

---

[151] Plutarch *Plutarch's Lives*. Chapter 17, section 4.

[152] Graham Wiley, "Pyrrhus Πολεμιστής". *Latomus*. April-June 1999, pp.306.

[153] H.H. Scullard, 1935. *A History of the Roman World 753 – 146 BC*. Chapter 5.

[154] Graham Wiley, "Pyrrhus Πολεμιστής". *Latomus*. April-June 1999, pp.306-7.

indicate a certain naivety at the bargaining table. The King of Epirus decided to offer the Roman gold as a bribe in order to further his overtures of peace, but Luscinus turned him down flat. His offer refused, Pyrrhus then attempted to frighten Fabricius into an agreement, and when tactic failed "privately invited him, in case he brought about the settlement, to follow his fortunes and share his life as the first and foremost of all his companions and generals"[155]. In refusing this final offer of friendship, Fabricius reportedly said: "Nay, 0 King, this would not be to thy advantage; for the very men who now admire and honour thee, if they should become acquainted with me, would prefer to have me as their king rather than thee"[156].

Peace negotiations were going nowhere unless Pyrrhus agreed to take his men and arms and return to his homeland, so he decided that he had little choice but to force the Romans to accept a truce by winning on the battlefield. He next came to face the Roman army again at the Battle of Asculum, where the rough and uneven ground hampered his forces and put him at a disadvantage. His army had a large contingent of cavalry and elephants, and the unfriendly terrain meant that they couldn't make full use of their mobility against the slower Roman infantry; the battle was bloody, and many were "wounded and slain"[157]. The fighting raged all day but was eventually abandoned as night fell and the two sides broke contact to cluster around their campfires and wait for the next dawn. During the next day's

[155] Plutarch, *Plutarch's Lives*. Chapter 20, section 4.

[156] Plutarch, *Plutarch's Lives*. Chapter 20, section 4.

[157] Plutarch, *Plutarch's Lives*. Chapter 21, section 5.

battle, Pyrrhus gained the upper hand when he was able to move onto an open plain where both his men and his elephants had more room to manoeuvre. Innovative in combat, the Romans tried several new tactics to effectively beat the lumbering elephants sent against their lines, but when the massive animals charged forward they pulled back and retreated to their fortified camp, "leaving Pyrrhus in possession of the field"[158]. It was another hard-won victory, and the losses on Pyrrhus' side were devastating; the king himself documented his losses at "thirty-five hundred and five"[159]. Winning such victories at the cost of losing virtually destroying his own forces is the direct origin of where the phrase "Pyrrhic victory" comes from. Pyrrhus himself was wounded in the fighting, and admitted: "If we are victorious in one more battle with the Romans, we shall be utterly ruined"[160].

Instead of pursuing his conflict with Rome, Pyrrhus decided to pursue a different project altogether and pulled out of Italy and to head to Sicily where he would become "hegemon over the Greek cities"[161]. For a brief period, he was able to establish himself as virtual ruler over the Greek-settled cities there, but his reign in Sicily was marked by brutality and bloodshed, and Pyrrhus proved Homer right in saying "that valour, alone of the virtues, often displays

---

[158] Graham Wiley, "Pyrrhus Πολεμιστής". *Latomus*. April-June 1999, pp.307.

[159] Plutarch, *Plutarch's Lives*. Chapter 21, section 8.

[160] Plutarch, *Plutarch's Lives*. Chapter 21, section 9.

[161] Graham Wiley, "Pyrrhus Πολεμιστής". *Latomus*. April-June 1999, pp.308.

transports due to divine possession and frenzy"[162]. Although Pyrrhus secured leadership over the Greeks of Sicily, he wasn't a popular ruler and enforced an army-style administration on the population that favoured his own men, demanding tribute money and dealing out harsh punishments to any that opposed him. Ambitious, ruthless and restless to achieve more glory, any pretence of unifying the countryside was dropped, and he became an unapologetic dictator. Even Plutarch, who generally has much good to say of Pyrrhus admitted: "he ceased to be a popular leader and became a tyrant, and added to his name for severity a name for ingratitude and faithlessness"[163].

With Sicily reasonably secured, Pyrrhus began to turn his attention back to dealing with the Romans, who seemed to be his primary obstacle in establishing territorial holdings in Italy. He didn't need to wait long and soon was asked to return to Italy and assist the Samnites and Tarentines, who had been turned out of their territories. Grateful for an excuse to withdraw from the tumultuous political climate of Sicily Pyrrhus returned to Tarentine with a considerable army, ready to take on the Roman army under the leadership of Curius Dentatus. Determined to surprise his enemy, Pyrrhus forced-marched his soldiers north along the Appian Way in the dead of night, only to find himself lost. His late arrival at the battlefield proved fatal and "at daybreak he was in full view of the enemy as he advanced upon them from the heights"[164]. The Romans, now used to fighting the

---

[162] Plutarch, *Plutarch's Lives*. Chapter 22, section 6.

[163] Plutarch, *Plutarch's Lives*. Chapter 23, section 3.

[164] Plutarch, *Plutarch's Lives*. Chapter 25, section 3.

elephants hurled javelins at the mighty animals until they were finally compelled "to wheel about and run back through the ranks of their own men, thus causing disorder and confusion"[165]. Pyrrhus was finally defeated, and his "hopes of the conquest of Italy and Sicily were finally demolished"[166]. His army was virtually shredded and scattered.

Pulling out of Italy, the Greek warlord showed no sign of slowing down decided that the time was right to lash out again at the Macedonians, presumably in an effort to refinance Epirus' coffers and make good all the money he had spent fighting in Italy and Sicily. Fighting now as a mercenary with no national army, the soldiers that Pyrrhus led were just a "nondescript body united only by trust in him personally"[167]. In search of glory primarily loot - Pyrrhus met his bizarre demise while fighting a series of small battles back in Greece. According to sources, during a chaotic encounter in Argos Pyrrhus was engaged in hand-to-hand combat with a young boy from the region in an uneven fight pitting the grizzled former king against an unskilled opponent. Like the other women in the town, the boy's mother was watching from the rooftops as the two forces clashed right below them. Upon seeing her son fighting for his life and clearly in trouble, she lifted a heavy tile from the roof and threw it down at Pyrrhus. According to Plutarch,

---

[165] Plutarch, *Plutarch's Lives*. Chapter 25, section 5.

[166] Graham Wiley, "Pyrrhus Πολεμιστής". *Latomus*. April-June 1999, pp.310.

[167] Graham Wiley, "Pyrrhus Πολεμιστής". *Latomus*. April-June 1999, pp.312.

"[i]t fell upon his head below his helmet and crushed the vertebrae at the base of his neck"[168]. As he lay on the ground blinded and helpless, a passing enemy soldier took out his sword and although fearful of the terrible look in Pyrrhus' eyes, "slowly and with difficulty ... severed the head".

This then was an unglamorous end for a man with the greatest aspirations for world conquest, dying instead at the feet of some of the poorest people in the countryside. Although Plutarch gives him much recognition for bravery and wrote that "men believed that in military experience, personal prowess, and daring, he was by far the first of the kings of his time', he also recognises his short-comings as he wrote that "what he won by his exploits he lost by indulging in vain hopes, since through passionate desire for what he had not he always failed to establish securely what he had"[169]. Pyrrhus was indeed a warrior, without a doubt. A military leader, unquestionably. An empire-builder, probably not. In the end, he measured as less than the man he aspired to be.

---

[168] Plutarch, *Plutarch's Lives*. Chapter 34, section 2.

[169] Plutarch, *Plutarch's Lives*. Chapter 26, section 1.

RICHARD THE LIONHEART

"The Warrior Soldier King"

In the case of England's Richard I, or Richard Lionheart as he was later popularly known, the mere act of being born was a political one. The product of a marriage that in itself carried dramatic political consequences, it seemed destined that Richard was to move "on a world stage where all who supported him could admire [him]... [and] where all who loathed him could see his arrogance and his ruthlessness"[170]. Born in 1156, Richard was the son of Henry II, King of England and the notorious Eleanora of Aquitaine. Previously married to King Louis VII of France, Eleanora was an influential woman who brought "a tremendous ascension of wealth and prestige to her new husband"[171] after they married. Although her previous marriage to Louis VII was annulled prior to her involvement with Henry, unsurprisingly the French king was "alarmed and angered" by her choice, considering France and England had been habitual enemies for generations. Having failed to

---

[170] John Gillingham, 1999, *Richard I*. Yale University Press, New Haven & London, pp.3.

[171] John Gillingham, 1999, *Richard I*. pp.25.

produce a male heir throughout the 14 years she was wedded to Louis, her fortune and profitable landholdings were now to be counted as part of Henry's family wealth following her marriage, and within the first five years, she managed to produce four children, three of whom were boys[172].

Perhaps there is a little irony in the fact that Henry barely saw his sons as they were growing up, spending his leisure time in the saddle, hunting, and his working time overseas "governing his continental dominions"[173]. Henry was so scarce that in 1160 the Archbishop Theobald of Canterbury wrote to the king to urge him to return to England, writing "Even the most hard-hearted father could hardly bear to have them out of sight for so long"[174]. Henry seemed to have what his French rival wanted, but seemed to care little for it. Beyond snippets such as these, little is known about Richard's upbringing and childhood other than he was primarily raised by Eleanora, and had a wet nurse by the name of Hodierna to whom he eventually awarded a generous pension[175]. When only a child he was betrothed to marry to cement a political alliance. In an effort to establish an allegiance with Raymond-Berengar IV, the then count of Barcelona King Henry agreed that "Richard should be betrothed to one of the count's daughters and that when married, they should be granted the duchy of Aquitaine"

[172] John Gillingham, 1999, *Richard I*. pp.27.

[173] John Gillingham, 1999, *Richard I*. pp.28.

[174] John Gillingham, 1999, *Richard I*. pp.28.

[175] John Gillingham, 1999, *Richard I*. pp.28.

thus marking the beginning of Richard's association with his mother's homeland[176].

Despite this early arrangement Richard I was again used as "a pawn in the diplomatic game"[177] before he reached the age of maturity, being promised in marriage to Alice, the daughter of Louis VII[178]. Although this marriage never took place, it would play an important role in shaping Richard's life and in terms of his relationships with Normandy and King Philip of France. Richard was betrothed to Alice for some 20 years, throughout which his intended bride was in the custody of his father[179]. Although the arrangement suited Henry well, giving him direct control over the provinces that acted as Alice's dowry, it probably wasn't a situation the young girl would have chosen. Even when her husband-to-be came of age, her guardian, the English king was unwilling to give up custody of her and allow the marriage to be consummated. By the time Alice turned 30, the situation had reached crisis point for Richard who by that time "was so far bound to her that he could not marry any other lady, and his father obstinately persisted in preventing his completing the marriage with her"[180]. Richard's private life proved to be as complex as his career,

---

[176] Jacob Abbott, 1902, *Richard I*. Harpers & Brothers, New York and London, pp.15.

[177] John Gillingham, 1999, *Richard I*. pp.28.

[178] Douglas Boyd, 2018, 8 facts about Richard the Lionheart. https://www.historyextra.com/period/medieval/8-things-you-probably-didnt-know-about-richard-the-lionheart/

[179] John Gillingham, 1999, *Richard I*. pp.5.

[180] Jacob Abbott, 1902, *Richard I*. pp.48.

and he ended up severing his relationship with Alice to marry Berengaria of Navarre in 1190; although this new bride took on the title of Queen of England, she never actually set foot in Richard's homeland[181].

As a young man, Richard was noted for both his good looks and his fighting ability with a sword and lance. According to one of the foremost chroniclers of the Third Crusade Richard de Templo, Richard was a tall man "of elegant build; the colour of his hair was between red and gold; his limbs were supple and straight. He had quite long arms which were particularly suited to drawing a sword and wielding it to great effect"[182]. Although we have no documented accounts of his training, it is certain that as a healthy, active prince Richard received military instruction and clearly excelled with hand-to-hand weapons. Certainly, the account of his prowess on the battlefield later in life is a testament to his prowess, and he was generally regarded as a fearsome and deadly warrior in personal combat.

With or without a sword in his hand, Richard carried himself with confidence and at the age of 14 he "was formally installed as Duke of Aquitaine"[183] as part of his father's plan to distribute his realms amongst his family prior

---

[181] Susan Flantzer, *Berengaria of Navarre, Queen of England*. http://www.unofficialroyalty.com/berengaria-of-navarre-queen-of-england/

[182] Frank McLynn, 2007, *Lionheart and Lackland: King Richard, King John and the Wars of Conquest*. Vintage, London, pp.24.

[183] John Gillingham, 1999, *Richard I*. pp.40.

to his death. In Henry's mind, by giving his sons different lands in his kingdom, they could "rule them in his absence, though still under his command"[184]. According to some, the subsequent "war without love"[185] was an inevitable result of King Henry's decentralisation of his kingdom and that "by dividing his domains and setting up his sons as rivals to his power... he was putting irresistible temptations in front of them"[186]. The stage was set for family infighting.

The first family squabble erupted in 1173 when Richard declared himself in rebellion along with some other nobles against his father, Henry having crowned him King of England in 1170[187]. Focused squarely on bringing his errant eldest son back under control, he overlooked the involvement of his other sons Richard and Geoffrey, and his own wife, Eleanora[188]. Although Henry II managed to quash the uprising and secure submission from his all his sons, it is hard to say whether Richard's subsequent role in Aquitaine acting "as his father's agent" was intended as a reward for his "obstinate resistance" or punishment for his rebellion[189]. Either way, it was a learning period for Richard and one in which he began to prove his capabilities as both a soldier and military leader. During the early 1180s, Richard was

[184] Jacob Abbott, 1902, *Richard I*. pp.42.

[185] John Gillingham, 1999, *Richard I*. pp.41.

[186] Frank McLynn, 2007, *Lionheart and Lackland*, pp.37.

[187] Frank McLynn, 2007, *Lionheart and Lackland*, pp.34.

[188] Dr. Mike Ibeji, 2011, *The Character and Legacy of Henry II*, http://www.bbc.co.uk/history/british/middle_ages/henryii_chara cter_01.shtml

[189] John Gillingham, 1999, *Richard I*. pp.52.

responsible for reclaiming the castles taken by the rebels, which included the "notoriously strong" Castillon-sur-Agen[190]. Richard commenced a two-month siege of the castle before finally securing the fortress and earning himself the title "Lionheart", in recognition of "his novel, brave and fierce leadership"[191].

Richard's star was rising, and he was fast becoming a force to be reckoned with, both politically and militarily, but his familial relations were a complicated distraction. In 1183, Richard was compelled to fight off an invasion of the Aquitaine lead by his brothers, Henry the Young and Geoffrey Duke of Brittany. It was much like young brothers fighting over their favourite toys, but in this case the profitable tax revenue of Richard's holdings meant real power and influence, and when they saw the opportunity to take it away from their brother Henry and Geoffrey raised private armies and attacked. Assisted by a military aide from his father, Richard managed to hold off his brothers' forces in a stalemate, but the conflict eventually ended when Henry the Young died of dysentery later that year[192]. With his elder brother's death, Richard became heir to the thrones of England, Anjou and Normandy and his father Henry II had a change of heart. He now decided that a redistribution of the family wealth and landholdings was in order, and insisted that the Aquitaine be handed over to Richard's younger

[190] Jann Tibbetts, 2016, *50 Great Military Leaders of All Time*, "Richard I of England". Alpha Editions, New Delhi.

[191] http://www.storiespreschool.com/richard_lionheart3.html

[192] Jann Tibbetts, 2016, *50 Great Military Leaders of All Time*, "Richard I of England".

brother John, "who had never had any territory to govern and was known by the unkind nickname "Lackland". Having just fought a series of battles to keep it, Richard was understandably reluctant to part with his mother's legacy and all that tax money. Richard sought the assistance of the new king of France, Louis's son Philip II with whom he would develop a long-lasting political allegiance and close personal relationship[193]. Phillip's late royal father had been humiliated both professionally and personally by Henry II, losing both land and his wife to the English king. Louis was only too happy to have an opportunity to not only take back some French prestige but also to win a score an emotional blow by helping Richard undermine and defeat his own father.

With Philip and his considerable military forces on his side, Richard challenged his father and defeated him in battle in 1189, securing his position as heir to the throne of England. He might have saved himself the effort, as Henry II ended up dying just days after the battle leaving Richard to be crowned King of England in 1189[194]. While fortunate for the Lionheart, this coronation would prove less auspicious for his nation. Soon after his ascension to the throne, Richard "turned his immense energies to preparations for a crusade"[195] in the Holy Lands of the Middle East, with the objective of ejecting the Moslems that had just captured Jerusalem. While it is "unlikely that anyone ever went on

---

[193] Melissa Snell, 2018, *Richard the Lionheart*.
https://www.thoughtco.com/richard-the-lionheart-1789371

[194] Melissa Snell, 2018, *Richard the Lionheart*.
https://www.thoughtco.com/richard-the-lionheart-1789371

[195] David Miller, 2003, *Richard the Lionheart: The Mighty Crusader*, Chapter 2.

crusade in more extraordinary style than Richard did", nothing could deter him from his new military project despite the many pressing issues the new king should have been handling domestically. As historian John Gillingham suggested "the more prudent thing would have been to stay at home"[196], but Richard felt compelled to respond to the fall of Jerusalem and thereby win glory and fame for himself as well as the favour of God. His throne was far from secure, with his younger brother John plotting behind the scenes waiting eagerly for his own opportunity to seize power. At the same time, his relationship with King Philip of France was precarious, hanging in the balance based on his long-time betrothal to his sister. Richard decided to leave England anyway and invited King Philip along so he could keep an eye on him, leaving for Sicily in 1190 on the first leg of his campaign.

Before he could depart, however, he needed funds. Going on crusade with his army and followers was an extremely expensive affair, and Richard needed to drain the royal treasury, directing that "Ships were to be bought and equipped for the purpose of transporting the troops to the East. Arms and ammunition were to be provided, and large supplies of food. Then the princes, and barons, and knights who were to accompany the expedition required very expensive armour and costly trappings and equipment of all sorts"[197]. So desperate was Richard for funds that he is quoted as having said, "I would have sold London if I could

---

[196] John Gillingham, 1999, *Richard I*. pp.6.

[197] Jacob Abbott, 1902, *Richard I*. pp.77-8.

find a buyer"[198]. Although Richard spent only a year or so in the Holy Land, during that period he managed to bring England to its financial knees, treating it "as a bank on which to draw and overdraw in order to finance his ambitious exploits abroad"[199]. Not only did Richard neglect his kingdom and the administration of it during this period, but he was also accused of being "brutal and stupid" in conduct during his time overseas[200]. Far from the "valiant, wise, liberal, merciful, just and... religious"[201] man of legend, the real Richard the Lionheart of the crusades has been described as "'negligent', 'undesigning, impolitic and violent"[202].

Despite neglecting his kingdom, Richard enjoyed some significant diplomatic as well as military achievements during his crusade. The first occurred at Messina in Sicily – his first port of call with King Phillip. Here, within a matter of days, Richard managed to negotiate the release of his sister Joan, the dowager Queen of Sicily, and secure her fortune by attacking the city and taking hostages. Having gained control of Messina, Richard and Philip made it their base prior to heading into Israel in an attempt to reclaim Jerusalem for the Christians.

---

[198] Jann Tibbetts, 2016, *50 Great Military Leaders of All Time*, "Richard I of England".

[199] John Gillingham, 1999, *Richard I*. pp.13.

[200] John Gillingham, 1999, *Richard I*. pp.11.

[201] John Gillingham, 1999, *Richard I*. pp.11.

[202] John Gillingham, 1999, *Richard I*. pp.2.

Flushed with success, Richard set sail with his army in April 1190, for good measure bringing along his new fiancée Berengaria of Navarre, and his sister Joan. Terrible weather conditions scattered his ships, and some of his fleet was wrecked on the coast of Cyprus. Arriving safely onshore without him, Berengaria and Joan were taken prisoner by the Cypriots and held for ransom in the expectation that the new English king would pay huge sums for them. Instead of paying up with gold, an enraged Richard gave the island cold steel and led "an impromptu and bloody conquest of the Christian island of Cyprus"[203] defeating the island's tyrannical leader Isaac Komnenos, in the process. It was a brutal and bloody campaign, and neither Richard's violent conquest of the island nor his subsequent sale of Cyprus painted him as a virtuous and noble leader; these were only two of the many controversies regarding his participation in the crusade[204]. This unfortunate distraction of killing and enslaving fellow Christians didn't curtail Richard's enthusiasm for killing and enslaving Moslems, and in the following year he finally arrived safely in front of Acre, ready to capture the city with his ally King Philip. Richard was reportedly very sick, but this didn't stop him from participating in the siege of Acre with gusto. Legend has it that although so sick with scurvy he couldn't walk, Richard "picked off guards on the walls with a crossbow, while being

---

[203] John D. Hosler PhD, 2015, *The Military Legacy of Richard the Lionheart: Constructed Heroism and Selective Memory in Modern English Historiograph.* Delivered at the Annual Meeting of the Society for Military History in Montgomery, AL (April 2015), pp.6.

[204] John Hosler, Encyclopedia of War, "Richard I, King [of England] 1157-99. pp2.
https://www.academia.edu/11812444/Richard_I_king_of_England

carried on a stretcher"[205] which if true speaks volumes about his determination to carry his expedition forward.

In addition to his military forces arrayed on the battlefield, Richard also attempted to use his charm and negotiation skills to end the siege of Acre and requested a meeting with the Muslim leader Saladin, Sultan of Egypt and Syria. His overtures at talking things out were ultimately met with rejection, with Saladin responding "Kings meet together only after the conclusion of an accord"[206]. Arbitration attempts thwarted, Richard had no choice but to win on military grounds – a challenge that he embraced with all the passion and enthusiasm of a man whose enemies described him as "the most remarkable man of the age"[207]. What followed was the bloody siege of Acre, in which thousands of men on both sides as they fought for control of the city. While not as costly as Pyrrhus' victories over Rome, the siege of Acre cost Richard dearly in terms of his friendship and political alliance with Philip as well as his own reputation[208].

At Acre, Philip fell ill with a fever that caused "so fierce a heat... that every nail fell off his fingers and all the

---

[205] Hela Tamir, Israel, 1995, *History in a Nutshell: Highlighting the Wars and Military History*. The Lockman Foundation, pp.38.

[206] John Man, *Saladin: The Life, the Legend and the Islamic Empire*. Transworld Publishers, London, pp.278.

[207] John Gillingham, 1999, *Richard I*. pp.16.

[208] John Hosler, Encyclopedia of War, "Richard I, King [of England] 1157-99. pp2.

hair from his brow"[209]. The French king had reached his breaking point and wanted to quit the expedition and return to France, and soon Philip and Richard found themselves pursuing very different agendas. Once their relationship deteriorated into open hostility, the two kings agreed that Philip would depart and head home, after promising that he would not "do any harm to his [Richard's] men or lands so long as King Richard continued his pilgrimage"[210]. After Philip set sail home, Richard continued his peace negotiations with Saladin, but the Sultan kept changing the terms of the agreement and delaying the moment when prisoners would be exchanged. Frustrated by what seemed like endless postponements and delays to buy time, Richard retracted his promise to release all his prisoners into Saladin's care, instead of ordering that they brought before him at the foot of Mount Ayyadieh. The prisoners "numbered more than three thousand and were bound with ropes", and as soon as they arrived Richard set his soldiers on them, and they "flung themselves upon them all at once and massacred them with sword and lance in cold blood"[211]. Spectacularly merciless and bloody, the slaughter of the unarmed and tied prisoners is generally overlooked in popular histories of Richard, but at the time did much to enhance his fearsome reputation while at the same time being ruthlessly practical as he ensured he wouldn't have to care for the large numbers of enemy prisoners or leave them behind[212]. To modern eyes, it

[209] Thomas Andrew Archer, 1889, *The Crusade of Richard, 1189-92*. G.P. Putnam's Sons, pp.117.

[210] Thomas Andrew Archer, 1889, *The Crusade of Richard, 1189-92*, pp.120.

[211] Thomas Andrew Archer, 1889, *The Crusade of Richard, 1189-92*, pp.130

[212] Unknown, 2018, *The Massacre at Ayyadieh – Richard the Lionheart not so lionhearted*. https://thehistoryjar.com/2018/08/20/the-massacre-at-ayyadieh-richard-the-lionheart-not-so-lionhearted/

is difficult to correlate Richard's behaviour towards his prisoners in this episode with his reputation as a man who "had fortitude as well as courage, coolness as well as daring, skill as well as valour"[213]. Certainly there was not much valour or courage required to cut down the helpless men that day.

Following the slaughter at Acre and the loss of his ally King Philip, Richard was still determined to continue his crusade although it is hard to say for what purpose. According to some, Richard's primary goal had never been to reclaim Jerusalem at all, but instead he wanted "to raid Egyptian territory" although in doing so he "was setting a dangerous precedent of turning crusade armies toward targets far removed from Jerusalem"[214]. Other historians suggest that Richard showed admirable restraint in declining to attack Jerusalem, choosing instead to inflict on Saladin and his men "a blow which should disable them for a long period"[215]. Perhaps, in the final analysis, the English King was seeking a combination of glory as well as religious fulfilment. Although the Third Crusade is one of the highlights of Richard's life and career, it was far from the resounding success Richard may have anticipated and expected. Certainly he had faced and defeated the formidable Saladin; he had won some impressive victories

---

[213] George P.R. James cited in John D. Hosler PhD, 2015, *The Military Legacy of Richard the Lionheart*, pp.4.

[214] Michael Markowski, 1997, "Richard Lionheart: bad king, bad crusader?" USA Journal of Medieval History, Vol 23, No. 4, pp.355.

[215] John D. Hosler PhD, 2015, *The Military Legacy of Richard the Lionheart*, pp.7.

thanks to his capacity for martial strategy, but as a result back home his kingdom was in crisis, and his personal relationships were in shambles. Far from the Middle Eastern battlefields, his brother John and former ally King Philip were poised to attack England, and Richard had little choice but to reach an agreement with Saladin and head for home with a complete victory over the Muslim forces out of reach.

Eventually packing up and sailing back to Europe, Richard's ships were battered by bad weather and shipwrecks, leading to his humiliating capture and his imprisonment in Vienna where he was locked up and held for ransom. It was up to his subjects back home to secure his release at great cost; heavy taxes were imposed to raise the necessary money to have him set free. According to some reports, the "people of England undertook the task not only with willingness but with alacrity, raising nearly a million dollars to rescue their king[216]. This is somewhat surprising given that Richard has been repeatedly referred to as "an ill son, an ill father, an ill brother and a worse king"[217] in some contemporary texts. Despite his critics, Richard appears to have been much-loved by his countrymen and continued to rule over England and Normandy for some five years before his death in 1199, during which open warfare had finally broken out between England and France. Right up until he died, Richard persistently battled his former ally Philip, and it was while he was laying siege to a French castle that he was struck in the shoulder by a crossbow arrow. Although the wound itself was superficial, it soon became

[216] Jacob Abbott, 1902, *Richard I*. pp.330.

[217] John Gillingham, 1999, *Richard I*. pp.12.

infected and "death drew nigh" and "he was overwhelmed with remorse, and he died at length in anguish and despair"[218]. The Lionheart was no more.

As a man Richard has been described as "vain... devious and self-centred"[219], and as a king, it has been said he was neglectful and as a son and husband, selfish and ruthless. As a warrior, however, "Richard is certainly entitled to rank amongst the most distinguished of ancient or of modern times"[220]. Certainly King Richard earned the title "the Lionheart", and although he may not have really been a particularly likeable man or the most beloved of English monarchs, all in all during his lifetime he lived up to his name until the very end.

---

[218] Jacob Abbott, 1902, *Richard I*. pp.335.

[219] Michael Markowski, 1997, "Richard Lionheart: bad king, bad crusader?", pp.352.

[220] John D. Hosler PhD, 2015, *The Military Legacy of Richard the Lionheart*, pp.3.

TOMOE GOZEN

"Samurai Woman Warrior"

An introduction to the story of Tomoe Gozen means a journey back in time to the Heian period of Japanese history. Recalled as the country's Golden Era, the Heian period was a long and peaceful one, lasting from 794 BC until the 12ᵗʰ century. Political power was firmly in the hands of the Fujiwara clan who carefully controlled who took on the role of Emperor, generally preferring a child ruler to an adult as it enabled them to orchestrate the nation's affairs more effectively as "the power behind the throne". Although the Fujiwara were challenged by rival family clans from time to time, it was, for the most part, a quiet and prosperous time in Japanese history. This was a period that allowed for the development of Japanese as a written language and the proliferation of cultural achievements, from novels to art and fashion[221].

Women of all classes had certain freedoms during the Heian era that would be denied them in later times, and

---

[221] https://www.ancient.eu/Heian_Period/

could appeal for divorce and remarry afterwards; they were also entitled to their own property[222]. As Buddhism became increasingly influential in Japanese society, so the position of women would be quickly diminished until the religion's fundamental conviction that women were evil and needed to be dominated reduced them to an entirely submissive and subordinate status[223]. Tomoe Gozen was fortunate to be born at a time when women still enjoyed some freedom, although exactly when that was is hard to say, as there are few references to Gozen from her lifetime. She, like many of the *"onna-bugeisha"* or women warriors, of the period has been all but written out of history[224].

The Samurai emerged as a new social class during the Heian period, and women who were Samurai wives or were destined to become Samurai brides were trained in the art of war and weapons so they could defend their homes and livelihoods while their husbands were away fighting. Tomoe Gozen was one of this new breed of woman. In addition to military training, Gozen would also have been taught how to perform the complex duties of a housewife, including everything from how to manage an estate to how to conduct a tea ceremony[225]. In terms of her military training, Gozen

[222] https://study.com/academy/lesson/women-in-heian-period-japan.html

[223] http://www.inquiriesjournal.com/articles/286/women-in-ancient-japan-from-matriarchal-antiquity-to-acquiescent-confinement

[224] https://broadly.vice.com/en_us/article/a383aj/female-samurai-onna-bugeisha-japan

[225] Margaret Everton, 2014. *Lady of Legacy: Tomoe Gozen.* https://darlingmagazine.org/lady-of-legacy-tomoe-gozen/

would have learnt how to wield a *naginata*, a curved sword at the end of a long pole which when handled correctly could keep the enemy well beyond arm's length while delivering a fatal blow[226]. When fully armed, Gozen probably also carried a small dagger called a tanto, which looked a lot like a tiny sword although it's unlikely that Gozen had it on display as "the traditional female costume allowed many possibilities for concealing weapons"[227].

While the women of the imperial court whiled away their days coddled in kimonos, composing poetry, the women of the evolving Samurai class were more like the pioneers of America's Wild West. Alongside their husbands, they settled new lands and fought for them as necessary[228]. Belonging to the Samurai or *bushi* class gave these women noble standing and the ability to advance in military rank. As in the case of Gozen, they could rise as high as to command an army as a general. Tomoe was an exceptional example of this; however; most Samurai women were trained only to the degree necessary to ensure they could protect their homes and families. These women were known as *onna-bugeisha,* and Gozen is often referred to as such, although she actually belonged to a more elite group, known as *onna-musha.* These

---

[226] Ibid.

[227] Stephen Turnbull, 2010. *Samurai Women 1184-1877.* Osprey Publishing, Oxford, UK, pp.22.
https://books.google.co.za/books?id=X7GHCwAAQBAJ&printsec=frontcover&dq=tomoe+gozen&hl=en&sa=X&ved=0ahUKEwiolc-C67jgAhVileAKHTOsD1cQ6AEIWjAI#v=onepage&q=dagger&f=false

[228] Ellis Amdur, 2002. Women Warriors of Japan: The Role of the Arms-Bearing Women in Japanese History. *Journal of Asian Martial Arts,* vol. 5, no. 2, 1996. https://koryu.com/library/wwj1.html

are women who fought alongside the Samurai in offensive battle, rather than staying at home to defend their families and holdings in their husband's absence.

As Gozen studied and matured, so her connection to the powerful family of Minamoto, or Kiso, no Yoshinaka would shape her destiny. Gozen's mother was wet-nurse to Kiso, which was considered a significant honour and also gave Gozen's family considerable political influence, which might explain Gozen securing the unusual position as an *onna-musha*. As the family of Kiso's wet-nurse or *menoto*, Gozen would have profited from the influence she had over Kiso as he became a man and would probably have also enjoyed a close relationship with her "milk sibling"[229]. While Kiso was born in competition with his blood siblings, Tomoe was no threat to his political power, and the close proximity of the two children could have easily developed into a close bond. The exact nature of the relationship that developed between Gozen and Kiso is unclear although there are certain indications that suggest they never married, but more on that later.

Certainly, Gozen's relationship with Kiso is an integral part of her story and her abilities as an archer, swordswoman, and horsewoman stood her in good stead to be by his side through the most traumatic events of his life - of which there were many. Kiso was a key player in the

---

[229] Tomas D. Conlan, "Thicker Than Blood: The Social and Political Significance of Wet Nurses in Japan, 950-1330". *Harvard Journal of Asiatic Studies*. Vol. 65, No.1 (June 2005), pp.

Genpei War which raged between two rival clans between the years 1180 and 1185. During the Heian period, the imperial court had been dominated by the Fugiwara clan but, as emperors were particularly fertile (some produced up to 50 children), the royal family became too large and unwieldy, not to mention expensive to maintain. As conflict within the clan emerged, so the rival factions enlisted the assistance of distinguished Samurai warriors, one side recruiting the Minamoto family and the other side the Taira[230].

The rivalry between these two clans had been raging for some years already. As far back as 1159, fueled by jealousy over Taira no Kiyamori's growing prestige following the Heiji Disturbance, Minamoto no Yoshitomo had seized the throne in Kiyamori's absence. Taira soon rectified the situation, killed Yoshimoto in the process and establishing his own clan as the most powerful in all of Japan[231]. Over the next few years, Kiyamori's position became increasingly unsustainable as his important allies, like Go-Shirakawa, began to fall by the wayside. In 1180, Kiyamori placed his toddler of a grandson, the two-year-old Antoku, on the throne. The Minamotos were furious and with the help of Go-Shirakawa's son Mochito, launched a full-on offensive against the Kiyamoris, marking the beginning of the Genpei War[232].

---

[230] https://www.britannica.com/place/Japan/The-Heian-period-794-1185

[231] https://www.ancient.eu/Genpei_War/

[232] Ibid.

While the main focus of the conflict raged on between the Taira and the rebel army led by Minamoto no Yoritomo, Kiso was leading his own rebellion. Declaring himself SEII TAISHOGUN or a general of the highest possible rank, Kiso was something of a loose cannon and even his cousin, the Minamoto clan leader Yoritomo, was thinking over strategies for quelling his enthusiasm for battle and bringing him back under control, if not outright having him killed. While his own kin was considering his assassination, Kiso continued his offensive against the Taira, with Gozen at his side[233]. While Kiso planned his military strategy, Yoritomo was involved in some fairly convoluted political negotiations which saw him ally with Go-Shirakawa, who he believed would not only help him subdue the Taira but also assist him in containing his zealous cousin[234].

The only historical document describing Tomoe Gozen and her role in the Genpei War is that of *The Heiki Monogatari*, an epic story of the War compiled from Japanese oral accounts. According to the Heike, Tomoe Gozen was one of two women who accompanied Kiso into battle, but her participation became unique after her fellow warrior, Yamabuki, fell sick and remained behind in the capital. The Heiki describes Gozen as a beautiful woman and "fearless rider" who could handle a sword so effectively that "she was

---

[233] https://en.wikipedia.org/wiki/Battle_of_Kurikara

[234] Stephen Turnbull, 2016. *The Gempei War 1180-85: The Great Samurai Civil War*. Osprey Publishing, Oxford, UK, pp.46

a match for a thousand warriors"[235] which was high praise indeed. Nevertheless, several sources confirm that she was present at the Battle of Kurikara, loyally supporting Kiso as he engineered a cunning victory.

The Taira army had divided into two, with the main body of 70,000 men crossing over the mountains into modern-day Ishikawa. They far outnumbered Kiso's troops, and the general predicted that due to their large numbers, the Taira would attempt a "decisive battle"[236]. The odds did not favour Kiso in a direct engagement against such superior numbers, so Kiso considered and then implemented a master plan of deception to both convince his enemy that his own force was even larger than theirs, as well as keep them immobilised on higher ground. When this was accomplished, Kiso planned to then ambush the Taira and "under cover of darkness I will drive their whole army over into Kurikara valley below"[237]. He then sent soldiers carrying 30 white banners to the top of Kurosaka hill, where they would be seen. His plan worked and the Taira, "imagining themselves to be confronted by superior force" decided to avoid the risk of being out-flanked and rested in the mountains of Tonami[238].

---

[235] *The Heiki Monogatari*, 1918. Asiatic Society of Japan. Vol XLVI, part II, pp.121.

[236] Ibid, pp.25-26

[237] Ibid, pp.25-26

[238] Ibid, pp.25-26

While the Taira rested, Kiso positioned his army and organised his forces into three units, each of which overlooked the treacherous valley. Following the Battle of Kurikara, this valley would become known as Hell Valley[239]. The units were commanded by Kiso's most trusted and skilled generals, including Tomoe Gozen herself. Kiso kept the Taira engaged in traditional samurai conflict but was "careful not to let the fight develop into an all-out melee"[240]. Kiso was biding his time, waiting for night to fall to launch his attack. As dusk descended, he sent one of his divisions to surprise and attack the Taira army on their left flank while their right side was compromised by a herd of enraged oxen. According to Turnbull, evidence suggests that Kiso and his men tied torches to the horns of 100 oxen. When they heard the clash of the unit attacking the left of the Taira forces, the torches were lit, and the cattle stampeded straight at the enemy forces; the frantic herd rampaged right into the Taira army[241]. Having restricted the Taira on both sides, Kiso then launched a frontal attack to drive the Taira back into Hell Valley.

As the Taira were forced to flee, night had fallen to the extent that they could no longer see the road in front of them and the soldiers stumbled into Kiso's trap with "horses and men falling on top of one another and piling up in heaps". According to *The Heiki Monogatari*, the Battle of Kurikara ended with some "seventy thousand horsemen of

---

[239] Stephen Turnbull, 2016. *The Gempei War 1180-85: The Great Samurai Civil War*, pp.47.

[240] Ibid, pp.48.

[241] Ibid, pp.48.

the Heiki perishing, buried in this one deep valley". The next confrontations between Kiso and the Taira would not be so easily won, but Kiso could be certain of one thing – the undying loyalty of his attendant/lover/concubine/wife, Tomoe Gozen.

As little as we know of Gozen's martial achievements, we know even less about her marital ones. Although many sources refer to Gozen as Kiso's wife, there is no documentary proof for this, but there is evidence to suggest that it's probably not true. Some Japanese texts suggest that Gozen actually married another Samurai named Wada Yoshimori, while others indicate that she was the lover of another general who fought at the Battle of Kurikara, Higuchi Kanemitsu[242]. Although these stories are less prevalent than the one about her marriage to Kiso, they are in some ways more believable. After all, if Yoshimori had a son it stands to reason that he needed a wife; if anyone were going to bestow legendary fighting powers onto Wada's son Asahina Saburō Yoshihide, Gozen would be a popular choice. Not only was Asahina Yoshihide celebrated for his prowess as a warrior, but he was also believed to have superhuman powers that enabled him to perform incredible feats. Irrespective of what her actual personal relationships were Gozen lived, fought and died for Kiso, although he denied her right to die by his side.

---

[242] Stephen T. Brown, 1988. "From Woman Warrior to Peripatetic Entertainer". *Harvard Journal of Asiatic Studies*, Vol. 58, No. 1 (June 1998), pp. 186.

Kiso fought his last battle at Awazu, but it wasn't against the rival Tairu clan. Instead, it was against his own family. After his victory at the Battle of Kurikara, Kiso marched his forces to the capital of Kyoto where the Tairu clan were protecting their young emperor, Antoku. The Tairu fled, taking the child emperor with them. Kiso's troops were advancing quickly on Kyoto from the north, while another Minamoto force was rapidly approaching from the east[243]. Yorimoto had sent a unit forward under the leadership of Yukiiye. Although Yorimoto's motives weren't entirely pure and he was both suspicious and jealous of his cousin Kiso and his victories, he was welcomed into Kiso's camp as one of his own. Yukiiye was by many accounts "an unscrupulous schemer" however, and plotted to goad the two cousins until they were set on a collision course that would destroy them both, leaving him the spoils of their war[244].

At this time in Japanese history, the country was rife with political scheming, and Yukiiye wasn't the only one hatching plots to increase his personal power. Emperor Go-Shirikawa, who had defected to the Minamoto side of the two warring factions, ordered Kiso and Yukiiye to join forces. This hadn't been part of Kiso's plan – he wanted to secure Kyoto for himself in the hopes that it would give him the advantage he needed to take control of the Minamoto

---

[243] Sir George Bailey Sansom, *A History of Japan to 1334*. Volume 1, pp.294. https://books.google.co.za/books?redir_esc=y&id=t2c4t4yw21gC &q=Yoshinaka+#v=onepage&q=Kurikara&f=false

[244] Frank & Kilkuchi Brinkley, "Fall of Yoshinaka", *A History of the Japanese People From the Earliest Time to the End of the Meiji Era*. Library of Alexandria, USA.

clan himself. According to some sources Kiso and Yukiiye
did discuss possible collusion and possibly even planned to
set up a "government in their own northern provinces"[245]. It
seems that Yorimoto had made a wise choice when he
selected Yukiiye though, and he duly reported Kiso's
ambitions of power Go-Shirikawa. While the emperor
pretended his support for Kiso was unwavering, behind his
back he was "privately relying on Yorimoto"[246].

Not only did Go-Shirikawa immediately report Kiso's
possible plan to seize power for himself rather than support
the Minamoto clan to Yorimoto, but he also "appointed him
the high office of sei-i tai-shogun (barbarian-subduing
generalissimo)" and gave him control over all the lands
previously held by the Tairu[247]. Given his status, Yorimoto
couldn't ignore the threat that Kiso's ambitions posed,
especially when combined with his cousin's arrogance and
inherent rebellious nature. Upon receiving the news of a
possible conspiracy against him from the emperor, he sent
his two younger brothers and "myriads of men" to confront
and subdue Kiso's rebellion[248]. Kiso found himself in a
dangerous situation. Not only was the majority of his own
army far away fighting the threat of the turncoat Yukiiye, but
he also happened to be headquartered in a city whose
inhabitants despised him while his own clansmen were
advancing against him. With the forces of Yoshitsune and

---

[245] Sir George Bailey Sansom, *A History of Japan to 1334*. Volume 1, pp.296.

[246] Frank & Kilkuchi Brinkley, "Fall of Yoshinaka".

[247] Ibid.

[248] Sir George Bailey Sansom, *A History of Japan to 1334*. Volume 1, pp.296.

Noriyori fast advancing on his position, Kiso made a

desperate and fateful decision on what he should do next –
he fled for his life.

Kiso, Gozen and four other famous generals said to
be Gozen's brothers launched an attack to capture Go-
Shirikawa and headed south. The Battle of Awazu wouldn't
be Gozen's first fight; according to *The Heike Monogatari*,
"[M]any times had she taken the field... and won matchless
renown in encounters with the bravest captains"[249]. Kiso
was in good company with his most trusted and capable
warrior officers.

Fortune had turned back in the Tairu clan's favour,
and with his own clan marching against him Kiso provided
them the time they needed to reorganise and regroup for the
next decisive battle. Meanwhile, Yoshinaka was joined by
Imai Kanehira, his "milk brother", generally assumed to
actually be Gozen's full brother by blood. The two were
firm friends and cohorts and according to *The Heike
Monogatari*, greeted each other joyfully. It is during this
reunion that Kiso gives his reason for abandoning the fight
at Mizushima[250] saying "I was so anxious about you that I
did not stop to fight to the death in the Rokujo Kawara, but

---

[249] *The Heiki Monogatari*, 1918. Asiatic Society of Japan. Vol XLVI, part II,
pp.121.

[250] Sir George Bailey Sansom, *A History of Japan to 1334*. Volume 1, pp.296.

turned my back on a host of foes". Imai replied that he similarly, had left a battle unfinished in order to aid Kiso. It seemed that the two friends and allies were destined to die in

battle together, and Gozen was there for the glorious family affair.

With just a tiny force of just 300 samurai warriors facing Noriyori's attacking army of 6,000 soldiers, Kiso led Gozen and his men into battle, likely knowing it would be his last fight. Regardless, Kiso cried joyfully to his men that they should be inspired by the prospect of noble and bloody death. He encouraged them on with the battle cry "if we must die, what death could be better than to fall outnumbered by valiant enemies? Forward then!"[251] Although ridiculously outnumbered, Kiso's troops charged into the battle like wild men; with flailing swords and attacking furiously. The force of their charge managed to break through the first line of Noriyori's defence, hacking their way into the densely packed ranks of the enemy where they kept on moving forward, pushing into Noriyori's second line of troops. As they surged on, Kiso's forces were swallowed by the sheer mass of the enemy around them, and as they began to die they were reduced quickly from 300 to just 50, then just five men left. Among Kiso's last men standing was the valiant Gozen. During her part of the battle she had managed to kill a samurai known as Uchida Ieyoshi. Little is known of this man, although one source refers to him as "a gigantic warrior",[252] and his main claim to

[251] *The Heiki Monogatari*, 1918. Asiatic Society of Japan. Vol XLVI, part II, pp.123.

[252] Frank & Kilkuchi Brinkley, "Fall of Yoshinaka".

fame seems to have been meeting his death at the hands of this legendary woman warrior in single combat.

Looking around his remaining five samurai, Kiso knew the battle was lost and urged Gozen to leave saying "As you are a woman, it were better that you now make your escape. I have made up my mind to die, either by the hand of the enemy or by mine own, and how would Yoshinaka be shamed if in his last fight he died with a woman?"[253] Assuming that this account is fundamentally true, it is this that indicates the true status of the relationship between Kiso and Gozen. Had they been married, Gozen would have stayed by his side and if Kiso has committed suicide - she would have died at his side as well[254]. Despite Kiso's insistence, Gozen refused to leave him and drew her horse to one side to wait. Although most sources attest to the fact that it would have brought shame on a samurai to have a woman present at his death, one American historian suggests that Kiso probably feared that she would die a more glorious death than he and that this was his motivation for sending her away[255].

As Gozen sat and waited, another force of enemy reinforcements arrived on the battlefield, consisting of 30 mounted warriors led by "a strong and valiant samurai" known as Onda-no-Hachiro Moroshige[256]. Gozen didn't

[253] *The Heiki Monogatari*, 1918. Asiatic Society of Japan. Vol XLVI, part II, pp.123.

[254] https://en.wikipedia.org/wiki/Seppuku#Ritual

[255] Stephen T. Brown, 1988. "From Woman Warrior to Peripatetic Entertainer", pp.188.

[256] Ibid.

hesitate as she saw the horsemen arrive and launched herself at the leader, dragging him from his horse. Pinning Moroshige's head to the pommel of her saddle, Gozen promptly beheaded him while the enemy soldiers stared in amazed disbelief. Her enemy dead, she stripped off her armour and finally followed Kiso's order and moved away, leaving him to die. Rather than wait for one of his many enemies to kill him, Imai urged Kiso to go off into the forest and find a quiet place where he could take his own life. Although the tradition of seppuku or hari-kari suicide would only become well-known in the 17th century, it was not uncommon before this for samurai to take their own lives in order to avoid being taken captive and potentially tortured by the enemy[257]. Kiso refused, proclaiming that he didn't turn his back on his adversaries at Rakuji-kawara to die alone. He insisted to his friend that he and Imai stay and die together. Concerned for his friend' honour, Imai burst into tears and pleaded with Kiso not to risk an "unworthy death... at the hands of some low retainer".

Before his enemies moved in for the kill, Kiso capitulated and rode through the opposing warriors into the forest while Imai created a diversion, leading the oncoming Minamoto force away from Kiso with the words "so take my head and show it to him [Yoritomo], anyone who can!"[258]. Certainly they tried to accommodate him, but Yorimoto's men failed to kill Imai as his armour proved too thick for their arrows. Riding away, he was able to escape unharmed

---

[257] https://en.wikipedia.org/wiki/Seppuku#Ritual

[258] *The Heiki Monogatari*, 1918. Asiatic Society of Japan. Vol XLVI, part II, pp.124.

while Kiso was left to wander through the forest as night fell across the battlefield. The evening was cold, and everything was covered in a thin layer of ice, making it impossible for Kiso to distinguish a trail through the boggy ground. Eventually his exhausted horse stumbled into the mud of a rice field, sinking up to his neck and floundering to get out. Kiso urged him on, but soon his enemies caught up to him and the drowning horse. Kiso's ambitions of power were ended with an arrow shot into his face[259], after which he was beheaded. Upon hearing that Kiso's head was now a trophy and his friend was truly dead, Imai flung himself from his horse to fall on his sword in grief.

Some sources suggest that Kiso wanted Gozen to survive his last battle so she could tell the story of his death and "hold memorial services for the repose of his departed spirit". In this version of events, having removed her armour, Gozen went directly to Shinano to inform Kiso's family of his demise. Having completed this final act of service to Kiso, most believe Gozen went immediately to a monastery where she lived out the rest of her days as a nun, "devoting the rest of her days to prayers for his spirit[260]. Although this is the most popular story relating to Gozen's life after Kiso's death, others believe that she was forced into service as a prostitute when her future husband Wada Yoshimori, attacked her with a club and made her his concubine. According to this version of events, it was only after her son Asahina Saburō Yoshihide died in 1213 that she became a nun and remained one until her death at the

---

[259] Ibid, pp.124.

[260] Frank & Kilkuchi Brinkley, "Fall of Yoshinaka".

great age of 91[261]. One other account suggests that Tomoe first avenged Kiso's death, murdering his enemies one by one before taking his head and walking out into the ocean with it, thus getting her final wish of dying by his side[262]. Clearly the woman has inspired many and varied legends.

Although documentary evidence of Gozen's life and deeds may be thin and limited, it hasn't dulled her impact on her importance as a historical figure in Japan where she continues to be the inspiration for many theatrical productions, books, and video games. The mystery that surrounds her upbringing and lifetime make her all the more appealing as a representative of "female resilience and courage".[263] There are some historians that may doubt that Gozen actually lived and that if she did she wasn't the mythical warrior figure that she has become. Others point to the rich, storytelling traditions of the Japanese people as being fundamentally based on real historical accounts and that the legends of Gozen the warrior samurai grew out of the events of her lifetime, even if their proportions now have reached almost "superhero" status. Whatever the truth really is, it seems that "whether she lived or not may not be important; her loyalty, bravery, and strength make her an important role model"[264].

---

[261] Stephen Turnbull, 2010. *Samurai Women 1184-1877*, pp.37.

[262] https://www.ancient-origins.net/history-famous-people/tomoe-gozen-fearsome-japanese-female-warrior-12th-century-002974

[263] https://darlingmagazine.org/lady-of-legacy-tomoe-gozen/

[264] https://sites.google.com/site/floresworldhistory7/the-rise-of-the-warrior-class-in-japan/reading-further-tomoe-gozen--history-or-legend

JULIUS CAESAR

"The First Roman Caesar"

Thousands of years after he lived, the name Julius Caesar still echoes through history as one of history's greatest figures even if most people today aren't exactly sure who he was or what he did. Arriving into the world in 100 BC to a noble Roman family, Caesar was not born directly into political power. Although his people the Julii Caesares were members of the aristocracy as a result of their lineage, his father wielded little power or influence[265]. The *Historia Augustus* suggests that Caesar's name derived from the fact that "he was brought into the world after his mother's death and by an incision in her abdomen"[266], but in reality, his mother Aurelia Cotta played a significant role in his life and lived with him until her death in 54 BC[267]. His father

---

[265] Arnold Joseph Toynbee, "Julius Caesar: Roman Rule", *Encyclopaedia Britannica*, https://www.britannica.com/biography/Julius-Caesar-Roman-ruler

[266] Aelius Spartianus, Iulius Capitolinus, Vulcacius Gallicanus, *Historia Augusta*, "The Life of Aelius", pp.86 http://penelope.uchicago.edu/Thayer/E/Roman/Texts/Historia Augusta/Aelius*.html

[267] Richard A. Billows, 2009, *Julius Caesar: The Colossus of Rome*. Routledge, London, pp.34.

GAIUS Julius Caesar had much less opportunity to influence his son's life, dying when Caesar was just 16 years old[268]. As a member of the Roman elite and leading families, Caesar received a classical education and learned to read and write both Latin and Greek, while focusing on the art of rhetoric, of which his tutor M. Antonius Gnipho was an acknowledged master[269]. This was a fortunate investment into his future career as a politician, as Caesar seems to have decided on entering public life at an early age and would come to rely on his "ability to speak fluently, effectively and persuasively"[270]. Julius Caesar would go on to become one of the most effective leaders of men in history.

As Caesar was growing up from a child into young man, he would have been observing and learning of the political ramifications that surrounded the social and civil wars of the time which undoubtedly made a significant impression on him, shaping both his perspective and his character[271]. Republican Rome had been ravaged by civil war, eventually won by the brutal General Sulla. Victorious at last, Sulla began the customary Roman practice of clearing out his remaining political enemies, generally by either having them assassinated or exiled. The young Caesar just happened to be married to the daughter of one of Sulla's

[268] C. Suetonius Tranquillus, *The Lives of Twelve Caesars*. Loeb Classical Library, 1913, pp.4.
http://penelope.uchicago.edu/Thayer/E/Roman/Texts/Suetoniu s/12Caesars/Julius*.html

[269] Richard A. Billows, 2009, *Julius Caesar: The Colossus of Rome*, pp.34.

[270] Richard A. Billows, 2009, *Julius Caesar: The Colossus of Rome*, pp.34.

[271] Richard A. Billows, 2009, *Julius Caesar: The Colossus of Rome*, pp.38.

bitterest political opponents, which wasn't particularly favourable for any prospects of long life or successful career advancement in the new regime. Caesar went before Sulla personally, and his intelligence and charm impressed the dictator to the point where he decided not to have Julius executed after all. Instead, he insisted that Caesar set aside his wife Cornelia, thereby severing his association with the family of his enemy Cinna. Despite his youth, Caesar refused to be bullied by the dictator, staying faithful to his wife and risking everything. Staying loyal to Cinna's family, Caesar "was held to be one of the opposite party"[272] and although allowed to live, Sulla compelled him to give up both "his wife's dowry, and his family inheritances".

To escape his precarious personal situation, Caesar enlisted in the Roman military and left Rome's political intrigues behind until "his near kinsmen Mamercus Aemilius and Aurelius Cotta" managed to persuade the brooding Sulla to allow him to return to Rome. After much lobbying, Sulla agreed reluctantly and gave what could be construed as a "shrewd forecast" when he responded to their pleas with the words "Have your way and take him; only bear in mind that the man you are so eager to save will one day deal the death blow to the cause of the aristocracy"[273]. Sulla may have been a brutal military strongman, but he was an excellent judge of character and saw in Julius Caesar an even greater threat to the Roman Republic than he himself was.

---

[272] C. Suetonius Tranquillus, *The Lives of Twelve Caesars*, pp.4.

[273] C. Suetonius Tranquillus, *The Lives of Twelve Caesars*, pp.5.

His security won by his family, Caesar returned to Roman and became more politically active, where he "acquired a reputation as a bit of a dandy" and "lived in the grandest style"[274]. After Sulla's death, Caesar committed himself to advancing his political aims through a legal career and became a criminal prosecutor. In 77 BC, Caesar was instrumental in the prosecution of one Cornelius Dolabella, who was charged for extortion. Caesar faced one of Rome's most experienced and impressive orators, defence attorney Q. Hortensius. The trial did not go Caesar's way, but although Dolabella was subsequently acquitted Caesar's prosecution speech "remained long in circulation as a literary classic"[275]. Still a political hotbed of ruthless politics, Julius found himself the target of an angry Roman public for his failure to indict Dolabella and again decided it might be best to leave the city before something nasty happened to him. Packing up, he left for a school in Rhodes where he wanted to study under the famous Greek rhetorician, Apollonius Molo[276]. On route to his scholarly destination, Caesar was to have an encounter that would illustrate much about his character.

While sailing across the Mediterranean Sea, Caesar's ship was intercepted and captured. At the time, an organised group of pirates virtually controlled the eastern sea and were known to be ruthless with how they treated Roman nobility, who were generally taken prisoner and ransomed for large sums back to their wealthy families. Some elite prisoners

[274] Richard A. Billows, 2009, *Julius Caesar: The Colossus of Rome*, pp.63.

[275] Richard A. Billows, 2009, *Julius Caesar: The Colossus of Rome*, pp.62.

[276] C. Suetonius Tranquillus, *The Lives of Twelve Caesars*, pp.7.

would "invoke the protection of Rome" by proclaiming that as Roman citizens they should be released immediately. The pirates had a simple method of compliance with any hostages that claimed this protection – they would "release" the prisoner to the sea and the sharks by throwing them off the ship without delay or fanfare. Caesar knew better and quietly went into captivity at the pirates' island stronghold.

The pirates interviewed Julius about his family, their holdings and their wealth so that they could determine an appropriate ransom demand for his release. When he was told that he was worth 20 "talents" of silver (approximately 1700 kilograms) to them, "Caesar reportedly laughed at this demand, telling the pirates... he was worth at least 50 talents"[277]. Pleased but sceptical, the pirates sent out messengers to meet with Caesar's family with the promise that if they didn't come up with the money, he would be executed. Weeks passed, and as his family and entourage scrambled to raise the money for his ransom, Julius spent his time as a prisoner becoming a favourite guest celebrity at the pirate base, entertaining his captors with lectures on the law, politics and history and reportedly won large audiences and admirers. He also learned all he could about where their base was while openly teasing them that once he was free, he would certainly return and have every last one of them executed by crucifixion.

---

[277] Richard A. Billows, 2009, *Julius Caesar: The Colossus of Rome*, pp.64.

Although it almost bankrupted his family and friends, the ransom was eventually raised, paid and Caesar was soon released. Ferried to Miletus and set free, he soon made his way to the nearest Roman garrison and "once he was set on shore on payment of fifty talents, he did not delay then and there to launch a fleet and pursue the departing pirates, and the moment they were in his power to inflict on them the punishment which he had often threatened when joking with them"[278]. Commandeering both soldiers and ships, he arrived at the far side of the pirates' island base at night and led his men to attack their camp overland. Taking them by complete surprise, he destroyed the base and captured the majority of the outlaws he found there and had them imprisoned in the fortified prison of Pergamum. When the local governor delayed issuing permission for the prisoners to be executed, Caesar simply showed up at the prison with his soldiers and demanded to see the jailer. Taking full responsibility for their executions, he promptly had them crucified in small groups of 15, slitting their throats after they had been hung up so that the crosses could be made available for the next batch of unlucky pirates to be brought out. Working methodically, he was able to complete the executions of all the pirates within a day, keeping his promise to them that he would see them all brought to justice.

Although Caesar did eventually arrive at Rhodes and spent several months there studying, his episode with the pirates tells us more about his character than his study of philosophy does. After returning to Rome, he promoted the incident as a great military victory, reporting he had

---

[278] C. Suetonius Tranquillus, *The Lives of Twelve Caesars*, pp.7-8.

destroyed "a Mithridatic force operating, apparently unchecked, in Asia"[279] again revealing his "decisiveness and force of personality"[280]. Gathering admirers, he continued to climb in popularity as he ascended in political rank, spending profusely as he went. By the time he was elected as aedile, he had thrown a gladiatorial contest that "entertained the people with three hundred and twenty single combats"[281], winning the hearts of the people as he did so. Some of his critics thought that throwing money away in an attempt to buy popularity, that Caesar would "change a solid good for what would prove but short and uncertain return"[282], but Caesar knew that fame in ancient Rome was the forerunner of real power and what he was buying was worth more than gold.

Popularity aside, Caesar was proving himself to be a worthy politician and effective military leader and in 62 BC was elected to his first formal post. In his official capacity as *propraetor*, Caesar was sent to Spain although his departure from Rome was almost prevented by the many people he owed money to "who, as he was going off, came upon him, and were very pressing and importunate"[283]. According to

---

[279] Richard A. Billows, 2009, *Julius Caesar: The Colossus of Rome*, pp.66.

[280] Richard A. Billows, 2009, *Julius Caesar: The Colossus of Rome*, pp.67.

[281] Plutarch, *The Parallel Lives*. Edited by A.H. Clough. Project Gutenberg, 1996. "Caesar". http://www.gutenberg.org/files/674/674-h/674-h.htm

[282] Plutarch, *The Parallel Lives*. Edited by A.H. Clough. Project Gutenberg, 1996. "Caesar".

[283] Plutarch, *The Parallel Lives*. Edited by A.H. Clough. Project Gutenberg, 1996. "Caesar".

Plutarch, this was the beginning of Caesar's alliance with Crassus. Reportedly the wealthiest man in Republican Rome, Crassus had his own political ambitions and recognised the younger Julius as being a talented operator that could help him. He was willing to assist Caesar with "those creditors who were most uneasy to him", in exchange for "Caesar's youthful vigour and heat" which would strengthen Crassus's cause against his rival, Pompey[284]. Caesar later revealed the extent of his art of negotiation when he managed to convince these two powerful men "who had been enemies since their consulship" to make peace and agree "that no step should be taken in public affairs which did not suit any one of the three"[285]. The trio went on to form the First Triumvirate – a political alliance that enabled Julius, Pompey and Crassus to "to bypass the Senate, obstruct the normal political process, and help each other". According to Livy, the First Triumvirate was nothing more than "a conspiracy against the state by its three leading citizens"[286], but it worked effectively for Caesar, giving him the financial backing of Crassus and the support of political powerhouse, Pompey the Great.

Now one of the most powerful men in the Republic, Caesar chose Gaul as his province to administrate, a move that Suetonius suggests was both financially and politically shrewd as it was "the most likely to enrich him and furnish

[284] Plutarch, *The Parallel Lives*. Edited by A.H. Clough. Project Gutenberg, 1996. "Caesar".

[285] C. Suetonius Tranquillus, *The Lives of Twelve Caesars*, pp.25.

[286] http://www.livius.org/articles/concept/triumvir/first-triumvirate/

suitable material for triumphs"[287]. Over the course of the next few years, Caesar showed himself "to be a soldier and general not in the least inferior to any of the greatest and most admired commanders", subduing 300 states and killing a million men in the process[288]. While fighting the united Gaelic tribes under the talented Vercingetorix, he achieved their complete subjugation following his stunning victory at Alesia. Once Gaul was secure, Caesar continued flexing his military muscle and "did not let slip any pretext for war, however unjust and dangerous it might be"[289]. Seeking battle further afield, Caesar crossed the Rhine to attack the Germans and "invaded the Britons too, a people unknown before, vanquished hem and exacted money and hostages"[290]. Conquest meant slaves to sell, war booty and popularity back at home, and Caesar's support amongst the common people in Rome continued to swell, to the consternation of his political opponents.

Marcus Claudius Marcellus was one such opponent and saw Caesar's attempts at self-promotion as reckless use of Rome's resources and the lives of their fighting men. When it became known that Caesar was going to seek election to high position of consul, he opposed it. Marcellus argued that Caesar should be replaced as governor of Gaul before his term ended as "peace was established, and the victorious army ought to be disbanded". Marcellus also

---

[287] C. Suetonius Tranquillus, *The Lives of Twelve Caesars*, pp.30.

[288] Plutarch, *The Parallel Lives*. Edited by A.H. Clough. Project Gutenberg, 1996. "Caesar".

[289] C. Suetonius Tranquillus, *The Lives of Twelve Caesars*, pp.33.

[290] C. Suetonius Tranquillus, *The Lives of Twelve Caesars*, pp.34-5.

made sound legal argument against the candidacy, contending that since Caesar would not be present at the elections in person, he should also be debarred from the election process[291]. Caesar pleaded with the senate to intervene on his behalf, but they refused, and he was eliminated from participating. He was summoned back to Rome to face the charges levied by his political enemies of "waging an unjust war", but he refused to return and disband his army. Declared a traitor and an enemy of the Roman Republic, a civil war was begun with Caesar and his supporters on one side and the forces of the Roman Senate on the other, led by his former ally Pompey the Great.

Suetonius suggests that Caesar had been itching for the opportunity to declare a civil war and this disagreement simply gave him the perfect excuse[292]. After several skirmishes, Caesar took on the strongest of Pompey's forces who were in Spain at the time being commanded by three lieutenants. As he left, Caesar declared "I go to meet an army without a leader, and I shall return to meet a leader without an army"[293]. Despite having few supplies and being delayed by the siege of Massilia, Caesar "nevertheless quickly gained a complete victory"[294]. Next, he turned and fought a series of battles with Pompey and his forces before finally defeating him after a brilliant campaign in Greece. Seeking a complete elimination of his opponents, he went on to

---

[291] C. Suetonius Tranquillus, *The Lives of Twelve Caesars*, pp.40.

[292] C. Suetonius Tranquillus, *The Lives of Twelve Caesars*, pp.43.

[293] C. Suetonius Tranquillus, *The Lives of Twelve Caesars*, pp.48.

[294] C. Suetonius Tranquillus, *The Lives of Twelve Caesars*, pp.49.

subjugate the remainder of Pompey's forces in Africa before defeating his sons[295]. Returning to Rome victorious Caesar "displayed among the show-pieces of the procession an inscription of but three words, "I came, I saw, I conquered," not indicating the events of the war, as the others did, but the speed with which it was finished[296].

With Pompey dead Caesar was declared dictator for life and applied himself to the administration of Rome, introducing critical reforms and even changing the calendar, so it ran according to the sun's course[297]. He also reorganised the Romans into guilds according to their trades, thereby dissolving the traditional division between Sabine and Roman, and creating a situation that "became a source of general harmony and intermixture"[298]. As a statesman, Caesar was as exceptional as he was a brilliant tactician and he helped to transform the Roman Republic by relieving debt and changing the structure of the Senate to ensure it better represented the people and ruling that "half of the magistrates should be appointed by the people's choice"[299]. Caesar's reforms weren't popular with the traditional elite, and his enemies were keen to tarnish his reputation at every opportunity, saying that "he behaved more haughtily" as a result of the honours that had been bestowed upon him.

---

[295] C. Suetonius Tranquillus, *The Lives of Twelve Caesars*, pp.51.

[296] C. Suetonius Tranquillus, *The Lives of Twelve Caesars*, pp.52.

[297] C. Suetonius Tranquillus, *The Lives of Twelve Caesars*, pp.56.

[298] Plutarch, *The Parallel Lives*. Edited by A.H. Clough. Project Gutenberg, 1996. "Caesar".

[299] C. Suetonius Tranquillus, *The Lives of Twelve Caesars*, pp.57.

As a man, Caesar's character was far from flawless, and he was a renowned lady's man who "seduced many illustrious women"[300] and according to some, a male king or two along the way. In his earlier years in the military, Caesar had been serving in Egypt when he became romantically involved with Nicomedes, king of Bithynia[301]. Although he was just 19 when this happened, word of the affair would haunt him for the rest of his life as fodder for his political enemies. Once while he was addressing the senate, he mentioned his obligations to King Nicomedes only for Cicero to stand up and shout "No more of that, pray, for it is well known what he gave you, and what you gave him in turn"[302]. Despite the derision of his peers "Caesar seems to have been completely unaffected by this mockery... nor did his youthful affair with the king detract from his political stature"[303]. In fact, it seems his political stature was such that it sparked jealousy amongst his peers and rivals alike, inciting them to conspire against him.

Many residents of Rome thought of Caesar as a king and even "called out the title 'Rex' to Caesar as he passed by

---

[300] C. Suetonius Tranquillus, *The Lives of Twelve Caesars*, pp.70.

[301] James Neill, 2009, *The Origins and Role of Same-Sex Relations in Human Societies.* McFarland & Company Inc., London, pp.200

[302] C. Suetonius Tranquillus, *The Lives of Twelve Caesars*, pp.69.

[303] James Neill, 2009, *The Origins and Role of Same-Sex Relations in Human Societies*, pp.200.

on the streets of Rome"[304], although Caesar himself repeatedly refused the honour. Cassius Dio writes that many extravagant honours were bestowed upon Caesar "some in a spirit of exaggerated flattery and others by way of ridicule"[305]. His military rivals crushed and his political rivals marginalised, it was said that he began to gain an arrogant, aloof attitude that gave his detractors reason to begin plotting against him, believing that he was planning on declaring himself a monarch. One particular incident was revealing, during which a group of elite Roman senators came to meet him in the Temple of Venus and found him waiting for them. Convention and political protocol required that he rise from his seat and greet them as equals, but he remained seated and beckoned to them to sit around him as subordinates. This was a particular habit of royalty, and "aroused so great indignation among them all, not only the senators but all the rest, that it afforded his slayers one of their chief excuses for their plot against him"[306]. Offered later as a justification, Caesar's supporters claimed he was suffering from diarrhoea and "remained where he was in order to avoid a flux"[307], but no one believed this excuse. Clearly no fan of Caesar, Cassius Dio writes that "although he pretended to shun the title [of king], in reality he desired to assume it"[308]. The Roman elite could not tolerate any idea of a monarchy and plans to assassinate Julius Caesar

---

[304] https://www.unrv.com/fall-republic/caesar-the-king.php

[305] Cassius Dio, *Roman History*. Loeb Classical Library, 1916. Book 44, pp.320.
http://penelope.uchicago.edu/Thayer/E/Roman/Texts/Cassius_Dio/44*.html

[306] Cassius Dio, *Roman History*. Book 44, pp.322.

[307] Cassius Dio, *Roman History*. Book 44, pp.322.

[308] Cassius Dio, *Roman History*. Book 44, pp.326.

started to move forward in earnest.

A core cadre of Roman nobility met secretly to discuss how they might act "on behalf of the Roman people", who despised the idea of giving up their representative government for one-man rule. The conspirators talked over several different options but hesitated "for they stood in awe of him, for all their hatred of him, and kept putting the matter off, fearing, in spite of the fact that he no longer had any guard, that they might be killed by some of the men who were always with him".[309] Although news of the plot never reached Caesar's ears, he was nonetheless warned by "unmistakable signs" that something was amiss. Shortly before he was to be assassinated he was offering a sacrifice to seek good omens from the gods when a soothsayer warned him "to beware of danger, which would come not later than the Ides of March"[310]. The night before his rendezvous with destiny, Caesar's wife awoke from a dark dream and felt that it portended danger for her husband, and begged him to stay home and not go out in public that day. Caesar hesitated, but then said his goodbyes before heading out to the senate-house on 15th March, 44 BC. On his way, he was handed a note telling him of the plot to kill him "but did not read it, thinking it contained some indifferent matter of no pressing importance"[311]. As he neared the senate he passed the same priest that had warned him of danger, and as Dio reports Caesar laughed at the soothsayer, pointing out that the Ides of March "is come and that I am alive", to which the soothsayer responded "Ay, it is come but is not

---

[309] Cassius Dio, *Roman History*. Book 44, pp.332.

[310] C. Suetonius Tranquillus, *The Lives of Twelve Caesars*, pp.108-110.

[311] Cassius Dio, *Roman History*. Book 44, pp.337.

yet past"[312]."

As he came into the building and began talking with the mingling senators, the conspirators gathered around him. Impulsively one grabbed his shoulders, while another lunged forward and "stabbed him from one side just below the throat"[313]. Galvanised to action, his murderers surrounded Caesar with drawn daggers and he "was stabbed three and twenty wounds".[314] Although it's likely that he died "uttering not a word", most of us prefer Shakespeare's version in which Caesar turns to Brutus with the dramatic question "Thou, too, my son?"[315] Caesar drew his last breath, leaving his assassins to defend their actions to the public gathered in the Forum that "they had killed him... not to secure power or any other advantage, but in order they might be free and independent and be governed rightly"[316]. The vast majority of Romans felt a little differently and appreciated most of the developmental reforms that Caesar had introduced. When his lieutenant Mark Anthony spoke movingly at his funeral, he declared "by reason of the greatness of his virtue he undertook correspondingly great deeds, and was found to be equal to them"[317].

Anthony's speech was written to appeal to the

---

[312] Cassius Dio, *Roman History*. Book 44, pp.337.

[313] C. Suetonius Tranquillus, *The Lives of Twelve Caesars*, pp.112.

[314] C. Suetonius Tranquillus, *The Lives of Twelve Caesars*, pp.112.

[315] Cassius Dio, *Roman History*. Book 44, pp.339.

[316] Cassius Dio, *Roman History*. Book 44, pp.341.

[317] Cassius Dio, *Roman History*. Book 44, pp.380.

sympathies of the common Roman man, and concluded with "though you enacted many laws that men might not be killed by their personal foes, yet how mercilessly you yourself were slain by your friends! And now, the victim of assassination, you lie dead in the Forum through which you often led the triumph crowned; wounded to death, you have been cast down upon the rostra from which you often addressed the people"[318]. After Anthony had finished speaking, Caesar's body was moved to a pyre in the Campus Martius where soldiers worked tirelessly to prevent the destruction of the surrounding buildings as the crowd threw more and more material to build the fire ever larger. As his body burned, so the heavens opened and according to Dio "inasmuch as he had been slain in Pompey's edifice and near his statue which at that time stood there, he seemed in a way to have afforded his rival his revenge"[319]. While Caesar's assassins may have been anticipating "a quick restoration of the traditional Republic", this was not the turn history took and instead Caesar's death "let slip the dogs of war"[320]. Instead of a restored republic, what followed after years of turmoil and factional conflict was exactly what the conspirators had wanted to avoid – all meaningful political power held in the hands of one man. One of history's greatest warriors was gone, but in his place emerged a new leader that would go on to create the Roman Empire – Augustus Octavian.

---

[318] Cassius Dio, *Roman History*. Book 44, pp.399.

[319] Cassius Dio, *Roman History*. Book 44, pp.402.

[320] Michael Parenti, 2003, *The Assassination of Julius Caesar: A People's History of Ancient Rome*. The New Press, New York, pp.179

LEONIDAS OF SPARTA

"Immortal Spartan King"

One would expect great things of a man rumoured to be descended from the Greek demigod- hero Heracles, and the legendary King Leonidas certainly doesn't disappoint. Born to a supposedly barren mother in Sparta around 540 BC, Leonidas' birth marked the end of a political crisis amongst his people. His father Anaxandridas had been ruling Sparta for at least 20 years by the time Leonidas was born and his inability to produce a male heir was causing great consternation among the ephors who formed the elected council that assisted the king in ruling the country. In this patriarchal society, it was imperative that the monarch should produce a male heir as quickly as possible, and the political pressure on his father was immense as the ephor councilmen worried about what would happen if no prince could be borne by the queen. According to Plutarch "the institution of the ephors... strengthened the civil polity"[321]. The ephors feared that with no son, not only would there be no successor to the throne, the line of the mythical founder

---

[321] Plutarch, *The Parallel Lives*. Loeb Classical Library, 1914. "Life of Lycurgus", pp.297.

of Sparta Eurysthenes would die out, from which Anaxandridas was descended. Such was the concern that they pleaded with the king to set aside his barren wife and find another who would be capable of bearing him children, particularly a healthy son that could follow him on the throne. The king was genuinely in love with his wife, so when he refused the ephor council compromised and "very much against Spartan custom"[322] said, "Since thou art so fond, as we see thee to be, of thy present wife, do what we now advise... We ask thee not now to put away thy wife to whom thou art married- give her still the same love and honour as ever – but take thee another wife beside, who may bear thee children"[323]. One can only wonder what the queen thought of this idea.

Anaxandridas agreed to the terms set out by the ephors and married a "child of the people" – a woman descended from Chilon the Wise[324]. Doing his husbandly duty by his second wife, she soon became pregnant and bore him a son named Cleomenes. It was shortly after this that Anaxandridas' first wife miraculously became pregnant herself. Few were convinced that is was a genuine royal offspring though, suggesting that "fearing the embarrassment of not being able to produce an heir and jealous of the second wife, was only pretending to be

[322] Helena P. Schrader, "Leonidas: Childhood and Youth", *Sparta Reconsidered*, http://www.spartareconsidered.com/childhood-and-youth.html

[323] Herodotus, 440 BC, *The Histories*. Trans. George Rawlinson. Book 5, Chapter 40. http://classics.mit.edu/Herodotus/history.5.v.html

[324] Helena P. Schrader, "Leonidas: Childhood and Youth", *Sparta Reconsidered*,

pregnant"[325]. To prevent rumour and speculation when the time came for the queen to give birth, the ephors council was shuffled into the room so that they could witness the event to ensure she didn't sneak another woman's child into the room and subsequently claim it as her own. Evidently, trust was in short supply in ancient Greece when it came to royal childbirth. However, the truth of her pregnancy was soon proven by the arrival of Leonidas' elder brother, subsequently named Dorieus. The timing of the births of the king's first two sons would mean a lifetime of rivalry between the two, with Dorieus believing he was the rightful heir to the throne because he was born to Anaxandridas' first wife, and Cleomenes claiming his right as the first son.

Despite being heirs to the throne, when they reached the age of seven, both Leonidas and his brother were admitted into the rigorous Spartan education system known as the *agoge*[326]. The system was integral to the concept that all citizens were equal before the law[327] and all male citizens went through the experience, with the exception of the firstborn[328]. Young Cleomenes remained at home with his father while the other two brothers entered into the agoge system "which sought to turn boys into elite soldiers,

[325] Ian MacGregor Morris, 2004, *Leonidas: Hero of Thermopylae*. The Rosen Publishing Group, New York, pp.26-7.

[326] Ian MacGregor Morris, 2004, *Leonidas: Hero of Thermopylae*, pp.29.

[327] Ian MacGregor Morris, 2004, *Leonidas: Hero of Thermopylae*, pp.35.

[328] Unknown, "Do You Have What It Takes to Be One of The Strongest & Most Mentally Tough Citizens on Earth?" https://bengreenfieldfitness.com/article/fitness-articles/spartan-agoge/

disciplined and loyal"[329]. In several respects, this was fortuitous for Cleomenes who has been described as dull-witted, if not completely crazy and "was not in his right mind and really quite mad"[330]. Dorieus, on the other hand "was first among all of his peers and fully believed that he would be made king for his manly worth"[331]. During the course of their education, Leonidas and his sibling underwent a harsh regime of deprivation and physical training in the Spartan tradition. Sleeping in dormitories on "mattresses made from rushes", the boys had little to eat beyond "a porridge-like broth"[332].

These hardships were not only designed to create strong and loyal soldiers and citizens but also to create durable bonds between the boys that would last into their adulthood. "A common upbringing, shared hardships and follies... create a sense of belonging... that bridges political differences"[333]. Unlike the oldest brother who "surpassed all his co-mates"[334], Schrader speculates that Leonidas was more "one of the boys" who "might have become obsessively

---

[329] Ian MacGregor Morris, 2004, *Leonidas: Hero of Thermopylae*. The Rosen Publishing Group, New York, pp.30.

[330] Herodotus, *The Histories*. Trans. A.D. Godley. Harvard University Press, 1920. Book V, chapter 42, section 1.

[331] Herodotus, *The Histories*. Trans. A.D. Godley. Harvard University Press, 1920. Book V, chapter 42, section 1.

[332] Ian MacGregor Morris, 2004, *Leonidas: Hero of Thermopylae*. The Rosen Publishing Group, New York, pp.31.

[333] Helena P. Schrader, "Leonidas: Childhood and Youth", *Sparta Reconsidered*

[334] Herodotus, 440 BC, *The Histories*. Trans. George Rawlinson. Book 5, Chapter 40.

loyal, the quintessential 'team player'"[335].   This aspect of
both his upbringing and his personality would have stood
him in good stead for leadership, meaning he could "count
upon not only the loyalty Spartans owed their kings as
descendants of Heracles and demi-gods, but also upon the
more visceral, emotional, blind loyalty of his comrades"[336].
However, the throne was a long way off for Leonidas, with
two brothers in line ahead of him. When Anaxandridas died
in 540 BC, it was Cleomenes who succeeded him, and for a
few years, Dorieus struggled under his rule before leaving
Sparta with a group of followers to colonise Cinyps now
known as Wadi Qaam or Wadi Kaim. According to
Herodotus, Cinyps "has not its equal in all Libya", but
Dorieus's time there was short-lived, and he was "driven in
the third year by the Macians, the Libyans, and the
Carthaginians"[337].

Rather than returning to the country ruled by his
detested half-brother, Dorieus decided to make a new
beginning and set off to "found the city of Heraclea in
Sicily"[338]. Sadly, the young leader never accomplished this
fresh start; he stopped in Italy along the way to assist his
allies the Sybarites, who were engaged in their own border
conflicts with invaders and requested his help. It was an

[335] Helena P. Schrader, "Leonidas: Childhood and Youth", *Sparta Reconsidered*

[336] Helena P. Schrader, "Leonidas: Childhood and Youth", *Sparta Reconsidered*

[337] Herodotus, 440 BC, *The Histories*. Trans. George Rawlinson. Book 5, Chapter 40.

[338] Herodotus, 440 BC, *The Histories*. Trans. George Rawlinson. Book 5, Chapter 40.

unfortunate choice, as he and many of his men "fell in a battle wherein they were defeated by the Egestaeans and Phoenicians"[339]. Dying when he did, he missed his chance to inherit his rightful throne when events gained momentum; "Cleomenes, after reigning no great length of time, died without male offspring, leaving behind him an only daughter, by name Gorgo"[340]. Although something of a tyrant and "war criminal", Cleomenes pursued what he believed to be Sparta's best interests with "a single-minded ruthlessness"[341]. Various power struggles had led Cleomenes into conflict with his neighbours and despite initially securing some impressive victories, his efforts to expand the territories and holdings of Sparta were frustrated by his co-king Demaratus. In the way of his territorial ambitions, Cleomenes had managed to have Demaratus eventually deposed after claiming that his co-ruler was not the "rightful king of Sparta, since he was not the true son of Ariston"[342]. Returning to Sparta following his military campaigns, he was not so much a victorious warrior king but more of a rambling madman. His political rivals soon exposed his in discrediting Demaratus and undermining him to remove him from the throne. In the end, he himself was denounced and deposed and exiled to neighbouring Arcadia.

---

[339] Herodotus, 440 BC, *The Histories*. Trans. George Rawlinson. Book 5, Chapter 40.

[340] Herodotus, 440 BC, *The Histories*. Trans. George Rawlinson. Book 5, Chapter 40.

[341] Nigel M. Kennedy, 2010. *Spartans: A New History*. Wiley-Blackwell, UK. Chapter 4.

[342] Herodotus, 440 BC, *The Histories*. Trans. George Rawlinson. Book 6.

In Herodotus' account of Cleomenes' descent into madness and subsequent death, he states that the king's insanity "proceeded not from any supernatural cause whatever, but only from the habit of drinking wine unmixed with water"[343]. Despite this testimony, some historians have suggested that Leonidas and possibly Cleomenes' own daughter Gorgo, were instrumental in driving him insane. Herodotus states that "his kindred imprisoned him, and even put his feet in the stocks"[344], which Schrader suggests means these "relatives could have been none other than his only surviving child, Gorgo and/or his half-brothers Cleombrotus and Leonidas"[345]. While imprisoned, Cleomenes asked his keeper for a knife and began to mutilate himself, "cutting gashes in his flesh, along his legs, thighs, hips, and loins, until at last, he reached his belly, which he likewise began to gash, whereupon in a little time he died"[346]. A sad ending for a Spartan king with great dreams of military conquest.

With Dorieus's body already cold in the ground, Leonidas had much to gain from his brother's death, which is why some historians have explored the possibility that Cleomenes might have had a familiar helping hand on his way to eternity and that Leonidas and Gorgo were indeed behind his downfall. Dr. Nic Fields, author of Thermopylae

---

[343] Herodotus, 440 BC, *The Histories*. Trans. George Rawlinson. Book 6.

[344] Herodotus, *The History*, Book 6,
https://ebooks.adelaide.edu.au/h/herodotus/h4/book6.html

[345] Helena Schrader, 2012, "Leonidas and Gorgo", *Sparta Reconsidered*.
http://elysiumgates.com/~helena/Leonidas.html

[346] Herodotus, *The History*, Book 6,
https://ebooks.adelaide.edu.au/h/herodotus/h4/book6.html

480 BC: Last stand of the 300 claims that Herodotus' version of Cleomenes death is unbelievable as "the Spartans were notoriously abstemious". Instead, he suggests "It seems more likely that Cleomenes' reign was cut short [sic] by murder, arranged and hushed up, on the orders of the man who succeeded him on the Agiad throne"[347]. Schrader suggests that those who remain unconvinced by Herodotus' account of Cleomenes' death "lack the imagination to believe him", saying they "cannot believe that anyone would try to flay themselves alive"[348]. Modern sources suggest that Cleomenes' reported self-mutilation is "consistent with a paranoid schizophrenic suicide"[349]. What really happened to bring Leonidas to the Spartan throne will never really be known, but what is certain is that history had special plans him when he arrived there.

Since the Ionian Revolt in 499 BC, the Persians under Darius I were eager to punish the Greek people of Athens and Eretria for supporting the rebellion against their rule, while at the same time certainly wanted to capture more Greek territory to add to their empire. Although Darius died before he could achieve these goals, his son Xerxes succeeded him and began planning for the Greek invasion in earnest; Schrader suggests that Xerxes "appears to have become obsessed with the idea of humiliating the Greeks"[350].

---

[347] Helena Schrader, 2011, "Leonidas the Murderer?", *Sparta Reconsidered.* http://spartareconsidered.blogspot.com/2011/05/leonidas-murderer.html

[348] Helena Schrader, 2011, "Leonidas the Murderer?", *Sparta Reconsidered.*

[349] Helena Schrader, 2011, "Leonidas the Murderer?", *Sparta Reconsidered.*

[350] Helena Schrader, 2012, "Leonidas and Gorgo", *Sparta Reconsidered.*

He gathered a massive Persian army and began the long march to invade Greece from the north. Having recently become King of Sparta from his brother, Leonidas recognised that only a coalition of the Greek states could hope to defeat the huge army of invaders. While the other city-states began to muster their forces, Leonidas decided to buy time by blocking the only narrow land passage into mainland Greece that the Persians were heading for at Thermopylae. Impassable on one side by sea cliffs and on the other by mountains, there was a natural bottleneck through which the enemy would have to funnel. There, the huge advantage that the Persians had in numbers would be would nullified by being forced to fight on a narrow front. Preparing to meet the Persians, he gathered a force of 300 men "but not the three hundred youths who usually accompanied him to the field, but the same number of men who had sons living"[351]. With the prophecy that "either a Spartan or a Sparta king must perish" ringing in his ears, Leonidas was anxious to ensure no soldier's family would be destroyed in the event of his death[352]. As the leader of the Greek coalition's land force, Leonidas was instructed to defend and hold Thermopylae at all costs.

As in the previous Battle of Marathon, which the Spartans had largely missed due to it being their holy season[353]the Greeks were heavily armed, making it difficult

---

[351] C.W.C. Oman, 1898, *A history of Greece from the earliest times to the death of Alexander the Great.* Longmans, Green & Co., New York, pp.199.

[352] C.W.C. Oman, 1898, *A history of Greece from the earliest times to the death of Alexander the Great,* pp.199.

[353] C.W.C. Oman, 1898, *A history of Greece from the earliest times to the death of Alexander the Great,* pp.198.

for their opponents to make headway with their "dart and scimitar and wicker shield"[354]. Nevertheless, "[t]he fight which followed was a fierce one"[355] , and Xerxes resorted to sending in The Immortals "who were reputed to be pre-eminent among the entire host for their deeds of courage". However, not even the Immortals could make an impression on Leonidas' force and "as night fell, they ceased from battle, the barbarians having lost many dead and the Greeks a small number"[356]. Although the Persian army massively outnumbered the defenders, they could not breakthrough, and the numbers of Persian dead were staggering. It has been said that frustrated and impatient to continue the invasion, Xerxes, offered Leonidas the opportunity to join his army and become the Persian governor of Greece. Leonidas refused, however, "saying that it was better to die for the freedom of the Greeks than to live and rule them"[357].

What Xerxes' forces had trouble winning by brute force they were to win by subterfuge and the betrayal of a Greek looking to secure a rich reward. A local man named Epialtes offered to show the Persians hidden trails through what were thought to be impassable mountains, thereby cutting around the Spartan's positions to surround them.

[354] C.W.C. Oman, 1898, *A history of Greece from the earliest times to the death of Alexander the Great*, pp.202.

[355] Diodorus Siculus, *The Library of History*, Loeb Classical Library, 1946. Book XI, pp.140.
http://penelope.uchicago.edu/Thayer/E/Roman/Texts/Diodorus_Siculus/11A*.html

[356] Diodorus Siculus, *The Library of History*, pp.142.

[357] Philip de Souza, *The Greek and Persian Wars 499-386 BC*. Routledge, New York, pp.51.

Dazzled by the scale and size of the invading forces, Epialtes was brought before Xerxes himself "and told of the path leading over the mountain to Thermopylae"[358]. This would be the act that would fulfil the prophecy Leonidas made when confronted by the ephors council prior to his departure for Thermopylae. According to Plutarch, the ephors challenged Leonidas saying "you lead but few to Thermopylae" to which Leonidas responded, "They are many... considering on what design we go." When asked to elaborate, the Spartan king replied: "I pretend to go to hinder the barbarians' passage, but really to die fighting for the Greeks"[359]. By following Epialtes' advice and guidance, Xerxes was able to send "a detachment of Persians... to intercept the retreat of Leonidas and attack him in the rear"[360]. Warned in advance that he was about to be surrounded, Leonidas sent away the allied troops that he had with him from Corinth and Arcadia, fearing that as "they were not bound by the iron bonds of Spartan discipline and Spartan [they] might retreat without disgrace from a hopeless field"[361]. It was better, he reasoned that they should live to fight another day and spread the word about the Persian invasion than remain with him in what was now going to be a hopeless fight. Bound by duty and honour himself, Leonidas was resolute in his defence of Thermopylae and

---

[358] Herodotus, *The Histories*. Trans. A.D. Godley. Harvard University Press, 1920. Book VII, chapter 213.

[359] Plutarch, *Apophthegmata Laconica*. Trans. by Ed Goodwin. "Of Leonidas the Son of Anaxandridas".
http://www.perseus.tufts.edu/hopper/text?doc=Perseus%3Atext%3A2008.01.0198%3Achapter%3D51

[360] Samuel Griswold Goodrich, 1846. *Pictorial History of Greece, Ancient and Modern*. Sorren & Ball and Samuel Agnew, Philadelphia, pp.175.

[361] C.W.C. Oman, 1898, *A history of Greece from the earliest times to the death of Alexander the Great*, pp.204.

declared that he and his remaining Spartans would stay and fight to the last man. On the third and last day of battle, King Leonidas, a small number of allied Thespiaean troops and his "300" Spartans lined up for battle.

In the mountains, Phoenician troops guarding the upper pass around the Spartans' flank braced for battle when they saw the Persian forces approach. Before any fighting actually started the Greek commander there ordered his soldiers to move off the pass, thinking to gain better cover and more defensible ground. Unfortunately, this left the road open to encircle Leonidas; the Persians promptly by-passed right by them "along the evacuated pass... leaving them to regret at leisure the unhappy and imprudent movement by which they had afforded him [Hydarnes] a free passage"[362]. The Spartans and their allies below were now surrounded and doomed.

Knowing he would be fighting to his death, Leonidas lead his men out further than on previous days to meet the Persians where many "were trampled alive by each other" while the Greeks fought on "recklessly and desperately"[363]. The battle raged all day, and the fighting finally died down when the light faded at dusk. The next morning, only a handful of Greeks remained on their feet to oppose them. In the early morning light, the carnage of the battlefield could be clearly seen, and mindful of the horrific casualties

---

[362] Samuel Griswold Goodrich, 1846. *Pictorial History of Greece, Ancient and Modern*, pp.176.

[363] Herodotus, *The Histories*. Book VII, chapter 223.

that they had taken already the Persians avoided close conflict. Instead, they gathered around the flanks of the Greek forces "and shooting arrows and hurling javelins at them from every direction they slew them to a man"[364]. The last defenders of the pass were dead, and the road was open for Xerxes to continue his invasion southward towards Athens.

In this way, the Pythia's prophecy before the battle was fulfilled. Prior to their soldiers leaving Sparta to meet the Persians, the priestess who was believed to channel divinations from the Greek god Apollo had told the Spartan leaders "Either your great and glorious city must be wasted by Persian men, or if not that, then the bound of Lacedaemon must mourn a dead king, from Heracles' line"[365]. The death of King Leonidas was mourned, but possession of his dead body had been bitterly contested during the fighting. When the battle was over and the last Spartans killed, the Persian king was "so enraged with... the Spartan king's defiance" that he had it "impaled and decapitated"[366]. Leonidas' mutilated corpse was taken back to Sparta some 40 years later and reburied under a stone lion in recognition of his name "son of the lion"[367].

---

[364] Diodorus Siculus, *The Library of History*, pp.150.

[365] Herodotus, *The Histories*. Book VII, chapter 220.

[366] Philip de Souza, *The Greek and Persian Wars 499-386 BC*, pp.57.

[367] https://en.wikipedia.org/wiki/Leonidas_I

The Battle of Thermopylae had carried a heavy price for both sides; the Persians had lost at least 20,000 men, and Sparta had lost their king. Psychologically, there was lasting damage to the invaders. Although they had won the battle, from that day on the Persians perceived every Greek warrior to be "a reckless hero, careless of life, and only bent on slaughter"[368]. They would never face a Greek army again without remembering the horrors of the Battle of Thermopylae and what it had cost them in lost lives. For the Spartans, despite losing the battle and their warrior king Leonidas gained the "laurels of the hero" and became a long-term "symbol of the defence of Democracy against tyranny, and a reminder of the need for sacrifice in order to win that victory"[369]. A legendary hero and fearless warrior who lead from the front to willingly sacrifice his own life for the freedom of Greece, Leonidas died leaving behind an enduring legacy and "a crown/ of valour mighty and undying fame"[370].

---

[368] C.W.C. Oman, 1898, *A history of Greece from the earliest times to the death of Alexander the Great*, pp.207.

[369] Helena Schrader, 2012, "Leonidas and Gorgo", *Sparta Reconsidered*.

[370] Diodorus Siculus, *The Library of History*, pp.154.

ARTEMISIA OF CARIA

"The Opportunist Queen"

Every little girl dreams of being a princess, isn't that true? Our next warrior from the pages of history was indeed a Greek princess of royal blood, but in 500 BC, life in classical Greece wasn't much of a fairy tale. Artemisia of Caria was born to King Lygdamis, the ruler of Halicarnassus, the capital of Caria. At the time, Caria was a Greek city-state that was geographically in modern-day Turkey, ruled by the Achaemenid or First Persian Empire[371]. Of her family, little is known other than her mother was from Crete, and she grew up as a Greek, the princess of the royal line. We can assume that she grew up in a patriarchal society where she would have been afforded a basic education that would have included elementary mathematics, reading and writing. Most likely she was also exposed to some poetry in the Hellenistic tradition. Certainly, her male counterparts would have been given more comprehensive schooling, but she was probably given some physical training in the way of athletics and dancing until she reached the accepted age for marriage, around 13 or 14.

---

[371] https://en.wikipedia.org/wiki/Artemisia_I_of_Caria

As a princess, Artemisia would have been married off to a man of her father's choosing to cement or further his political ambitions. From this moment on, she would have been subservient to her husband and expected to acquiesce to his every whim, living under his protection and authority[372]. Women were very much considered second-class citizens in Ancient Greece, even those born to parents in high places or in royal households. Given that this was the usual and traditional trajectory of a woman's life at the time, it makes it all the more remarkable that Artemisia managed to acquire the military skills she was to demonstrate later in her life.

Artemisia first tasted a large measure of personal freedom after her husband died. Her father, having died earlier, she was suddenly no longer answerable to any male figure for the first time and found herself as the ruler of her people. Tradition dictated that she should hand over the reins of power to her "young son"[373], perhaps serving as regent until the young prince reached the age of adulthood himself, but Artemisia didn't see it quite that way. Instead, she assumed the role of Queen of Halicarnassus and never looked back. As sole ruler, she earned a reputation as a brave but shrewd leader, an excellent sailor, and someone not afraid to speak her mind[374].

---

[372] https://www.ancient.eu/article/927/women-in-ancient-greece/

[373] Herodotus, *The Histories*. Ed. A.D. Godley. Harvard University Press, Cambridge, 1920. Book 7, Chapter 99, Verse 1.

[374] https://scottmanning.com/content/the-artemisia-of-herodotus-was-complex/

Most of what we know of Queen Artemisia comes from the Halicarnassus-born historian Herodotus, with little other documentary evidence available to corroborate or contradict his version of history. What really is most interesting is that he documents her contribution in his account of the Battle of Salamis, which is the focus of his narrative. That she appears at all in his historical account carries great significance and suggests that she was responsible for an important episode in the Greek victory over the Persians.

Some have suggested that Herodotus possibly mentioned Artemisia in his histories because they were both from Halicarnassus, or because he found it "a great marvel that a woman went on the expedition against Hellas"[375]. Alternatively, Artemisia could have been singled out because the events of her life illustrate Herodotus' consistent themes of how both intelligence and chance can influence events and the uncomfortable experience of being forced to make a useful, but not necessarily moral, decision[376]. Certainly, Artemisia gains some distinction simply by her gender, standing out in the male-dominated world of Persian military leadership. After all, the Greeks reasoned – she was only a woman.

---

[375] Rosaria Vignolo Munson, "Artemisia in Herodotus". *Classical Antiquity*, Vol. 7, No. 1 (Apr., 1988), pp. 91-106. University of California Press, pp.92.

[376] Ibid, pp.105-6.

Although Herodotus only documents Artemisia's involvement in the battles associated with the second Persian invasion of Greece, it is believed that she personally led five warships to war at the Battle of Artemisium. This naval battle occurred concurrently with the famous Battle of Thermopylae where a massive invading Persian army won a tough victory after overwhelming the tiny force of ferocious Greek forces, led by King Leonidas and his Spartans. Although the Persians were victorious on land, their forces fighting offshore at the Battle of Artemisium fared less well, and the battle was inconclusive. When the defending Greek navy received news from shore that the fight at Thermopylae had ended in defeat, they disengaged and pulled back from the Persians, retreating in good order. Watching the Greeks sail away the Persians had little to celebrate, having lost hundreds of their ships to gales and storms, not to mention their battle casualties. The battle had raged for three days, and during the last hours of the fighting, both sides had suffered heavy losses, which probably was the most significant reason that the much smaller Greek fleet pulled back when they did.

The Greeks headed back into the narrow waters of the straits of Salamis, where they believed their lighter ships would have an advantage over the heavier vessels of the Persians. Themistocles, the leader of the Athenian fleet, devised a plan to try and encourage both Artemisia's Carian fleet and the Ionian Greeks to desert the Persians and join forces with the Greek allies. Taking the "seaworthiest Athenian ships", Themistocles went to every place where there was available drinking water and engraved a message on the rocks for the Ionians and Carians to read. According to Herodotus, the message read "Men of Ionia, you do wrongly to fight against the land of your fathers and bring slavery upon Hellas. It were best of all that you should join yourselves to us; but if that be impossible for you, then do you even now withdraw yourselves from the war, and entreat the Carians to do the same as you"[377]. To Herodotus' mind, these messages had two purposes. First, to try and strengthen the Greek allied fleet and the second should the first fail, to instigate doubt in the mind of King Xerxes, leader of the Persian forces. If Themistocles couldn't wrest the Carians and Ionians away from the Persians, he might succeed in creating some tension and disunity within the Persian fleet[378].

Themistocles' efforts proved fruitless, but the aftermath following the Battle of Artemisium influenced Artemisia's thinking when summoned to a meeting just before the Battle of Salamis. The Persians had marched deeper into Greece following their victory at Thermopylae, burning and looting as they went until they reached and captured Athens itself. After the city was taken, King Xerxes gathered his military leaders together to discuss their next move. The Greeks were not beaten, and their small navy still needed to be hunted and destroyed before a Persian victory and conquest could be declared. The Greeks allies bided their time, hopeful that they could lure the invaders into a sea battle in the narrow straits of Salamis, where they expected to have a significant advantage. Fighting there, the greater numbers of Persian warships would not count, as

---

[377] Herodotus, *The Histories*. Book 8, Chapter 22.

[378] Herodotus, *The Histories*. Book 8, Chapter 22.

they simply could not all manoeuvre in such a confined space of the straits; this combined with the fact that the Greek ships were lighter and more nimble vessels would place the Persian fleet at a significant disadvantage[379]. Overconfident and eager to win a complete victory over the Greeks, the general consensus between Xerxes and his allied leaders meeting at Athens was that the conflict was all but over and "gave their united voice for offering battle at sea"[380] to finish off what remained of Greek resistance. Only one person present stood up to voice a difference of opinion – Artemisia. She openly disagreed with her male counterparts when they dismissed the Greek navy as a threat, and rather than acquiesce, she spoke up, loudly and clearly declaring that a new sea battle would be a mistake. Artemisia well recalled the superiority of the Greek fleet at the Battle of Artemisium and knew that they would continue to fight hard.

Artemisia's advice to Xerxes was to "spare your ships, and offer no battle at seas; for their men are as much stronger by sea than yours, as men are stronger than women"[381]. Pointing out that Xerxes had already secured Athens, she questioned what was to be gained from a sea battle. Rather than set sail and engage the Greek navy, Artemisia advised Xerxes to stay on land and suggested a possible advance into Peloponnese to destroy Greek resistance there. By remaining on land, she advised that Xerxes could "easily gain that end wherefor you have

---

[379] Herodotus, *The Histories*. Book 8, Chapter 68.

[380] Ibid.

[381] Ibid.

come"[382]. She reasoned that since the Greek allies were isolated and regrouping on the island of Salamis without any source of supplies, the Persians could easily take Peloponnese without any fear of significant resistance, and that a victory there would damage the Greek position substantially enough as a result that "they will have no mind to fight sea-battles for Athens"[383].

The leaders of the Egyptians, Cyprians, Cilicians, Pamphylians, and others were no doubt offended by her speech most likely because a woman disagreeing with men in military matters was scandalous, but also due to her unflattering references to them as "evil slaves... in whom is no usefulness".[384] However, they were secretly pleased as they were convinced that Xerxes would turn against her as a result of her advice. Instead, he was impressed by her knowledge and understanding of their military position and held her in even greater esteem than before. In the end, this was not enough to prevent him from heeding the advice of the male majority and opting to pursue a decisive victory at sea. Herodotus suggests that this decision was influenced by Xerxes' belief that his absence at the previous confrontation had led to his men being "slack fighters" and that they would up their game if he was present[385].

---

[382] Ibid.

[383] Ibid.

[384] Ibid.

[385] Ibid.

The decision made, Artemisia herself was under no obligation to fight personally in the coming battle. In fact, it was expected that as a mother with "a son in his twenties" she could easily have sent him in her place[386], but the Queen of Caria threw her full weight and energy behind the Persians, contributing her force of five ships to the Persian fleet of over 1,000 triremes and war galleys[387]. Artemisia's significance and importance in the Battle of Salamis came less from her military contribution than from her mere presence in person. Not only was Artemisia the sole woman directly in the fighting, but she was also the only commander present with a price on their head. Following the Battle of Artemisium, the Greeks were offering a "ten thousand drachmae" reward to anyone who could take Artemisia alive. The Greeks wanted Artemisia captured very badly, simply for the reason that "there was great wrath that a woman should come to attack Athens"[388]. This is unsurprising really, and few of the Persians themselves were comfortable with the notion of female commander in their ranks but kept their thoughts to themselves in deference to Xerxes' admiration of the Greek queen. It was a man's world, after all.

Time began to become Xerxes greatest enemy, not the Greeks. The coming Battle of Salamis was now vital for Xerxes as the momentum of his invasion of Greece slowed

---

[386] Barry Strauss, 2004. *The Battle of Salamis: The Naval Encounter that Saved Greece and Western Civilization.* Simon & Schuster Paperbacks, New York, pp.96.

[387] Herodotus, *The Histories.* Book 8, Chapter 48.

[388] Ibid, chapter 93.

down. His forces on land were now meeting with stronger and stiffer resistance, and the Greek allies had secured the Isthmus of Corinth by blocking the Scironian Road[389]; Persian luck and time was running out, and the sheer size of the invading forces was making it difficult to secure sufficient supplies to feed all the soldiers. If Xerxes could destroy the Greek allied navy, he would improve his position considerably and substantially increase his chances of securing a total Greek surrender. A final showdown was imminent, but from the morning the battle commenced nothing would go in Xerxes' favour, proving the wisdom of Artemisia's earlier advice "Spare your ships, and offer no battle at sea"[390]. Indeed, Artemisia wasn't the only one who warned of the dangers of this naval battle, with Herodotus interpreting the prophecy of Bacis as a prediction of the Persian defeat at Salamis: "Raging in dreadful wrath and athirst for the nations' destruction,/Utterly perish and fall"[391].

It has often been said that "all is fair in love and war", and certainly the Greeks took this to heart as they baited the Persians with subterfuge. First, before the battle started the Greeks sent a messenger to the Persian leaders informing them that infighting and discord about strategy was unravelling morale in the Greek navy and that their alliance was about to break apart. According to the message, the Greeks were ready to flee, and the Persians had to act

---

[389] Ibid, chapter 71.

[390] Ibid, chapter 68.

[391] Ibid, chapter 77.

immediately if they were to "suffer them not to escape".[392] Believing the information to be true, the Persians began their preparations and committed to give battle. They stationed men on the islet of Psyttalea that runs between mainland Greece and Salamis, while encircling Salamis itself and positioning ships as far out to sea as the Cynosura peninsula of the island of Salamis. Herodotus reports that these strategic manoeuvres took place under cover of darkness, but others contend that the Persian ships entered the straits only on the morning of the battle[393]. Watching these preparations, Artemisia was unmoved and continued to try to persuade her Persian allies that they should surround but not engage the Greek ships directly.

As she had warned, the Greeks were superior sailors and were better fighters at sea than their Persian counterparts but Xerxes and his fellow leaders believed they were merely going to be finishing off a demoralised and divided enemy that was ready to flee. The Persians were unpleasantly surprised when they sailed their warships into the Strait of Salamis that morning, expecting only token resistance but finding the Greeks "stood out to sea in full force". The battle began in earnest as the two navies began to ram and shower each other with spears and arrows. After some brief fighting, many of the Greek allies looked to withdraw, convinced that they couldn't win against such a large and powerful force coming at them. Credit for rallying

---

[392] Ibid, chapter 75.

[393] William W. Goodwin, 1906. "The Battle of Salamis". *Harvard Studies in Classical Philology*, Vol 17, pp.74-101, Department of the Classics, Harvard University.

them back to the fighting is given to the Athenian Aminias of Pallene who ridiculed their cowardice before a "vision of a woman" and berated them for their retreat[394]. The idea of a female commander standing on the bow of her own warship was hard enough for both Greeks and Persians to accept, but Aminias shouted to his men that sending a mere woman against them "delivered a crushing message: the Greeks were so effeminate in the eyes of the King of Persia that he could afford to field a mere woman against them"[395]. The message worked, and the Greeks roared back into the battle.

The superior ability of the Greek ship crews and the inability of the Persians to manoeuvre and bring their greater numbers to bear soon began to tell. Ship after ship on the Persian side were sunk or set afire with orderly precision, leaving those that remained disordered and with their commanders in disarray. Personally brave, they were overmatched, and the Persian navy began to break apart, losing all cohesion as the formations began to scatter. In the ensuing confusion, Artemisia found herself the target of an aggressive enemy ship from Attica, heading straight for her vessel with its ram positioned to sink her vessel. As she moved her ship to flee the threat, she found her escape route blocked by several Persian ships. Rather than surrender to the enemy, Artemisia took a great risk and ordered her ship to ram the closest Persian ship in her way. That ship carried King Damasithymus of Calyndus, a long-time ally and

---

[394] Herodotus, *The Histories*. Book 8, Chapter 48.

[395] https://www.telegraph.co.uk/history/10672838/Swords-and-sandals-epics-This-classics-lover-is-all-for-them.html

personal friend of Xerxes and his headquarters staff and officers. There were rumours suggested by Herodotus later that Artemisia may have had some personal quarrel with that king, but whether or not she decided to aim her ship at his on purpose or simply because it was in her way history will never know. In any case, Artemisia ploughed her warship into its side, sinking it and all its men[396]. One wonders what King Damasithymus thought in his final moments as he realised that his ally Artemisia was about to kill him and all his crew.

For most, destroying a friendly ship and killing everyone on board would probably provoke some consequences from one's king, if not swift retribution when one of the victims is a personal friend of the monarch. Somehow, Artemisia escaped any punishment and instead "the very harm which she had done won her great favour". From the Xerxes perspective, it was impossible to establish whether the ship Artemisia had destroyed was Persian or Greek, so Xerxes simply assumed it belonged to the enemy. On the Greek side, the ship that had been pursuing Artemisia promptly stopped, assuming that she had changed sides and she was now fighting against her former allies. As strange as this may sound in a modern-day context, it was surprisingly common to switch sides mid-battle during this era and is a recurring theme in the works of Herodotus. Indeed in his version of the post-battle events at Salamis, Herodotus asserts that the Athenian leader Themistocles himself was ensuring his bread was buttered on both sides. Not only had it been Themistocles who devised the plan of

---

[396] Herodotus, *The Histories*. Book 8, Chapter 87.

sending the Persians a message regarding the collapse of the Greek allies, but in his counsel address at Andros afterwards, Themistocles again covered his own back even as the Greek forces pursued the remnants of the enemy fleet as the fled.

Initially, Themistocles urged his Athenian crews to sail to the Hellensport and destroy the bridge there, cutting off one of the main Persian escape routes. When this suggestion was opposed, Themistocles quickly changed his tune and agreed that they should rather leave the bridge intact and drive the Persians out of the country, allowing the Greeks to turn their attention to their homes and crops. Once this plan of action had been agreed, Themistocles sent word to Xerxes that he personally had prevented the destruction of the bridge, thereby representing himself as sympathetic to the Persians "so that he might have a place of refuge if ever (as might chance) he should suffer aught at the hands of the Athenians; and indeed it did so happen"[397]. Similarly, Artemisia is shown to have carefully assessed her actions by weighing up the consequences in terms of both public and private good. This perspective is comparable with the premise of Athenian hegemony, that each individual works towards a common goal in order to receive a personal benefit. In other words, even by resorting to treason "for the sake of self-preservation", Themistocles' actions were considered acceptable in the political climate of the time. With Athens experiencing a period of ethical and political flexibility, the common view was that the ends justified the means. Even in Artemisia's case, where she turns her ship against her allies, she emerges victorious and respected.

[397] Ibid, Chapter 109.

From this, we can speculate that Herodotus, if not the Persians and the Greeks themselves valued self-preservation as much as he admired patriotic zeal.

After their defeat at the Battle of Salamis, the Persian general Mardonius comforted his king. Herodotus notes that Xerxes was "greatly distressed", but Mardonius assured him that he would stay behind with three hundred thousand men and attack Peloponnese, while Xerxes returned to Asia with the rest of the troops. Xerxes considered the plan, but before he agreed he sought the opinion of Artemisia. Following his military disaster at the Battle of Salamis, he had never forgotten that it was she alone that had counselled against fighting at all and had discerned the best course of action. With typical open-mindedness and her predilection for deception, Artemisia recommended that Xerxes take Mardonius' advice, pointing out that should Mardonius be successful Xerxes would take the credit and conversely should he fail "it is no great misfortune". Not only would Xerxes be safe, but she also pointed out that he would "be marching home after the burning of Athens, which thing was the whole purpose of your expedition"[398].

Xerxes quickly departed, fearing that the Greeks might indeed decide to destroy the bridge at Hellesport. Before he left, he was careful to place his sons into Artemisia's care, asking her to take them to safety in the city of Ephesus and provide for their safety. In Herodotus' writings, this is the

---

[398] Ibid, Chapter 102.

last we hear of Artemisia, and it appears that she took no further part in the Persian invasion, nor its eventual defeat. The next historical reference to Artemisia is attributed to the Greek author Ptolemy Hephaestion, who alleged that the queen fell in love with a man named Dardanus of Abydos. According to Ptolemy, "a writer who mixed up many fables with some truth"[399] when Artemisia discovered that Dardanus did not return her affections, she plucked out his eyes before throwing herself off the Lovers Leap at the promontory of Leucas[400]. Hardly a fitting end to a life that had been marked by Artemisia's rejection of the traditional woman's role and her ability to perform as an equal in the male-dominated world of politics and war.

Few historians have paid much attention to Artemisia and unlike many of our other warriors, even less has been said about her in contemporary works. If it wasn't for the movie "300" and its equally historically dubious sequel "300 2: Rise of an Empire" very few people would have any idea who Artemisia was or what she stood for. Her movie portrayal has painted her unkindly, as "a peasant girl brutalised by years of rape... who has malevolently blossomed into Bondage Nymphomaniac Revenge Barbie"[401]. Having said that, there are some background elements "Rise of an Empire" managed to get right. It is true that Artemisia was a cunning military strategist who

---

[399] http://www.thelatinlibrary.com/historians/notes/artemisia.html

[400] *Barker's Lempriere Abridged.* 1843, Longman, Brown, Green, and Longman's, London, pp.91

[401] https://www.theguardian.com/film/filmblog/2014/mar/12/300-rise-of-empire-reel-history-persians-greeks-salamis

wasn't disinclined to safeguarding her own survival at the cost of the common cause. The Macedonian author Polyaenus notes that whenever Artemisia set sail, she carried the flags of both the Persian Empire and the Greeks. When chasing a Greek ship, she would raise the Persian colours, but if she were pursued by a Greek, she would raise the Greek colours[402].

While she may have been an opportunist and of dubious loyalty, she was certainly personally brave and although we know little of what happened to her after the Battle of Salamis, the fact that her grandson later ascended the throne at Halicarnassus as king we can assume she stayed in power and assured her family dynasty. Although Artemisia disappears from history after the Battle of Salamis, she reemerges some years later as the mother or grandmother of the Halicarnassus satrap, Lygdamis II. Curiously, it was as a result of Lygdamis' tyranny that Herodotus was forced from his homeland and sent into exile on the island of Samos[403].

Despite her sudden fade from history, we have some evidence to suggest that Artemisia was acclaimed and celebrated for both her bravery and cunning at the Battle of Salamis. Over 500 years after the battle, the geographer and explorer Pausanius described an impressive statue of

[402] http://www.attalus.org/translate/polyaenus8B.html

[403] http://ehbed.witnesstoday.org/index.php/religion/46-reference/history/world-history/greco-roman/philosophers/375-herodotus

Artemisia that had been erected in the centre of Sparta. The pillars of the Persian portico were purportedly built from white marble purchased with the spoils of the Persian wars and on each one was a carved figure. One pillar bore the likeness of Mardonius, while another the figure of Artemisia, remembered for voluntarily joining Xerxes and distinguishing herself at the Battle of Salamis.

While the legend of Artemisia's namesake Artemis is likely to live on in memory forever as the goddess of the hunt, Artemisia's small contribution to world history was forgotten almost before it was remembered. Nevertheless, she characterises a different type of woman warrior to those we have come across already and are still set to encounter. With no great religious allegiance, Artemisia wasn't reported as favoured by gods or endowed with special powers. Instead, Artemisia is remarkable for her basic human qualities, being flawed, deceitful as well as a wife and mother. Throughout history, magic and supernatural powers have been attributed to powerful female figures as a way to excuse their strengths and abilities while maintaining the "natural" hierarchy of a patriarchal system. The Greeks had no need for such manipulations; however, as the myth of the Amazons gave women as much strength and capacity for war as men. In many ways, Artemisia epitomised the Amazon women – an independent and strong woman who by her very existence, threatened the future of Athens by undermining what was then the "natural order" of things.

Although there may be little room for Artemisia in contemporary culture, her name will live on in the world of natural medicine. The herb Artemisia Artemis is known to act as a natural insect repellent as well as having the capacity to treat a range of women-specific problems, including stopping menstrual bleeding and inducing abortion. Insofar as these two actions are associated with distancing a woman from her biological role in reproduction, so Artemisia's status as a masculinised woman capable of performing as a man on the battlefield lives on. Although her only forays into the military arena ended in defeat, Artemisia emerged triumphant, building a world for herself in which "the women are 'men' and the men are 'women' and 'slaves'[404]. This was the legacy Artemisia passed on to those who followed in her wake, including Artemisia II who similarly proved her capabilities as a naval commander and strategist[405].

---

[404] Rosaria Vignolo Munson, "Artemisia in Herodotus". *Classical Antiquity*, Vol. 7, No. 1 (Apr., 1988), pp. 91-106, pp.93.

[405] https://en.wikipedia.org/wiki/Artemisia_II_of_Caria

BASIL II

"The Bulgar Slayer"

"Some are born great, some achieve greatness, and some have greatness thrust upon them. Thy Fates open their hands. Let thy blood and spirit embrace them"[406]. Basil II was born into greatness insofar as he made the Emperor of the great Byzantine kingdom before he reached the age of 6, and achieved greatness in that during his reign he extended his domain beyond the realms of imagination. If you'd had the opportunity to sit down and chat with this impressive warlord; however, he would probably have claimed that he was a humble man that simply had greatness thrust upon him.

Basil was born in 958 BC to the power couple of Emperor Romanus and his rather controversial wife, the Empress Theophano. Described by one historian as "a woman of base origin, masculine spirit and flagitious

---

406 William Shakespeare, Twelfth Night, Act 2, Scene 5.

manners"[407] his mother was descended from a lowly wine merchant, and universally unpopular with her subjects who thought her elitist and scheming. Theophano was reportedly very beautiful and elegant, but she was the subject of vicious rumours and judged to have married above her station. It had long been rumoured amongst the Byzantines that Theophano knew no limit to her ambitions for power, and was instrumental in the deaths of both her father and her first husband[408]. When her son Basil II was thrust onto the emperor's throne at the tender age of five, it was under a heavy cloud of suspicion, and it was his mother who was actually the manoeuvring events to her benefit. Although he officially shared the throne with his brother Constantine, the latter appeared more concerned in following in his father's footsteps than taking on the rule of Byzantium, leaving the more serious work to Basil.

Emperor Romanus, father to both Basil and Constantine, had been known as a kind and fair leader but "indulged in every species of pleasure with an eagerness that ruined his health and reputation..."[409] The same lifestyle was true of Constantine so, while the young Basil was prepared for his future as emperor Constantine was allowed to "enjoy a life of luxury, hunting and country life".[410] Obviously, as a

---

[407] Edward Gibbon, 1898, *The History of the Decline and Fall of the Roman Empire, Volume 5*. Cosimo Classics, New York, 2008, pp.221

[408] Edward Gibbon, *The History of the Decline and Fall of the Roman Empire, Volume 5*, pp.221

[409] George Finlay, 1877, *A History of Greece: From its Conquest by the Romans to the Present Time*, Volume 2. Oxford at the Clarendon Press, pp.231.

[410] The World in the Year 1000 pp.259.

child of five Basil was in no position to take over the reins of the vast and extensive Byzantine Empire but because of his father's complete lack of interest in all things administrative a talented pool of military officers and state bureaucrats had formed around the royal family that would ensure that the essential functions of government could be maintained and preserved, no matter who was in charge. Shortly after her husband's demise Theophano swiftly married one Nikephoros Phokas, with whom she was rumoured to already have a dalliance with prior to Romanus's death[411].

History continued to repeat itself as events led up to the beginning of Basil's reign, and it is easy to speculate that the behaviour of his mother Theophano, probably did more to shape the character of our warrior than any instruction from his advisors or elders. As Theophano moved from man to man, she continued to exercise great influence and power over the Byzantine Empire. Not only was Theophano implicated in the death of her father-in-law and subsequently her husband, but she was also linked to Nikephoros's untimely demise. He was purportedly killed by his own nephew John Zimisces, who not only enjoyed the status of a general but also "ranked among the numerous lovers of the Empress"[412]. Unsurprisingly, after Nicephorus's death Zimisces took over the reign of the Byzantine Empire, and it was only after his demise - strangely also "strongly marked with the suspicion of

---

[411] Edward Gibbon, 1898, *The History of the Decline and Fall of the Roman Empire*, pp.212.

[412] Edward Gibbon, 1898, *The History of the Decline and Fall of the Roman Empire*, pp.213.

poison" did the two lawful emperors, Basil and Constantine finally ascend to the throne.

Much of Basil's life and his accomplishments were recorded by writer and the Byzantine philosopher and historian Michael Psellos, who describes him as "a villain in wartime, more of an Emperor in time of peace.[413]" Although a little on the short side, Basil cut an impressive figure on horseback and his eyes "shone with a brilliance that was manly". While not a verbose man Basil was famous for his loud, expressive laugh which "convulsed the whole of his body". Regardless of his physical appearance, the Byzantine people were probably just relieved that at last, there was an emperor on the throne who wasn't likely to be seduced by Theophano.

Once Basil claimed the throne for himself, he indulged his brother's title of co-emperor but had little desire to share his power or "accept advice on the conduct of public affairs". As a young man of 18 to 20 years old, Basil had no experience of civil administration nor military tactics, leaving him full of aspirations but with little skill. Acutely aware of his limitations, Emperor Basil turned to another Basil to help him outrun the government. The Lord Chamberlain Basil was, in fact, Basil's uncle, but, as he had been born out of wedlock to a concubine, he had been castrated to prevent

---

[413] Michael Psellos, *Chronographia*
https://sourcebooks.fordham.edu/basis/psellus-chrono01.asp,
Book One, paragraph 35.

him from making any claims to the throne[414]. The Chamberlain was an adept administrator and was admired for "his depth of intellect", making him the perfect advisor and assistant to the young Emperor Basil.

According to Psellos, prior to assuming the full responsibility of the Byzantine throne, Basil the Emperor had been a fun-loving youth whose main concern was banqueting and spare time "was spent in the gay, indolent atmosphere of the court". Once on the throne, however, things started to change, and Basil became more focused and mindful of his new duties, committing himself to the serious life of court politics and the even more important priority of holding onto his throne[415]. Basil had little time to prepare himself before the first challenge to his rule. Inexperienced and youthful, Basil looked like an easy target, and a rival sensed an opportunity to depose the new Emperor. A member of a leading Byzantine family of noble blood named Sclerus stepped forward and made a bid for the throne. At the same time, another contender emerged in the person of Bardas Phocus. Both were powerful men, and both happened to be nephews of the late and unlucky Nikephoros, eager to advance their family names.

Basil decided to pit both his rivals against each other, and so had his Chamberlain appoint Bardas Phocus in charge of the Byzantine army as it prepared to battle the

---

[414] Michael Psellos, *Chronographia*, Book One, paragraph 3.

[415] Michael Psellos, *Chronographia*, Book One, paragraph 4.

rebel Sclerus and the force of soldiers that he had raised. Phocus accepted the command, thinking that this would be an excellent opportunity to gain fame and glory amongst the people. Challenging Sclerus to single combat in order to avoid the bloodshed of a big battle, he handily defeated him in a duel and thereby ended the challenge to Basil's rule but quickly realised that he had been tricked into doing the Emperor's dirty work for him. Soon after the rebellion was put down, Phocus was shunned at court and rumours began to reach him that Basil was claiming all the credit for the victory over Sclerus for himself. Disgruntled, he soon decided to create a new revolt of his own and began to recruit an impressive army from "the leading and most powerful families". Defeated but still very much alive, Sclerus decided it was in his own best interests to join forces with his former rival[416] , and soon the two were allied against Basil and the Imperial forces still loyal to the Emperor. In response, Basil recruited a "band of Scythians" to assist him and began to hire an army of mercenaries to add more soldiers to his banner. Training alongside his men, Basil "was learning the art of war from experience in actual combat" with his brother by his side[417].

Eventually the two opposing armies met in battle, and as they clashed Phocus spied Basil on the battlefield and galloped "straight for the emperor with a wild war-cry, his sword uplifted in his right hand, as if he intended to kill the emperor there and then" while Basil stood calmly at the head of his men, clutching an image of the Virgin Mary for

---

[416] Michael Psellos, *Chronographia*, Book One, paragraph 10-13.

[417] Michael Psellos, *Chronographia*, Book One, paragraph 10-14.

protection. As Phocus thundered toward the emperor, he suddenly slipped from his horse and fell to the ground. Psellos explains that reports diverge at this point, with some saying the rebel leader was dead before he hit the ground, having been injured by a javelin while others maintain he had been poisoned. However it happened, Basil's brother Constantine claimed "the proud distinction of having slain the rebel" and the two brothers watched on as their army descended on the dead Phocus "and chopped him in pieces with repeated sword-blows"[418]. Having secured victory in the face of two rebellions, Basil did not celebrate but instead became more paranoid of all those around him. There were no feasts of triumph or dancing, women or wine. Instead, Psellos tells us that the emperor's character changed forever and "he became suspicious of everyone, a haughty and secretive man, ill-tempered, and irate with those who failed to carry out his wishes"[419].

Having finally established himself securely on his throne, Basil threw himself into the administration of the state but not before exiling his right-hand man. The Lord Chamberlain Basil claimed some of the credit for pitting his emperor's two worst enemies against each other and unwisely began to boast that it was he, not his sovereign that came up with the winning strategy. Unsurprisingly this reached the ears of the Emperor and the Chamberlain suddenly out of favour unwelcome at court. His attempts to impress Basil with his political shrewdness had done just that, to the extent that his nephew now felt keenly

---

[418] Michael Psellos, *Chronographia*, Book One, paragraph 17.

[419] Michael Psellos, *Chronographia*, Book One, paragraph 18.

embarrassed and threatened. Not only was he nominally sharing the Byzantine throne with his brother, but the possibility of any rumours spreading that "the emperor was greatly indebted"[420] to his Chamberlain needed to be eliminated. After wrestling both feebly and briefly with his conscience, Basil dismissed the older Basil and shipped him off into exile[421]. The Chamberlain was happy to flee and left abruptly before things could get any worse for him.

With the throne finally to himself, Basil was eager to prove himself and put his military training to the test. Having filled his coffers from the properties of the rich and powerful and "surrounded himself with favourites who were neither remarkable for brilliance of intellect, nor of noble lineage, nor too learned", Basil felt ready to embark on a campaign of conquest to make a name for himself and legitimise his leadership. He set his sights on the lands to the west, and in 981 set off with his army to invade Bulgaria, ruled by King Tzar Samuel. The Bulgarian ruler was a worthy opponent described as "invincible in power and unsurpassable in strength".[422] While Basil had little military experience, he was confident that he could out-general his Bulgarian opposite and began a series of campaigns into enemy territory with a deliberate methodology that mirrored how he lived his monastic life. Breaking with tradition, Basil ignored military convention at the time and decided not to wage his war only during the "warring season" of warm

---

[420] Michael Psellos, *Chronographia*, Book One, paragraph 19.

[421] Michael Psellos, *Chronographia*, Book One, paragraph 19.

[422] Paul Stephenson, 2003, *The Legend of Basil the Bulgar-Slayer*. Cambridge University Press, pp.16.

weather. Instead, he and his army invaded Bulgaria in the spring and stayed, with no intention of returning home as the summer drew to a close. Prepared to face both hot summers and freezing winters, "all his natural desires (were) kept under stern control...the man was as hard as steel"[423].

What Basil lacked in experience, he made up for in his attention to detail and made it his business to study even the most mundane of military tasks; he learned each rank and position of his own soldiers, as well as the tasks allocated to those ranks. Basil commanded his troops in the brutal Roman fashion, punishing them harshly if they disobeyed an order even if insubordinate actions ended in victory for his side. Despite doing all he could to prepare, Basil's first engagement with Samuel's Bulgarian army ended in disaster and his "ineffective siege" of an enemy city merely irritated the Bulgarians rather than posed any real threat. Embarrassed by the inadequacy of his forces to take the city, Basil ordered his men to begin the desultory march homeward and withdrew his soldiers. Heads bowed and with morale at a low ebb, his army trudged their way right into an ambush set by Samuel in a mountain pass through which the Byzantines were moving. The trap was sprung, and the result was a massacre for Basil's men; the Emperor returned home to Constantinople safely, but very few of his soldiers survived. Embittered and ashamed of himself, Basil "swore a solemn oath that he would have his revenge on the entire Bulgarian nation"[424].

---

[423] Michael Psellos, *Chronographia*, Book One, paragraph 32.

[424] John Julius Norwich, 1998, *A Short History of Byzantium*. Penguin Books, 1998, pp.

The skirmishes between Basil and Samuel continued annually over the next 20 years or so, culminating in the Battle of Kleidion in 1014. Over the intervening years, Basil had slowly but surely conquered the eastern half of the Balkans for his empire and continued to destroy "one Bulgarian outpost after another"[425]. Systematic and relentless, he had made it his entire life's mission to eradicate Samuel and the kingdom of Bulgaria from the map. Several decades of continuous assaults by Basil's forces had encouraged Samuel to construct a series of wooden fortifications along the Struma Valley to slow down and hinder any Byzantine invading force. In the summer of 1014 at Kleidion, Basil had arrived again and made several attempts to break through, but they all ended in failure and retreat. Frustrated and not yet prepared to go home, Basil entertained suggestions from his officers on what to do next. One of his men advocated a more cunning strategy than the simple direct assaults that had been tried before, and Basil so liked the idea that he immediately made it his own and put it into practice. While the Emperor led a new attack against the Bulgarian strongpoints, he sent a second force of his soldiers led by his general Nicephorus Xiphias to march over a mountain range and attack the Bulgarians from behind[426].

The plan was wildly successful, and the Bulgarian army had nowhere to run, trapped between the Byzantines behind them and their own walls in front. Surrender was inevitable,

---

[425] Richard Overy, 2014, *A History of War in 100 Battles*. Oxford University Press, pp. 217.

[426] Richard Overy, 2014, *A History of War in 100 Battles*. Oxford University Press, pp. 217.

and most of the Bulgarians laid down their arms and became prisoners, although Samuel managed to escape. It was reported in early Byzantine texts that between 14,000-15,000 Bulgarians were taken prisoner, but a late-medieval Bulgarian account suggests "little more than half this figure"[427]. According to legend, what happened next would cement Basil's reputation as an inhumane and ruthless enemy as well as earn him his unofficial title of "Bulgar Slayer". An unsubtle man, Basil decided to send a message to Samuel that he was not a man to be trifled with. With the Bulgarian soldiers helpless, the Byzantine Emperor gave orders that 99 out of every 100 prisoners be blinded, with the 100th man being left with one eye, so he could guide his men home[428]. This was done, and soon lines of blinded men were streaming back home. Supposedly, the Bulgarian King was so horrified that "[T]he shock of seeing his mutilated army killed Samuel"[429]. By today's standards, treating prisoners of war this way sounds barbaric but in Basil's time blinding was a common punishment for prisoners of war and "was also a traditional method of punishing the leaders of Byzantine revolts and political opponents"[430]. In this way, the Emperor was simply acting in accordance with common practice, although on a much larger scale than perhaps anyone had seen before.

---

[427] Richard Overy, 2014, *A History of War in 100 Battles*. Oxford University Press, pp. 217.

[428] Judith Herrin, *Byzantium: The Surprising Life of a Medieval Empire*, pp.21. https://erenow.com/postclassical/byzantium-the-surprising-life-of-a-medieval-empire/21.html

[429] Lynda Garland, 1999, "Basil II as Humorist" *Byzantion*, Vol. 69, No.2. Peeters Publishers, pp.322.

[430] Judith Herrin, *Byzantium: The Surprising Life of a Medieval Empire*, pp.21.

Further, modern conceptions of warfare and torture are vastly different to what was commonly acceptable during the Byzantine era, and war leaders especially were expected to be hard-hearted and ruthless, the better to achieve victory and earn respect. Word of what happened following his victory at Kleidion travelled fast, but Basil was still remembered as "having led a holy and chaste life, leaving behind a good memory of his life and deeds".[431]

In addition to the atrocities committed at Kleidion, it is also been claimed that in 1022, when confronted with a sea of mud that preventing him withdrawing from the battlefield Basil ordered that 13,000 of his own men be killed, perhaps so that they wouldn't be tempted to surrender and be taken alive by the enemy. It has been suggested that these men were actually sacrificed for a practical purpose - Basil's answer to Sit Walter Raleigh's red cloak episode and that by walking over the dead bodies of their comrades the rest of his troops were able to cross the perilous mud safely[432]. It would seem Psellos's observation that Basil was "a villain in wartime" was something of an understatement but his ruthlessness in war seemed to be taken into the larger picture of his capabilities as emperor and he has been said to be considered as "the greatest emperor ever... outshining even Constantine the Great"[433]. Of course, Basil had the advantage of learning how to govern over time, as he held

---

[431] Lynda Garland, 1999, "Basil II as Humorist" *Byzantion*, Vol. 69, No.2. Peeters Publishers, pp.323.

[432] Lynda Garland, 1999, "Basil II as Humorist" *Byzantion*, Vol. 69, No.2. Peeters Publishers, pp.323.

[433] John Carr, *Fighting Emperors of Byzantine*.

the throne longer than almost any other and ruled his kingdom for over 50 years[434].

King Samuel of Bulgaria was Basil's constant target for decades, but after his favourite opponent died the annual conflicts between Byzantium and Bulgaria continued for four more years after Samuel was succeeded on the throne by John Vladislav. It was only upon the death of Vladislav that the Bulgar wars ended in 1018[435]. Basil had finally tired of his old enemy and feeling at last secure in his victory, decided to make a pious pilgrimage to the Parthenon in Athens to give thanks[436]. Unlike most dynastic rulers at the time, Basil never married and lived a chaste and humble lifestyle, never said to be ostentatious in appearance or speech. According to Psellos, "He refused to make himself conspicuous in purple-coloured cloaks. He put away superfluous rings, even clothes of different colours"[437]. As he had never taken a wife or produced any heirs, Basil was reliant on his brother to provide a successor to the throne but "his failure to arrange marriages for his nieces and secure another generation of the Macedonian dynasty left the empire weaker".

Despite being widely recognised as the emperor who solidified the Byzantine nation, securing it against foreign

[434] Michael Psellos, *Chronographia*, Book One, paragraph 37.

[435] Judith Herrin, *Byzantium: The Surprising Life of a Medieval Empire*, pp.21.

[436] Judith Herrin, *Byzantium: The Surprising Life of a Medieval Empire*, pp.21.

[437] Michael Psellos, *Chronographia*, Book One, paragraph 22.

threats while also expanding its territories, Basil the Bulgar Slayer owed much of his actual success to a simple marriage contract. He secured stability in his nation primarily through the marriage of his sister Anna to Vladimir I of Russia[438] but failed to see the importance of arranging other influential political unions for his brother's children. Like many rulers, Basil's successes were due as much to luck as good judgement, although his capabilities as a careful strategist are documented. What sets him apart from his peers is his chaste lifestyle and dedication to duty, which continued up until his death. When Basil finally passed away at the great age of 72, he requested to be buried as a common soldier outside the walls of Constantinople. On his tomb are engraved the words "For from the day that the King of Heaven called upon me to become the emperor, the great overlord of the world, no one saw my spear lie idle. I stayed alert throughout my life and protected the children of the New Rome, valiantly campaigning both in the West and at the outposts of the East… O man, seeing now my tomb here, reward me for my campaigns with your prayers"[439].

A fearless, pious and religious man, Basil proved himself to be single-minded in his ruthlessness and dedicated to preserving his nation. As he achieved political security and assured his throne, he went on to devote all his energies to push forward the boundaries of his empire while never indulging himself in any personal pleasures, instead, living a simple soldier's lifestyle. From the moment he first

---

[438] Michael Psellos, *Chronographia*, Book One notes, no.11.

[439] Judith Herrin, *Byzantium: The Surprising Life of a Medieval Empire*, pp.21.

defended his right to rule against his rivals, he would go on to live his life as one of his people's greatest national warriors.

ERIC BLOODAXE

"The Bloody Brother"

Our next warrior from history has a particular distinction, in that his last name gives us no illusions that he is anything but a fighter. Somewhere between myth and man lies a wasteland of historical misinformation and confusion that makes it difficult to ascertain who Eric Bloodaxe really was. A rather vague article on Wikipedia takes on a rather sluggish meander through a plethora of Erics, Eiriks, and Eiríks before leaving us with little more than a stone stump and an old coin[440], but we'll come back to those a little later. The most reliable historical source of information about Eric, or Haraldsson as we should more formally call him is the *Anglo-Saxon Chronicle* which confirms that Eric was made king of Northumbria, which is consistent with our understanding of Eric Bloodaxe's life.

In 1902 historian W.G. Collingwood established the conventional premise that Eric, once king of Northumbria was the same man known to history as the Norwegian King

---

[440] https://en.wikipedia.org/wiki/Eric_Bloodaxe

Eirík Blóðøx (Eric Bloodaxe)[441]. Although this connection is controversial and difficult, for the purposes of this book, we're simply going to run with it and see where the myth and man begin to diverge. The earliest and most detailed accounts of Erik's life and accomplishments are the rather unreliable Icelandic sagas which are much like Blind Harry's epic poem, The Wallace about William Wallace; they tend towards the romantic rather than the factual. Nonetheless, according to the *Heimskringla* saga written by Snorri Sturluson around 1230, Erik was born to the King of Norway, Harald Fairhair and one of his many wives, named Bagnhild the Mighty[442].

"The most beloved and honoured" of all Harald's sons, when Erik turned 12 years old he was sent away to be fostered by a member of his mother's family. According to the Heimskringla, this move was preceded by the death of Erik's mother[443], and the foster father, Thorir Hroaldsson was selected because he was "on most intimate terms with the king"[444]. Hroaldsson was a *hersir*, a Viking leader with 100 men under his direct personal command and presumably selected because he supported Harald in his efforts to

[441] Clare Downham, *Viking Kings of Britain and Ireland: The Dynasty of Ivarr to A.D.1014.*

[442] Snorri Sturluson, 1230, *The Heimskringla*. Trans. Samuel Laing. https://archive.org/stream/heimskringlasag00andegoog/heimskri nglasag00andegoog_djvu.txt, pp.366.

[443] Snorri Sturluson, 1230, The Heimskringla. Trans. Samuel Laing. "Harald Harfager's Saga", Chapter 24.

[444] Leifur Eiriksson, (1220-1240), *Egils saga Skallagrímssonar*, Trans. Bernard Scudder, Penguin Books, 2002. Chapter 36.

centralise power and create a unified Norway[445]. While the *Egils saga* suggests that Erik remained with Hroalsson for some time before returning to his father's side and ruling with him, the *Heimskringla* suggests that Erik spent his years with Hroaldsson earlier on in his life and left his foster care at the age of 12 to embark on an expedition. Thanks to his father's gift of "five long-ships", Erik set out to try his hand at piracy sailing "first in the Baltic; then southwards to Denmark, Friesland and Saxland"[446].

After these first four years of his expedition, he returned home before setting out again, plundering the British Isles before heading north to Finland (Finmark) and onto Bjarmaland, which is now the Russian city of Arkhangelsk. While there, he met his wife, Gunhild. According to the account, while tucked away in a "Lapland hut", Erik and his men found a girl "whose equal for beauty they never had seen"[447] and for whom it would seem Erik was more than willing to bloody his axe. Gunhild explained to Erik's men that she was there to learn "sorcery from two of the most knowing Fins in Finmark", both of whom were exceptional hunters and desperate for her hand in marriage. Gunhild seemed less inclined to commit herself to a life of forest living but warned the Norwegians that these men were not only incredible trackers but also "hit whatever they take

---

[445] Gareth Williams, 2011, *Eric Bloodaxe*,
http://www.bbc.co.uk/history/ancient/vikings/bloodaxe_01.shtml

[446] Snorri Sturluson, 1230, *The Heimskringla*. Trans. Samuel Laing. "Harald Harfager's Saga", Chapter 34.

[447] Snorri Sturluson, 1230, *The Heimskringla*. Trans. Samuel Laing. "Harald Harfager's Saga", Chapter 34.

aim at, and thus kill every man who comes near them"[448]. Perhaps knowing that Erik was the son of the mighty Harald Fair-hair, Gunhild was happy to have Erik her get rid of two other suitors, so that he could request permission from her father, Ozur Tote of Halogaland for her hand in marriage.

Erik's men hid in the hut as the two unsuspecting Finish men returned and although they questioned Gunhild about "the traces close to the hut", she assured them that no one had been there. Knowing both the Fins were in love with her, Gunhild invited them to "lie down one on each side of me"; with her arms around each of them, they went straight to sleep and slept "so soundly that she scarcely could waken them"[449]. Taking advantage of their stupor, Gunhild took two large seal-skin bags and tied them tight over the men's heads and torsos, enabling the "king's men" to "run forth with their weapons, killing them"[450]. The next morning, they returned to the ship and presented Gunhild to Erik, who promptly sailed to Halogaland to get permission to marry the strange Lapland beauty.

In many respects, Gunhild has enjoyed greater renown and recognition than her husband which is something of a first in terms of the warriors we've explored so far, but not

---

[448] Snorri Sturluson, 1230, *The Heimskringla*. Trans. Samuel Laing. "Harald Harfager's Saga", Chapter 34.

[449] Snorri Sturluson, 1230, *The Heimskringla*. Trans. Samuel Laing. "Harald Harfager's Saga", Chapter 34.

[450] Snorri Sturluson, 1230, *The Heimskringla*. Trans. Samuel Laing. "Harald Harfager's Saga", Chapter 34.

so uncommon in the Norse sagas where there are numerous depictions of "strong, proud and independent women", albeit ones who were also portrayed as "wilful, manipulating and often uncompromising"[451]. Nonetheless, Gunhild seems to have been the brains behind the brawn when it comes to King Eric who in the *Egils Saga* is quoted as saying "Thou, Gunhilda, more than others provokest me to savageness"[452]. Certainly, the Heimskringla dedicates many more words to "the mother of kings"[453] then it does to Eric Bloodaxe although little of it is favourable. Throughout history, Gunhild has been portrayed as an evil witch who "seems to have had a bad influence" on Eric.[454] And yet, her reign of power lasted far longer than her husband's extending into the 970s thanks to her sons and subsequent marriages.

The *Heimskringla* declares this union occurred in 922, shortly after which it suggests that Erik returned to Norway to rule alongside his father. In keeping with the usual custom for his people King Harald had enjoying a polygamous life, marrying numerous women and "packed from out the place/the children born of Holge's race" according to his court poet Hornklofe. In other words, Erik

---

[451] Marit Synnøve Vea, *Viking Women*,
http://avaldsnes.info/en/viking/vikingkvinner/

[452] Leifur Eiriksson, (1220-1240), *Egils saga Skallagrímssonar*, Trans. Bernard Scudder. Chapter 48.

[453] Snorri Sturluson, 1230, *The Heimskringla*. Trans. Samuel Laing. "King Olaf Trygvason's Saga", Chapter 34

[454] Snorri Sturluson, 1230, *The Heimskringla*. Trans. Samuel Laing. "Hakon the Good's Saga", Preliminary remarks.
http://www.gutenberg.org/files/598/598-h/598-h.htm

was not the only son to inherit lands and titles upon the death of the King; in fact with the King had made provision to divide his territories amongst over 20 different sons[455]. However, his heirs "were in discord among themselves" prior to this distribution of lands, and the unrest continued as "new quarrels arose among the brothers... because they thought their dominions too little"[456]. As the favoured son however Erik had little to worry about according to the *Heimskringla* "with his father King Harald", suggesting he was given preferential treatment and was probably groomed as the primary successor to the throne. Initially, Erik was to inherit the valuable lands of "Halogaland, North More, and Raumsdal".[457]

Gareth Williams, the British Museum's curator of Early Medieval Coins, has suggested that Erik secured his succession to the throne only by bloodying his axe with the blood of his brothers. He posits that the epitaph refers to blood in the sense of 'blood relations' and points out that the early Latin text written by Theodoricus Monachus names Eric Bloodaxe as a "*fratris interfector*" or brother killer, saying "He had killed his brother Óláfr digrbeinn and Bjƒrn and others of his brothers. Thus, he was called blóðøx, because

[455] Gareth Williams, 2011, *Eric Bloodaxe*, http://www.bbc.co.uk/history/ancient/vikings/bloodaxe_01.shtml

[456] Snorri Sturluson, 1230, *The Heimskringla*. Trans. Samuel Laing. "Harald Harfager's Saga", Chapter 34.

[457] Snorri Sturluson, 1230, *The Heimskringla*. Trans. Samuel Laing. "Harald Harfager's Saga", Chapter 35.

he was a cruel and ruthless man"[458]. Indeed, the Heimskringla notes that when King Harald reached the age of 80, he could no longer operate effectively as king and "brought his son Eirik to his high-seat"[459] while naming Erik and Gunhild's son, Harald Greycloak as his successor. To say that the king's decision was unpopular would be a great understatement and his decree that Erik should have complete "power and command over the whole land" caused a "savage feud" that ended "in bloodshed on all sides, with Erik notoriously killing four of them [his brothers]"[460].

Three years passed, and Erik again became dissatisfied with his land holdings, despite having claimed the lands of his dead brothers. With his brother Olaf ruling all territories east of Viken and another brother Sigrod "all that of the Throndhjem country", Erik still wasn't contented and wanted more. Restless and ambitious, he felt entitled to rule all of Norway and believed that his father had bequeathed it to him[461]. Determined to fulfil what he saw as his destiny, Erik made plans to win "sole sovereignty" with force and forced a clash between him and his brothers at Tunsberg in the spring of 934. Leading a much larger army than his brothers could muster, Erik crushed his opposition and

[458] Theodoricus Monachus, A Twelfth-Century Synoptic History of the Kings of Norway. Edited and translated by M.J. Driscoll. Viking Society for Northern Research, University College, London, 2008. pp.9

[459] Snorri Sturluson, 1230, *The Heimskringla*. Trans. Samuel Laing. "Harald Harfager's Saga", Chapter 44.

[460] Snorri Sturluson, 1230, *The Heimskringla*. Trans. Samuel Laing. "Harald Harfager's Saga", Chapter 44.

[461] Snorri Sturluson, 1230, *The Heimskringla*. Trans. Samuel Laing. "Harald Harfager's Saga", Chapter 46.

"both brothers, Olaf and Sigrod fell there" leaving Erik to claim all of Norway as his own.[462]

Unfortunately, Erik was not a popular king despite being "a stout, handsome man, strong, and very manly" who was astute and successful on the battlefield. Sturluson describes him as being "bad-minded, gruff, unfriendly, and silent". Equally, Gunhild is praised for her cleverness and beauty, but these tributes are quickly undermined by the assertion that she was both "a very false person, and very cruel in disposition"[463]. With so many of his rival relations dead, there were few left to challenge Erik, with notable of his brother Hakon. Until 934 Hakon had remained in England where he had been fostered by Athelstan, the Anglo-Saxon king who ruled England from 924 to 927. Upon hearing of his father's death, Hakon immediately departed for Norway with the intention of claiming the throne for himself and putting an end to Eric's brutal sovereignty. After his arrival Hakon sought out Sigurd, the Earl of Hlader, who was reportedly "the ablest man in Norway" and secured his allegiance, promising him "great power" should he assist Hakon in securing sole sovereignty and overpowering the unpopular King Erik.

As Hakon made his way northward through the country, he was bombarded with tales of Erik's cruelty and

[462] Snorri Sturluson, 1230, *The Heimskringla*. Trans. Samuel Laing. "Harald Harfager's Saga", Chapter 46.

[463] Snorri Sturluson, 1230, *The Heimskringla*. Trans. Samuel Laing. "Harald Harfager's Saga", Chapter 46.

unpopularity. By comparison, Hakon was said to be much like his popular father, and Sturluson reports how people proclaimed "Harald Harfager is come again, grown and young".[464] Although Hakon was only 15 at the time, the people of Throndhjem welcomed him and acclaimed him king, with support for him growing as the news spread into the Uplands. By 935, Hakon had established enough of a following that he was ready to challenge his brother, whose popularity waned as Hakon's rose. Erik tried to raise an army to meet Hakon's forces, but day by day his brother's army grew in size as more and more of the landowners and local nobles flocked to his banner. Recognising that he could not prevail, he decided to pack up and flee the country, sailing first to Orkney and then onto Scotland and northern England.

It is here that the theory that Erik Bloodaxe was also the King of Northumbria emerges. According to the saga, back in England Athelstan as Hakon's foster father figure was still loyal to King Harald and sympathetic to all his family, and "therefore he would do kindly towards his sons"[465]. As a result, Athelstan offered the landless Erik Northumberland as a fiefdom, "which land he should defend against the Danes or other Vikings". The notion that Athelstan invited Erik to rule Northumberland has been contested by some scholars who refer to the Anglo-Saxon Chronicle, pointing out that he was (according to that

[464] Snorri Sturluson, 1230, *The Heimskringla*. Trans. Samuel Laing. "Hakon the Good's Saga", Chapter 1.

[465] Snorri Sturluson, 1230, *The Heimskringla*. Trans. Samuel Laing. "Hakon the Good's Saga", Chapter 3.

historical document) King of Northumbria only in 947 or 948, long after Athelstan's reign and his death. The Chronicle states that in "948 - this year king Edred ravaged all Northumberland because they had taken Eric to be their king..."[466] In support of the theory that Eric ruled Northumberland during Athelstan's reign is the 10th-century text, The Life of St Cathróe of Metz. This ancient account indicates that the author visited Eric and his wife in York sometime between 940 and 941, suggesting that the sagas are accurate and Eric did indeed rule under Athelstan. The saint suggests however that Eric's kingship was bestowed on him not because of his father's close relationship with Athelstan, but due to his wife being a "relative of the godly Cathróe".[467]

According to the *Heimskringla*, Northumbria had little wealth during Eric's reign and what it could provide was insufficient to keep Eric and his witchy wife in the manner to which they had been accustomed. There simply wasn't enough money to go around. To remedy the situation, Eric would go "on a cruise every summer and plundered in Scotland, the Hebrides, Ireland, and Bretland, by which he gathered property"[468]. Things would soon change for Eric, however, and when Athelstan passed away, his son Jatmund took over as King of England. Unfortunately for Eric, he

---

[466] Unknown, Anglo-Saxon Chronicle, G. Bell and Sons, Ltd., London, pp.77
https://archive.org/stream/anglosaxonchroni00gile/anglosaxonchroni00gile_djvu.txt

[467] Gareth Williams, 2011, *Eric Bloodaxe*,
http://www.bbc.co.uk/history/ancient/vikings/bloodaxe_01.shtml

[468] Snorri Sturluson, 1230, *The Heimskringla*. Trans. Samuel Laing. "Hakon the Good's Saga", Chapter 4.

"was in no great favour with him; and the word went about that King Jatmund would set another chief over Northumberland"[469]. Eric was not one to sit around and quietly wait for his estates to be taken away, however, and as he was "a man of great bravery and a victorious man"[470] set about gathering support, and managed to get another five kings to support him. Despite these new allies, sources suggest that Eric was heavily outnumbered when he confronted Jatmund at the Battle of Stainmore and facing "an innumerable mass of people", embarked on a "dreadful battle" at the culmination of which "King Eirik and five kings with him fell"[471].

Beyond this, there is very little information about the Battle of Stainmore, and other sources suggest that rather than dying valiantly on the battlefield Eric was actually ambushed and "by the treachery of Earl Osulf was slain by a nobleman named Macon, together with his son Henry and his brother Reginald in a lonely spot called Stainmore"[472]. Regardless of how Eric's death actually occurred, his demise marked the end of Scandinavian rule in England.[473] While

---

[469] Snorri Sturluson, 1230, *The Heimskringla*. Trans. Samuel Laing. "Hakon the Good's Saga", Chapter 4.

[470] From *Fagrskinna* as quoted in Paul B. Du Chaillu, 1889, *The Viking Age Vol I: The Early History Manners, and Customs of Ancestor of the English-speaking Nations*, Charles Scribner's Sons, New York. Chapter 29.

[471] Snorri Sturluson, 1230, *The Heimskringla*. Trans. Samuel Laing. "Hakon the Good's Saga", Chapter 4.

[472] Roger of Wendover, *Flowers of History*. Translated by J.A. Giles. Henry G. Bohn, London.
http://www.melocki.org.uk/wendover/Flowers1.html

[473]http://www.oxfordreference.com/view/10.1093/oi/authority.2011 0803100527185

little is known about the battle itself, Eric's death was commemorated in a poem included in the *Fagrskinna* saga. *Eiríksmál* was theoretically commissioned by Gunhild after her husband's death, and the poem recounts how the god Odin prepares the Valkyries for Erik's imminent arrival. When asked why it was Eric he was expecting, Odin replied: "In many a land.../Has he reddened the sword (moekir)/and carried the bloody blade".[474] At the end of the poem, Erik arrives saying he will name the other five kings who died at his side, but the poem ends without those names being revealed, suggesting that it remains unfinished.

Despite the mysteries and vagaries surrounding Eric's life and death, he is one of the most prominent Viking kings in history and legend suggests that the Rey (or Rere) Cross situated halfway between Penrith and Barnard Castle was erected to mark the place where Eric died. In 1990 archaeological excavations in the area were completed but found no indication of a burial of any importance, leaving Eric's final resting place as much a mystery as the rest of his life[475]. While he is often portrayed as a cruel and bloodthirsty man, it seems much of Eric's savagery can be traced back to his wife who continued to influence Norwegian politics through her sons, outliving them all. Gunhild was eventually killed by her own brother, Harald Bluetooth, who "decreed that, for her wickedness, she

---

[474] From *Fagrskinna* as quoted in Paul B. Du Chaillu, 1889, *The Viking Age Vol I*, chapter 29.

[475] https://www.flickr.com/photos/30591976@N05/4055952716

should be thrown into a bog and drowned"[476]. Had Eric not been so influenced by his wife, he may have been worthier of the title "warrior" and been revealed to be an adept and effective politician and ruler, rather than be mainly remembered for tyranny and ruthless ambition.

---

[476] https://www.historyanswers.co.uk/medieval-renaissance/8-haunted-castles-you-need-to-visit-in-this-life-or-the-next/

℩

MILTIADES

"Savior of Athenian Democracy"

After fumbling our way through the brutality of the
Vikings and the Bulgarian-slaying Basil, we return to a world
of military order and true personal leadership on the
battlefield. A more traditional warrior and hero than the
legendary, mythical men we looked at previously the Greek
Miltiades was born into one of the most famous families in
Athens around 550 BC; his people were known "for their
good education, success as politicians, and soldiers".[477]
Miltiades was the son of the famous Olympian chariot racer
Cimon Colalemos[478] who ran afoul of Hipparchus and
Hippias, the sons of Pisistratus, the ruler and tyrant of
ancient Athens at the time. Apparently jealous of him, they
decided to have Cimon killed to settle the matter, and
following the assassination of his father Miltiades was
essentially adopted into the family of his father's killers. This
kind of family dynamic might have been a little awkward for
some, but while some historians have asserted that Miltiades

---

[477] Natalia Klimcazk, 2016, *The Magnificent Helmet of Greek Warrior Miltiades*,
https://www.ancient-origins.net/artifacts-other-
artifacts/magnificent-helmet-greek-warrior-miltiades-006455
Oxford University Press, 1915, pp.6.

177

was treated with "favour and kindness" by Pisistratus' family[479] and raised well, others contend he was "vexed by the rule of Peisistratos"[480].

Miltiades was named after his father's maternal half-brother, who had left Athens years earlier to establish a Greek colony on what is now the Gallipoli peninsula of Turkey. The new colony flourished and grew, and became known as the Thracian Chersonese; this older Miltiades ruled as a semi-autonomous tyrant, supported and under the protection of Athens. When he died childless around 520 BC, his holdings were inherited by Stesagoras, Miltiades' brother. He didn't last long in power, however, and Herodotus records that he was killed unexpectedly by what must have been a common hazard in ancient times – an axe blow to his head. Back in Athens, Hippias was now in control following the death of his own father Pisistratus and decided that he could exert more direct control over the Chersonese colonists by sending Miltiades to claim his brother's estate and lands.

Miltiades left Athens and took over control of the Chersonese peninsula, and as the historian Creasy points out,

---

[479] Sir Edward Creasy, 1851, *The Fifteen Decisive Battles of the World, from Marathon to Waterloo*, pp.6.

[480] Herodotus, *The History of Herodotus, Volume II*. Translated by G.C. Macaulay, 2008. Book VI: The Sixth Book of the Histories, called Erato, pp.35. https://www.gutenberg.org/files/2456/2456-h/2456-h.htm

[480] Sir Edward Creasy, 1851, *The Fifteen Decisive Battles of the World, from Marathon to Waterloo*.

"it is with his arrival in the Chersonese that our first knowledge of the career and character of Miltiades commences"[481]. It would be 28 years later before he would evolve from mortal to legend and earn enduring fame at the Battle of Marathon, but even as a young and inexperienced soldier and politician Miltiades would distinguish himself with the same "resolute and unscrupulous spirit"[482] as he would demonstrate later at his great moment in history.

On arrival in Chersonese, Miltiades' first priority was to achieve complete control over holdings. He had learned that Stesagoras' brief time in power had been tumultuous and chaotic, marked by a series of wars and revolts by the local population against him. As soon as he arrived, he put the word out that he was deeply in mourning for his dead brother and remained "within his house, paying honours in all appearance to the memory of his brother Stesagoras".[483] This was only a performance, designed to lure the most important men from all the surrounding tribes, the very same men who had led revolts and insurrections against Stesagoras earlier. Eager to pay their respects (and possibly gain favour with the new man in charge) they all arrived at his house "in a body to console with him".[484] Miltiades had no intention of commiserating, however, and once he was satisfied that he had them all gathered together, he dropped

---

[481] Sir Edward Creasy, 1851, *The Fifteen Decisive Battles of the World, from Marathon to Waterloo*, pp.6.

[482] Sir Edward Creasy, 1851, *The Fifteen Decisive Battles of the World, from Marathon to Waterloo*, pp.6.

[483] Herodotus, *The History of Herodotus, Volume II*. Book VI, pp.39.

[484] Herodotus, *The History of Herodotus, Volume II*. Book VI, pp.39.

all pretence and promptly "made them all prisoners" and proceeded to stamp his "absolute authority" over the peninsula, "taking into his pay a body of five hundred regular troops"[485]. With all the potential leaders of rebellion locked up his personal prison and his own private army of armed enforcers, there was simply no one left that could oppose him. To further consolidate his hold on regional power, Miltiades went on to arrange a political marriage between himself and Hegesiple, the daughter of Oloros, the king of the Thracians. Now in absolute control of his lands, and supported by both Athens and Thrace, he was secure and in an unassailable position. Or at least that's the way it appeared until the Persian army showed.

Darius, King of Persia, arrived with a large army late in the 400s BC, looking for allies and sycophants that could contribute to his forces and supply him more troops as he moved to invade his neighbours. Miltiades realised that his best option to hold onto his territory was to go along, and he swore the appropriate oath of loyalty and submitted to Darius, becoming just "one of the numerous tributary rulers who led their contingents of men to serve in the Persian army in the expedition against Scythia"[486]. As a matter of self-preservation, it made sense, but Miltiades felt no loyalty to the Persian king and began to look for a way out. He saw his chance while on the campaign trail, and once the Persian army had crossed the Danube River and plunged into the

[485] Sir Edward Creasy, 1851, *The Fifteen Decisive Battles of the World, from Marathon to Waterloo*, pp.6.

[486] Sir Edward Creasy, 1851, *The Fifteen Decisive Battles of the World, from Marathon to Waterloo*, pp.7.

"wilds of the country that now is Russia" Miltiades came up with idea with one of his typically ruthless ideas. According to Creasy, Miltiades suggested to his fellow leaders that they destroy the bridge the Persians used to cross the mighty Danube "and leave the Persian king and his army to perish by famine and the Scythian arrows"[487]. The generals serving alongside the Chersonese leader were interested, but ultimately feared the Persian wrath if they weren't successful; in the end Darius and his men returned safely. Word of Miltiades' treacherous suggestion soon reached the Persian king, however, "and the vengeance of Darius was thenceforth specially directed against the man who had counselled such a deadly blow against his empire and his person"[488]. Miltiades was thereafter living on borrowed time.

Other political troubles continued to plague Miltiades' rule of Chersonese, and while his control of the peninsula was "precarious and interrupted" by rivals at home and abroad he managed to use the time he had to ingratiate himself back into Athenian society "by conquering and place under Athenian authority the islands of Lemnos and Imbros"[489]. It was as if he knew that he might need a place to flee if he had to make a run for it, and was trying to add favour to his name back in Athens. In 494 BC, the

---

[487] Sir Edward Creasy, 1851, *The Fifteen Decisive Battles of the World, from Marathon to Waterloo*, pp.7.

[488] Sir Edward Creasy, 1851, *The Fifteen Decisive Battles of the World, from Marathon to Waterloo*, pp.7.

[489] Sir Edward Creasy, 1851, *The Fifteen Decisive Battles of the World, from Marathon to Waterloo*, pp.7.

Phoenician army came calling under Persian control, sent to
Chersonese to claim it for themselves and punish Miltiades –
and if possible, capture him and drag him back to face
Darius. Miltiades didn't hang around to see what the
Phoenicians had to offer on the battlefield and "filled five
triremes with the property which he had at hand and sailed
away for Athens"[490]. While his son Metiochos was
eventually captured, Miltiades himself managed to escape
into the relative safety of his home town. The Athenians
were in "the full glow of their newly recovered liberty and
equality"[491], having finally expelled the dictator Hippias (the
last of Pisistratus's tyrannical family) from the city.

Certainly, Miltiades was expecting the Athenians to be
distracted by their celebrations after achieving hard-won
freedom from tyranny and simply leave him alone, but his
arrival provoked a very different response. Under the
influence of Miltiades' "enemies at Athens", the former ruler
of Chersonese was brought to trial "for having been a tyrant
of the Chersonese"[492]. While the charges weren't founded
on any specific laws or any reports of explicit cruelty to his
people, they were inspired by the general "horror with which
the Greeks of that age regarded every man who made
himself compulsory master of his fellow men"[493]. It was at

---

[490] Herodotus, *The History of Herodotus, Volume II*. Book VI, pp.41.

[491] Sir Edward Creasy, 1851, *The Fifteen Decisive Battles of the World, from Marathon to Waterloo*, pp.8.

[492] Sir Edward Creasy, 1851, *The Fifteen Decisive Battles of the World, from Marathon to Waterloo*, pp.8.

[493] Sir Edward Creasy, 1851, *The Fifteen Decisive Battles of the World, from Marathon to Waterloo*, pp.8.

this point that Miltiades' earlier political manoeuvring to curry favour finally paid dividends. His supporters among the Athenians "refused to convict him" in light of his successes in the islands of Lemnos and Imbros (and then giving the territories to Athens), instead electing him as one of their ruling generals for the forthcoming year[494]. It was this turn of events that set the stage for one of the greatest turning points in history and carried Miltiades along so that he was there in 590 BC with nine other generals as they gathered on a mountaintop to overlook the plains of Marathon. The council of war that they had there would change the course of the world.

The Greeks had watched with nervous anticipation as the "mighty empire" of Persia had expanded and invaded its neighbours over the preceding fifty years, "shattering and enslaving nearly all the kingdoms and principalities of the then known world".[495] Realising that they were likely next on the Persian list, the Athenians prepared themselves to defend their new democracy and Athens itself from what was at the time the largest and most powerful army in the ancient world. It seemed an impossible task, and the council of war was divided as they considered the vast numbers of enemy soldiers and resources that was going to come against them. Little help from their Greek neighbours and allies could be expected, and therefore the Athenians were heavily outnumbered on the battlefield. Although "Sparta, the great

---

[494] Sir Edward Creasy, 1851, *The Fifteen Decisive Battles of the World, from Marathon to Waterloo*, pp.8.

[495] Sir Edward Creasy, 1851, *The Fifteen Decisive Battles of the World, from Marathon to Waterloo*, pp.2.

war-state of Greece"[496] had promised their support, their
march was delayed for religious reasons, leaving the
Athenians with only the Plataeans as their active allies. This
supporting force amounted to only a mere thousand men,
but "the gallant spirit of the men who composed it must
have made it of tenfold value to the Athenians"[497]. Indebted
to the Athenians for protecting their independence from
Thebes some years before, the Plataeans' voluntary march to
Athens was never forgotten, and the people of this small
Boetian nation "were made the fellow countrymen of the
Athenians"[498].

Even with the reinforcements of their "weak but true-
hearted ally" the Athenian forces numbered "about eleven
thousand fully-armed and disciplined infantry"[499], with more
lightly-armed troops, slaves and inferior freeman armed with
cutlasses and javelins bolstering their ranks. Heroic in spirit,
the Athenian force's numbers looked paltry in comparison to
the massive invading Persian army; estimates vary, but there
is good evidence that the enemy numbered somewhere in
the region of 100,000. Considering that some of this
number would have been followers and sailors, it's possible
that the Persian force was only 50,000-strong – still five
times greater than the Athenians and with years of battle

[496] Sir Edward Creasy, 1851, *The Fifteen Decisive Battles of the World, from Marathon to Waterloo*, pp.5.

[497] Sir Edward Creasy, 1851, *The Fifteen Decisive Battles of the World, from Marathon to Waterloo*, pp.3.

[498] Sir Edward Creasy, 1851, *The Fifteen Decisive Battles of the World, from Marathon to Waterloo*, pp.3.

[499] Sir Edward Creasy, 1851, *The Fifteen Decisive Battles of the World, from Marathon to Waterloo*, pp.4.

experience and victories over the Greeks under their belts. This was the situation that day on the mountaintop at the council of Athenian generals, under the watchful eye of the Athenian War-Ruler, Callimachus. Tensions were high, tempers were short, and opinion was divided.

With his customary boldness, Miltiades "felt no hesitation as to the course which the Athenian army ought to pursue"[500]. He advocated immediate and swift action, favouring a ferocious surprise attack. He argued that by taking the offensive, the Greeks would catch the Persians unprepared and unable to bring their superior numbers to bear. With his military background and having been "[p]ractically acquainted with the organisation of the Persian armies", Miltiades was convinced that the Greeks could win a stunning victory "if properly handled". According to Creasy, it was not only Miltiades' military expertise that enabled him to accurately assess the situation, but also his capabilities as a shrewd political operator. Creasy advised that "with the military eye of a great general" and "as a profound politician" Miltiades was able to weigh up the possible consequences of action versus inaction and pleaded with the other generals and Callimachus to support and adopt his strategy to confront the Persians sooner rather than later.

The counsel was divided, as half the assembled generals "shrank from the prospect of fighting a pitched

---

[500] Sir Edward Creasy, 1851, *The Fifteen Decisive Battles of the World, from Marathon to Waterloo*, pp.4.

battle against an enemy so superior in numbers and so formidable in military renown"[501]. As War-Ruler, Callimachus had the deciding vote to break the deadlock, and Miltiades passionately pleaded with him, saying "With thee now it rests, Callimachus, either to bring Athens under slavery or by making her free". Miltiades continued his appeal to action, suggesting that should they choose not to fight immediately that he would "expect that some great spirit of discord will fall upon the minds of the Athenians", but if they "fight a battle before any unsoundness appear in any part of the Athenian people, then we are able to gain the victory in the fight, if the gods grant equal conditions"[502]. Miltiades' calculated words convinced Callimachus, and he cast his vote to fight; the Greeks began to plan a coordinated attack as soon as practical. The generals who had supported offensive action agreed that a strong, passionate leader was needed for their forces, and "gave over their commands to Miltiades"[503].

Encamped in the mountains overlooking the Marathon plains, the Athenians had the topographical advantage and "could watch every movement of the Persians on the ground below, while they were enabled completely to mask their own"[504]. Their positions also gave Miltiades the advantage of being able to choose the moment of attack;

---

[501] Sir Edward Creasy, 1851, *The Fifteen Decisive Battles of the World, from Marathon to Waterloo*, pp.5.

[502] Herodotus, *The History of Herodotus, Volume II*. Book VI, pp.109.

[503] Herodotus, *The History of Herodotus, Volume II*. Book VI, pp.110.

[504] Sir Edward Creasy, 1851, *The Fifteen Decisive Battles of the World, from Marathon to Waterloo*, pp.11.

Darius and his soldiers had fewer options unless they "were to attempt the perilous operation of storming the heights"[505]. Despite this disadvantage, Darius was confident of a decisive victory and already planning his next moves following the defeat of the Athenian force in front of him. His army was large, well-equipped and in good spirits; he took great satisfaction in noting that he was following in the very footsteps of the old Athenian dictator Pisistratus and his sons who had "won an easy victory over their Athenian enemies on that very plain"[506] some years before. While the Persians camped confidently on the plains below, in the mountains the Greeks and Miltiades prepared for the battle of their lives; the campaign that they were about to fight would decide the fate of the entire Greek civilisation, beyond Athens and her allies. According to Creasy, "if Athens had fallen, no other Greek state... would have had the courage to resist... the victorious Persians"[507]. The battle would decide whether the world's first democracy would survive or be crushed and its people returned to tyrannical, one-man rule.

The decision to attack seemed rash to some on the Greek side, as all their allies had not yet arrived on the battlefield. Miltiades' decision to attack without the support of the elite Spartan troops, in particular, appeared risky, but he had weighed the composition of the enemy carefully. He

---

[505] Sir Edward Creasy, 1851, *The Fifteen Decisive Battles of the World, from Marathon to Waterloo*, pp.11.

[506] Sir Edward Creasy, 1851, *The Fifteen Decisive Battles of the World, from Marathon to Waterloo*, pp.20.

[507] Sir Edward Creasy, 1851, *The Fifteen Decisive Battles of the World, from Marathon to Waterloo*, pp.20.

was intimately familiar with how the Persian army was organised, travelled and fought, and was certain he knew how to exploit the greatest weakness behind the appearance of Persian irresistibility. He "knew that the bulk of their troops... consisted of... unwilling contingents from conquered nations" while Miltiades himself "trusted the enthusiasm of the men under his command"[508]. He decided that an aggressive frontal assault might fracture the cohesion of the Persian lines, and gave the instruction to his men to make a change from the Greeks' usual tactics of advancing "slowly and steadily... in a uniform phalanx of about eight spears deep"[509]. Because the Marathon plains ranged almost two miles wide, Miltiades was forced to extend his lines to cover the full width of the area and prevent "himself from being out-flanked and charge in the rear by the Persian horse"[510]. Importantly, not only were the Greeks operating at a huge numerical disadvantage in men, they also had no cavalry or archers in their ranks while Darius has large numbers of both. As they formed their ranks and readied their weapons, the Greeks would be relying solely on the valour of their infantry and the strategic decisions of their leaders.

Upon Miltiades' order, 11,000 spear-wielding Greek heavy infantry soldiers roared their battle cries and raced

---

[508] Sir Edward Creasy, 1851, *The Fifteen Decisive Battles of the World, from Marathon to Waterloo*, pp.21.

[509] Sir Edward Creasy, 1851, *The Fifteen Decisive Battles of the World, from Marathon to Waterloo*, pp.21.

[510] Sir Edward Creasy, 1851, *The Fifteen Decisive Battles of the World, from Marathon to Waterloo*, pp.23.

down the hill, charging the Persians who upon "seeing them advancing to the attack at a run, made preparations to receive them"[511]. The Persians were confident, but the Athenian forces were ferocious and "fought in a memorable fashion".[512] The two forces smashed into each other, and initially, both sides seemed evenly matched with the Persians holding the centre and the Athenians and Plataeans moving to overpower the two wings of the enemy formation. As the defeated sections of the Persian army fled, so Miltiades combined his two wings and "led them against the Persian centre".[513] Armed with long, deadly spears the orderly Greeks had Persian infantry with "their shorter and feebler weapons"[514] at a significant and growing disadvantage. Although Darius directed his soldiers to "force a lane in the phalanx and to bring their scimitars and daggers into play" the Athenian formations held firm and despite "the fatigue of the long-continued action... the sight of the carnage that they dealt amongst their assailants nerved them to fight still more fiercely on"[515].

Finally, as dusk began to fall, the Persian forces had enough and started to break, first in small groups and then in

---

[511] Herodotus, *The History of Herodotus, Volume II*. Book VI, pp.112.

[512] Sir Edward Creasy, 1851, *The Fifteen Decisive Battles of the World, from Marathon to Waterloo*, pp.24.

[513] Sir Edward Creasy, 1851, *The Fifteen Decisive Battles of the World, from Marathon to Waterloo*, pp.26.

[514] Sir Edward Creasy, 1851, *The Fifteen Decisive Battles of the World, from Marathon to Waterloo*, pp.27.

[515] Sir Edward Creasy, 1851, *The Fifteen Decisive Battles of the World, from Marathon to Waterloo*, pp.27.

larger numbers until their entire army had turned and were running for their lives. The most obvious place to retreat seemed to be through their camp and to the beach, where their war galleys were anchored nearby in the water. Panicked, then terrified the Persians threw their weapons away and attempted to get to their ships while the Athenian warriors followed "striking them down" and attempting to capture the galleys. What followed was a slaughter, with thousands of Persian hacked down by the triumphant Greeks. According to Creasy, it was during this phase of the Battle of Marathon that the Athenians experienced their greatest losses including the War Ruler Callimachus and a number of other notable soldiers[516]. Still eager to achieve a victory, Darius sailed around "to the western coast of Attica" in the hopes of finding a foothold in the unprotected city of Athens. Miltiades had anticipated this very move, however, and night-marched his conquering army back to arrive before Darius had chance to disembark and land his forces, and the Persians had to choice but to withdraw and give up the expedition. Sailing away and back to Persia, Darius was forced to abandon all his hopes of European conquest and stamping out the fledgeling Athenian democracy.

Having conceived and achieved one of the greatest military victories of all time, Miltiades should have been entitled to a life of prosperity and popularity in retirement, but his ambitions were to be his undoing. Soon after his victory at Marathon, Miltiades proposed that the Athenians "should fit out seventy galleys, with a proportionate force of

---

[516] Sir Edward Creasy, 1851, *The Fifteen Decisive Battles of the World, from Marathon to Waterloo*, pp.28.

soldiers and military stress, and place them at his disposal".[517] Refusing to reveal his intentions, Miltiades assured the gathered Athenians that he would sail "to a land where there was gold in abundance to be won with ease"[518] and take his forces to punish nearby Greek islands that were deemed to have supported the Persian invaders. His true intentions were purely selfish, and he set out to attack the island of Paros, where he hoped to settle a personal score. One of the leading citizens of Paros was named Hydarnes, and he and Miltiades had been involved in a quarrel during Miltiades' period as prince of the Chersonese that the Athenian general was determined to punish with blood. According to Herodotus, the gods had different plans.

Miltiades led his Athenian fleet to Paros and landed his army, besieging the capital but not able to take it outright due to a determined resistance by the inhabitants. According to Herodotus, while considering his offensive options, Miltiades was approached by a woman named Timo who was "an under-priestess of the Earth goddesses", who offered him advice on how he might bypass the city's defences. Following her instructions, Miltiades attempted to break into the temple of the goddess Demeter Giver of Laws but as he struggled to enter the sanctuary, "a shuddering fear came over him", and he decided instead to retreat. As he leapt back over the wall he had scaled to enter the sacred property Miltiades was injured, either dislocating or breaking

[517] Sir Edward Creasy, 1851, *The Fifteen Decisive Battles of the World, from Marathon to Waterloo*, pp.31.

[518] Sir Edward Creasy, 1851, *The Fifteen Decisive Battles of the World, from Marathon to Waterloo*, pp.31.

his leg[519]. Wounded and psychologically disturbed by his experience, Miltiades called off the siege and the invasion. After 26 days, the Athenians sailed for home having laid waste to the island in their search for gold and booty.

Unsurprisingly, his return to Athens was met with a public outcry, and the "indignation of the Athenians was proportionate to the hope and excitement which his promises had raised"[520]. Miltiades once again found himself under arrest and in court facing charges "for the capital offence of having deceived the people"[521]. As Creasy asserts, "[h]is guilt was undeniable" but, with memories of his military triumphs still fresh in their minds, the Athenians reduced the sentence from death to "a fine of fifty talents" which was paid by Miltiades' son, Cimon.

Although he had escaped the death penalty, Miltiades didn't escape prison and would die there in 489 BC, probably as a result of gangrene infection from the injury he sustained on Paros. He died less than auspiciously, given his colourful career and all that he achieved in life but Miltiades' military and political accomplishments place him in the upper echelons of the greatest warriors in history. The part he played in the "critical epoch" that the Battle of Marathon became will never be forgotten, breaking as it did "the spell

---

[519] Herodotus, *The History of Herodotus, Volume II.* Book VI, pp.134.

[520] Sir Edward Creasy, 1851, *The Fifteen Decisive Battles of the World, from Marathon to Waterloo*, pp.32.

[521] Sir Edward Creasy, 1851, *The Fifteen Decisive Battles of the World, from Marathon to Waterloo*, pp.32.

of Persian invincibility" and securing "for mankind the intellectual treasures of Athens, the growth of free institutions, the liberal enlightenment of the Western world".

VLAD TEPES

"The Impaler of Wallachia"

The name Vlad Tepes isn't one you'd expect anyone outside of Romania to be familiar with, but the name Dracula has resonance with people from all over the world, bringing to mind images of a blood-thirsty, supernatural sadist who strikes fear into the hearts of all he encounters. Although some disputes that this ruler of Transylvania wasn't the inspiration for Bram Stoker's famous vampire lord[522], most accept that that the two are one and the same[523]. The real Vlad Tepes could be viewed as a cruel and psychotic tyrant or a hero dedicated to protecting his homeland from ruthless invaders, depending on your point of view. There is room for both interpretations as we explore a little of the life and times of Vlad the Impaler, who later became the most likely basis for the vampire Dracula.

---

[522] https://vamped.org/2016/05/26/great-dracula-swindle/

[523] Dr. Peter Dan, *Psycho-biographical considerations about Vlad the Impaler also known as Dracula*, pp.1. https://www.academia.edu/10342218/Psycho-biographical_considerations_about_Vlad_the_Impaler_also_known_as_Dracula

To get a clear understanding of the truth behind the myth, we need to draw on three different sources: Saxon, Russian and Romanian. According to Florescu, who dedicated his life to the story of Dracula and his co-author McNally, the Saxon narrative focuses on his cruelty, while the Russian one depicts him as "strict but just"[524]. The Romanians have little written reference to the man, but their oral history celebrates him as a leader who fought valiantly for his homeland and resisted the onslaught of the powerful Ottoman Empire[525]. Despite their disparate emphases, the three narratives are consistent in many of the facts and stories they present about this ruthless leader, lending validity to their perspectives and interpretations equally.

According to early sources, Vlad III was born in 1431 with most suggesting he drew his first breath in the mountains of Transylvania. However, medieval historian Prof. Florin Curta, disputes this, suggesting a more probable birthplace was that of Târgoviște – a city some 100 miles from Transylvania where his father ruled the principality of Wallachia. Although Vlad III's father held the position of ruler or "voivode" at the time of his birth, the title had been hard-won and wrested from Vlad II's cousin during the Draculesti-Danesti feud that raged throughout the early 1400s[526]. Here we get a hint of the Dracula connection which originated with Vlad II who in 1431 was inducted into

[524] Radu R. Florescu & Raymond T. McNally, 1989, *Dracula, Prince of Many Faces: His Life and His Times*. Hatchett Book Group, New York.

[525] Aurel Dănescu, *The Shadow of a Prince in History: The true Romanian story of Vlad the Impaler Dracula*, pp.5

[526] Marc Lallanilla, 2017, *The Real Dracula: Vlad the Impaler*,

the knightly organisation the Order of the Dragon, by King Sigismund of Hungary. As a member, Vlad adopted Dracul as his surname as it was derived from the Romanian word 'drac', meaning dragon. As his son, Vlad the Impaler became known as Drăculea, meaning 'son of Dracul'[527].

Vlad III didn't have the easiest of upbringings, although his earliest memories would have been of a court education focused on preparing him for knighthood. His father's political wrangling backfired when in 1437 "he pledged allegiance to the Sultan, Murad II"[528], but this declaration of loyalty didn't last long, and he soon swapped sides to support the rising Hungarian power, John Hunyadi. This understandably upset the Sultan who summoned Vlad to meet him in Gallipoli to answer for his treachery. On arrival in the city with his two young sons in tow, Vlad II was arrested but released after one short year in prison. His sons weren't so lucky, however, and remained behind as hostages in the fortress of Egrigöz "guaranteeing with their lives his good behaviour"[529]. While Vlad III's younger brother Radu adapted to the situation quite easily and became a loyal subject of the Sultan, "[captivity] irked Vlad"[530] and he became increasing suspicious and devious,

---

[527] Marc Lallanilla, 2017, *The Real Dracula: Vlad the Impaler,*

[528] Marc Lallanilla, 2017, *The Real Dracula: Vlad the Impaler,*

[529] Dr. Peter Dan, *Psycho-biographical considerations about Vlad the Impaler also known as Dracula*, pp.2.

[530] Marc Lallanilla, 2017, *The Real Dracula: Vlad the Impaler,*

while "harbouring a pervasive feeling of having been wronged"[531].

Life in Turkey wasn't all bad for the two brothers, and they were reasonably well treated while receiving excellent military training from the elite corps of warriors known as the Janissaries[532]. In the year 1448, Vlad and his brother were finally released by the Sultan, and while Radu opted to remain in Turkey, Vlad promptly packed up and returned home to Wallachia. Arriving in his native land, he was horrified to find "that his father had been assassinated and his older brother Mircea had been buried alive by the nobles of Târgoviste who had supported a rival claimant"[533]. Only 17 years old, Vlad had already made up his mind that he must win back his father's throne and set right to work to begin his career as "a great military strategist"[534]. The young prince was home, with a vengeance.

Physically, Vlad was far removed from the handsome royal figures of fairy tales. He was described as a short, burly man that projected an angry, ferocious air. One man that met Vlad left us a record; according to Nicholas Modrussa

[531] Dr. Peter Dan, *Psycho-biographical considerations about Vlad the Impaler also known as Dracula*, pp.9.

[532] Dr. Peter Dan, *Psycho-biographical considerations about Vlad the Impaler also known as Dracula*, pp.9.

[533] Dr. Elizabeth Miller, 2005, *Vlad the Impaler: Brief History*
http://www.ucs.mun.ca/~emiller/vlad.html

[534] Dr. Peter Dan, *Psycho-biographical considerations about Vlad the Impaler also known as Dracula*, pp.12.

the Wallachian royal had "a cruel and terrible appearance, a long straight nose, distended nostrils, a thin and reddish face in which the large wide-open green eyes were framed by bushy black eyebrow"[535]. Although Vlad managed to wrest his father's throne back from the reigning Vladislav II, his reign in 1448 didn't last long, and after a mere two months he was forced to flee when the Hungarians decided to reinstate Vladislav, supporting his claim to power with their army.

Over the next eight years, Vlad planned and plotted while hiding away in his uncle's Moldavian court until his uncle Bogdan I was assassinated in 1451. His patron and protector gone, Vlad was forced to flee again, this time to Transylvania with his cousin, Prince Stephen[536]. Vlad continued to campaign and advocate his return to power, and finally, in 1456 he convinced the Hungarians that he was the rightful heir to the throne and they threw their support behind his claim. He was put back in charge and was "once again the ruler of Wallachia, and the Sultan was his enemy"[537]. Having regained his position in his homeland, Vlad set about consolidating his grip on power by breaking "the political power of the boyars (nobles) who tended to support puppet (and often weak) leaders"[538] while

---

[535] Dr. Peter Dan, *Psycho-biographical considerations about Vlad the Impaler also known as Dracula*, pp.15.

[536] Dr. Peter Dan, *Psycho-biographical considerations about Vlad the Impaler also known as Dracula*, pp.14.

[537] Dr. Peter Dan, *Psycho-biographical considerations about Vlad the Impaler also known as Dracula*, pp.14.

[538] Dr. Elizabeth Miller, 2005, *Vlad the Impaler: Brief History*
http://www.ucs.mun.ca/~emiller/vlad.html

simultaneously staving off the threats of his rival claimants. His hold on the royal throne was precarious and under constant threat; this, coupled with his troubled childhood may have twisted his outlook on how he perceived the world. Dr. Dan suggests these elements may have "distorted his moral development",[539] and certainly Vlad took an extreme approach to law and order, inflicting severe punishment for the slightest indiscretion. A similar harsh attitude extended to his enemies and perceived rivals to such a degree that even "his most ardent defenders will concede that he took drastic measures to achieve his political, economic and military objectives"[540].

In the early 1460s, Vlad's pillaging and raids along the Muslim settlements on the other side of the Danube River provoked a war between himself and his number one enemy – the hated Turks. The Turkish forces heavily outnumbered Vlad and his small army, so he employed a series of clever if ruthless strategies to wrest every advantage he could. This included a rudimentary type of biological warfare, "sending victims of infectious diseases into the Turkish camps"[541] in the hope of eroding the enemy strength. In June 1962, Vlad led his soldiers on a famous and vicious "Night Attack", terrifying and scattering the Turks but failing to deter the Sultan from all-out invasion of Wallachia. Desperate, Vlad

[539] Dr. Peter Dan, *Psycho-biographical considerations about Vlad the Impaler also known as Dracula*, pp.7.

[540] Dr. Elizabeth Miller, 2005, *Vlad the Impaler: Brief History*
http://www.ucs.mun.ca/~emiller/vlad.html

[541] Dr. Elizabeth Miller, 2005, *Vlad the Impaler: Brief History*
http://www.ucs.mun.ca/~emiller/vlad.html

decided to up the stakes and ordered wholesale impalement of Turkish soldiers, starting with the dead and then moving on to include all the living prisoners he had captured. According to the Greek historian, Chalkondyles, as the Sultan and his army approached, they encountered a field across which a line of stakes extended "about three kilometres long and one kilometre wide"[542]. Upon these stakes were "the impaled bodies of men, women, and children, about twenty thousand of them"[543]. Horrified, the Turks retreated back from Wallachia; the Sultan quoted as saying "he could not conquer the country of a man who could do such terrible and unnatural things and put his power and his subjects to such use"[544].

Now a ruler both feared and dreaded, other stories of Vlad's cruel atrocities circulated throughout Europe. One tale, in particular, was told and retold that highlights not only his brutality but also marked him as merciless and emotionally detached from the suffering he could cause. According to German, Romanian and Russian sources, during Vlad's second reign he happened to notice a significant increase in the number of poor, vagrant and crippled people living in his kingdom, so he decided to do something about it. He promptly invited all the sick and poor of Wallachia to come for a feast in Târgoviste,

---

[542] Cited in *Vlad the Impaler: Brief History*
http://www.ucs.mun.ca/~emiller/vlad.html

[543] Cited in *Vlad the Impaler: Brief History*
http://www.ucs.mun.ca/~emiller/vlad.html

[544] Cited in *Vlad the Impaler: Brief History*
http://www.ucs.mun.ca/~emiller/vlad.html

"claiming that no one should hungry in his land"[545]. When the poorest and most desperate populace arrived, they were shown to a great hall where a lavish feast had been prepared for them. As they ate and drank Vlad personally addressed them, asking what else they wanted. He is said to have inquired "Do you want to be without cares, lacking nothing in this world".[546] Roaring their approval, the peasants took the bait and shouted that they dreamed of such a state. Satisfied, he ordered the doors and exits sealed to the hall and had it set on fire. He reasoned that this was the most sensible option for them, ensuring that those people "represent no further burden to others so that no one will be poor in my realm"[547]. Vlad it was said, practised his own brand of twisted and sadistic socialism.

This and other stories echoed throughout Europe, and he continued to add to the inventory of examples of his tyrannical barbarity. Probably the most savage episode of his biography took place in Brasov in 1459, when Vlad personally led an assault on the city after local merchants repeatedly refused to pay their taxes. To get his message across, Vlad "burned an entire suburb, and impaled entire families on Timpa Hill"[548]. Appalling from a modern-day perspective, "his defenders point out that his actions were no

---

[545] Dr. Elizabeth Miller, 2005, *Vlad the Impaler: Brief History*
http://www.ucs.mun.ca/~emiller/vlad.html

[546] Dr. Elizabeth Miller, 2005, *Vlad the Impaler: Brief History*
http://www.ucs.mun.ca/~emiller/vlad.html

[547] Dr. Elizabeth Miller, 2005, *Vlad the Impaler: Brief History*
http://www.ucs.mun.ca/~emiller/vlad.html

[548] Dr. Elizabeth Miller, 2005, *Vlad the Impaler: Brief History*
http://www.ucs.mun.ca/~emiller/vlad.html

more cruel than those of several other late-medieval or early-Renaissance European rulers such as Louis XI of France... and Ivan the Terrible of Russia"[549]. His brutality did win him some local support as a strong leader, and even today Romanians still speak of Vlad III as a victorious hero "who repeatedly defended his homeland from the Turks... and a leader who succeeded in maintaining law and order in what were indeed lawless and disorderly times"[550].

While little is known of the man behind the tyrant, it seems he practised private, as well as public cruelty in his personal relationships. One account of his private life tells of a mistress who informed Vlad that she was pregnant with his child. Vlad retorted that it was impossible and he accused her of making up the claim entirely. The woman persisted, and Vlad decided to settle the matter by cutting open her stomach and examining her entrails, saying "See you are lying. Let the world see where I have been"[551]. At some point, Vlad married and possibly had more than one wife during the course of his life. His first wife is believed to have been a noblewoman from Transylvania, about which another disturbing story has lived on in the oral history of Romania. According to the narrative, Vlad's wife was a "kind and humble" woman who became worried and distressed every time her husband left for battle. On one

[549] Dr. Elizabeth Miller, 2005, *Vlad the Impaler: Brief History* http://www.ucs.mun.ca/~emiller/vlad.html

[550] Dr. Elizabeth Miller, 2005, *Vlad the Impaler: Brief History* http://www.ucs.mun.ca/~emiller/vlad.html

[551] Dr. Peter Dan, *Psycho-biographical considerations about Vlad the Impaler also known as Dracula*, pp.18.

evening, while she was waiting for her husband's return an arrow flew through her bedroom window, putting out the candle. As she relit the candle, she discovered a letter attached to the arrow which stated that she and the fortress were surrounded by the Turks. When she looked out of the window the flickering lights encircling the castle confirmed the contents of the letter and "[t]hinking all was lost... she climbed up on the wall of the fortress and threw herself into the Arges River".

There is little documentary evidence of this first wife, whereas there is a little more to support the existence of his second wife, Ilona Szilagy. It is believed that Vlad met this future spouse during his imprisonment in Hungary which occurred at the end of his second reign in 1462. Ilona was the cousin of the King of Hungary, Matthias Corvinus and it was generally understood that the king offered Vlad a royal bride of his family to consolidate the allegiance he had sworn to Hungary. Some suggest that Ilona was a willing bride[552], but even if she was reluctant she didn't have to put up with Vlad for too long, as just two years after their wedding, he was killed on the battlefield. Between his two wives, Vlad had left behind three sons to continue his line. The eldest of which would go on to later rule Wallachian himself, employing just as much cruelty and sadism during his brief rule as his father had before him[553].

---

[552] Dirk Cameron Gibson, *Legends, Monsters, or Serial Murderers? The Real Story Behind an Ancient Crime*, pp.95.

[553] Dr. Elizabeth Miller, 2005, *Vlad the Impaler: Brief History* http://www.ucs.mun.ca/~emiller/vlad.html

Unsurprisingly, the exact circumstances surrounding Vlad's death are vague, but unlike his namesake Dracula, it is certain that he was indeed killed and did not rise from the grave. Around the end of 1476, Vlad was fighting with his soldiers in a skirmish, and he did not live to return from the battlefield. What actually happened to him in the Băneasa forest outside Bucharest no one really knows, but certainly a number of different theories have been posited over the years. According to Russian sources, Vlad was killed by his own men after they mistakenly took him for a Turk. Another variant suggests he was the victim of a planned ambush during which he was murdered under the instructions of his successor, Basarab Laiota. More recently, archaeologists and historians have debated a new theory in which instead of meeting his fate in the forest that day, Vlad was actually taken prisoner and "ransomed to his daughter in Italy and then buried in a church in Naples". This new hypothesis is based on the evidence provided by an ancient headstone found in Naples in the Piazza Santa Maria la Nova. The grave marker is decorated with the images of a dragon and two sphinxes, which scholars suggest literally spells out "the very name of the count Dracula Tepes". The tombstone itself was uncovered just recently, but its historical validity has yet to be substantiated[554].

So was Vlad the Impaler just a bloodthirsty tyrant or is he deserving of a place among the greatest warriors in history? Certainly, his capacity to use all his capabilities

---

[554] Esma Cakir, 2014, *Dracula's Tomb Discovered in Italy*. http://www.hurriyetdailynews.com/draculas-tomb-discovered-in-italy-67748

"including the ones born out of his pathology" to achieve his political goals is testament to a resolute and determined man. Without his capacity for cruelty, the psychological aspect of his war strategies would have been absent and subsequently, it can be argued that the victories he won may have turned in defeats. In terms of his unwavering commitment to "the independence of Wallachia, breaking the Boyars' grip on power, safeguarding Christianity from the onslaught of Islam", Vlad proved both valiant and victorious but to what degree this makes him a warrior is debatable.

According to Dr. Dan, Vlad must have been aware that his actions would mean "that history would not treat him kindly" and suggests his brutal approach to governing and warfare in retrospect was "an act of self-sacrifice".[555] While his capacity to strategise and win victories on his many battlefields was admirable, his complete lack of integrity or any kind of moral code makes it difficult to award him "warrior" class in the traditional sense. Generally in North American culture we celebrate a warrior as a noble hero stereotype, one who sacrifices himself for the good of others and fights for cause and higher purpose; certainly this description has resonance with the many warrior civilisations that have existed over the years, as well as with modern concepts. Looking back at the writings of Myamoto Musashi, who epitomised the qualities of integrity and honour in History's Greatest Warriors Volume One, the spirit of the warrior is summarised as "Today is victory over yourself of yesterday, tomorrow is victory over lesser

---

[555] Dr. Peter Dan, *Psycho-biographical considerations about Vlad the Impaler also known as Dracula*, pp.21.

men"[556]. Assessing the best evidence we have about Vlad suggests he never gained victory over himself in the Japanese sense, possibly because he was held prisoner "at the period in life, when ... the main developmental goals are establishing a sense of identity and a capacity for intimacy"[557].

While Vlad may be celebrated as a local hero by his people and a determined patriot who dedicated his life to his country, his cruel brutality, vicious mentality and ruthless approach to his rivals couldn't be more incompatible with the traditional warrior concept. However, as appalling as modern interpretations are of what he is said to have done, there is room for Vlad in the ranks of the greatest warriors in history. Never "a guardian of the ways of honour and courage", he was a single-minded and dedicated defender of his faith, his people and his kingdom against what must have seemed to be impossible odds against the Turks and his political rivals both at home and in Europe. Constantly under threat and never secure on his throne, he employed every resource at his disposal to win and to protect Wallachia from the Ottoman invaders and maintain his nation's independence. He well understood that the atrocities he committed would mean a horrible end for him and his family if he lost the struggle with the Turks, and he also knew how history would view him even if he were victorious, given the brutal methods he would need to use to win. In this sense, he sacrificed any noble legacy that might have been and

---

[556] Miyamoto Musashi, 1645. *A Book of Five Rings*. Translated by Victor Harris.

[557] Dr. Peter Dan, *Psycho-biographical considerations about Vlad the Impaler also known as Dracula*, pp.12.

traded it for victory for his homeland and his people, no matter what the cost. Weighing and then paying this price transforms Vlad into a warrior king worthy of respect for what he was able to achieve, if not for how he accomplished it.

DIHYA

"Algerian Warrior Queen"

While Joan of Arc stands out in the minds of most as
the most famous example of a brave and religiously-inspired
woman-warrior, few of us have heard of Dihya. A mighty
Queen Warrior, she was a kindred spirit to Joan of France
and defended her country and religion vehemently back in
the 7th century. Born in the mountains of modern-day
Algeria, Dihya is purported to have been a member of
royalty and destined to become the Queen of the Aurés.
Although little is known of her parentage, according to the
Arab historian Ibn Khaldun her mother was a member of
the Jrāwa tribe who went by the name of Tabita or Mathia
ben Tifan – daughter of Tifan[558.]

As a Jrāwa, Dihya would have been considered a
Berber, although this term has been rejected by the Amazigh
people throughout history. The Amazigh people populated
much of North Africa from as earlier as 5,000 BC and

[558] https://www.jpost.com/Magazine/Judaism/HisHer-Story-A-
Jewish-warrior-queen

commanded considerable respect for their military competence and excellence with horses. Calling themselves Amazigh, possibly meaning 'free men'[559] the Berbers integrated with the Phoenicians of Carthage, living alongside them in an uneasy peace for many years.

The Israeli writer and translator Nahum Slouschz suggests that Dihya was a descendant of a wealthy and noble family, deported from Judea. According to Slouschz's version of events, King Josiah instigated the Deuteronomic Reform, removing idols, destroying cults and establishing the Temple of Jerusalem as the focal point for all worship. In keeping with the Bible's Book of Deuteronomy, the reform stressed the notion that only one God should be worshipped, reinforcing the concept of monotheism.

Slouschz describes Dihya as "a descendant of a priestly family"[560]; as priests exist only in the Anglican, Catholic and Orthodox churches, her family didn't necessarily support the strict Judaism of Josiah, and this might have led to their deportation. Although some sources indicate that Dihya was Jewish by birth, it seems more likely that she converted to Judaism with the rest of her tribe earlier in the century. Historically the Amazigh people held a variety of religious beliefs, with some being Jewish, others

---

[559] https://en.wikipedia.org/wiki/Berbers

[560] https://mosaicmagazine.com/picks/2018/10/the-legendary-jewish-warrior-princess-of-the-berbers/

Christian and still others adhering to an ancient polytheist set of beliefs[561].

Although Dihya has been depicted as a leader faithful to the Judah religion, some claim she was a Christian who took strength from the image of the Virgin Mary. Others suggest that she practised an indigenous religion which worshipped the sun and moon which resonates with her reported prophetic powers better than either the Christian or Jewish religions. Whatever her beliefs, Dihya was brave and determined while facing the rise of Islam in Africa, perhaps partially due to the denigration of women within the Islamic religion which would have undermined her authority and status[562].

Little is known of her childhood, although there have been suggestions that she developed an early interest in desert birds. While this seems a trivial footnote in her life, her studies significantly advanced biological science in North Africa as well as contributed to her reputation during her lifetime as a sorceress who could foresee the future by speaking to the birds and animals[563]. As with everything relating to Dihya, there are many different versions of events that revolve around her; even her name is debated. Some

---

[561] Michael Klossner, 2015. "Tihya, Queen of the Berbers", https://theglobalculture.blogspot.com/2015/11/the-kahina-queen-of-berbers.html

[562] https://www.ancient.eu/Kahina/

[563] https://www.ancient.eu/Kahina/

refer to her as Dahiya while other scholars name her as Tihya or Dahra.

All the records we have of her life are often controversial and contradictory, full of legend and folklore with a few facts sprinkled in. Like her religious beliefs, Dihya's tribal origins are equally unclear with some suggesting she belonged to the Lūwāta tribe rather than the Jrāwa. Regardless of the lack of clarity regarding her origins, Dihya established herself as a powerful leader who united disparate Berber tribes to fight for their cultural and social independence, refusing to be subjugated[564].

Prior to leading her own army into battle, Dihya fought alongside Aksel, the king of Altava and chief of the Awraba clan; according to some sources he was her father[565]. During these battles, Dihya proved her capability as an adept soldier and astute military commander. Aksel led the Byzantine-Berber army into battle against the invading Arabs, plotting their defeat after pretending to join the Arab side. According to some, Aksel converted to Islam as a ruse to lure the Arabs into a false sense of security that enabled Aksel to ambush their weakening army[566]. It seems Aksel believed that converting to Islam would be profitable for

---

[564] Cynthia Becker, 2015. "Dihya: The Female Face of Amazigh History". *Amazigh World News.* https://amazighworldnews.com/dihya-the-female-face-of-amazigh-history/

[565] https://www.ancient.eu/Kahina/

[566] https://www.quora.com/Did-Arabs-invade-North-Africa-and-Berbers-lands

him, but as the Muslim influence and army grew in strength, Aksel's own position of sovereignty looked certain to come to an end, and he was encouraged to abandon his adopted faith and return to his religious roots.

The Berbers fought many invading forces over the years, and their violent response to the Islamic invasion was possibly not fuelled by religious beliefs. Fanatically independent, they had been subjected to Roman rule and were determined not to be conquered again. The invasion of the Arabs into their lands was resisted ferociously, and they saw the conflict with the warriors of Islam as a mere "continuation of a fight against the Romans"[567].

It is highly probable that Dihya joined the battle against the Arabs around the time of Aksel's reversion to Judaism, just as many of her fellow tribal members did. Ibn-Khaldun suggested that the conflict between the Arabs and the Amazigh was another form of the struggle between nomadic and settled people repeated throughout history, rather than a fight with origins in conflicting beliefs. Regardless of her motives, Dihya was a determined and effective soldier, earning herself widespread respect and authority.

---

[567] Abdelmajid Hannoum, 1997. "Historiography, Mythology and Memory in Modern North Africa: The Story of the Kahina", *Studia Islamica*, No. 85 (1997), pp. 88.

Late in the 7th century, chief Aksel was captured by Arab soldiers and forced to disband his army. After his release or escape, however, the king of Altava went right back to fighting and reformed his army to take on the Arabs once again. This time, he succeeded in defeating them and killing their leader, Uqba ibn Nafi. Upon his death, Aksel was succeeded by either his wife or another female relative, but the ruler of the successor was very brief. By around 690 AD, Dihya became commander of the Berber army.

Having already proved her worth as a soldier, Dihya cemented her reputation as a formidable military opponent. When the Islamic troops returned to invade again under the command of Hassan ben Naaman, they were prepared for renewed bitter fighting with the Berbers, but they didn't count on Dihya. Invading with 45,000 soldiers, Hassan was supremely confident of victory, especially so when he learned that he was opposed by a mere woman. Dihya first attempted to use diplomacy to neutralise the Arabs, but all offers of a negotiated peace were dismissed and refused. Instead, Hassan responded with his own ultimatum advising that he would grant peace only if Dihya converted to Islam and recognised the supremacy of the Muslim authorities. According to some sources, Dihya stalwartly refused with the declaration "I shall die in the religion I was born to"[568].

---

[568] https://www.bh.org.il/blog-items/queen-desert-amazing-story-jewish-khaleesi/

In an entirely polemic version of events, French historian Henri Garrot *suggests that Dihya actually converted to Islam rather than confront the mighty force of Hassan, but the Arab leader advanced to attack her army anyway. Mubarak Milli rejects this theory, claiming Garrot simply wanted to discredit the great Amazigh queen while suggesting that the Islamic invasion brought stability and prosperity to the region*[569].

Another source provides evidence consistent with this belief, suggesting that Hassan sent an envoy to Dihya demanding that she accept Islam as the religion of her people. When Dihya refused, Hassan's representative explained that they wanted to bring the Amazigh people into the light of Islam. Dihya again challenged him saying that she has read the Koran but found "nothing new in it" and that it seemed somewhat regressive "especially in regards to the relations between men and women"[570]. Inevitably this sparked a heated argument about the status of men and women, and reportedly Dihya angrily retorted "I am not inferior to you and you are not my equal!"

In this version of events, Dihya is as familiar with the premises of the Islamic religion as she is both Judaism and Christianity, although it is the latter that she has embraced. Hassan's envoy becomes enraged at her refusal to accept what she refers to as his "false prophet", and called her "a

---

[569] Bruce Maddy-Weitzman, *The Berber Identity Movement and the Challenge to North African States*. University of Texas Press, pp.45.

[570] https://aramaicherald.blogspot.com/2014/03/kahina-queen-of-berbers.html

witch and a sorceress". Her supporters counselled caution, but Dihya remained defiant and pointed out that if they converted to Islam, her people would lose both their lands and their freedom, which was ultimately the same fate they faced if they were defeated in battle. Declaring that they had nothing to lose and everything to win, she reasoned that the Berbers would need to fight.

It would seem that Dihya's faith, loyalty and her apparent ability to speak with animals and foresee the future swayed many of her people. Berbers from all over the region came together to join forces with the woman they called Kahina, meaning "the diviner, the fortuneteller"[571]. Although some have asserted that Dihya's reputation as a sorceress was bestowed on her by her opponents, others contend that her gift of prophecy gave her the capacity to predict the exact formation of opponents' troops, the direction of their attack and the source of their possible reinforcements. Inevitably this inspired her fellow Berbers and, although her victories were hard-won, they were nonetheless decisive.

Some accounts suggest that although her forces were significantly outnumbered by the Muslim army, Dihya was able to secure an unlikely victory by using her knowledge of the environment. Realising the untenability of her position, Dihya had ordered a retreat. However, as she perceived the strong winds blowing in the enemy direction she ordered

---

that large fires be set, sending great clouds of smoke at the Arab soldiers. This stopped the enemy advance, but also obscured her forces from Hassan and his men. Strategically, it also meant that to launch another attack the Arabs would have to cross a great swathe of burnt wasteland with no resources at hand. Hassan promptly retreated and spent the next five years in Egypt, licking his wounds and preparing for a second invasion.

There is evidence that indicates the success of her fire-brand approach inspired Dihya to instigate a scorched-earth policy that would, in time, prove disastrous both for her and for her people. Believing that the Arabs were primarily after the riches her land had to offer them, Dihya decided that by destroying everything of worth she would dissuade the Arabs from further invasions. Historian Edward Gibbon records the Berber Queen as urging her people to destroy all their precious metals and raze their cities so that "when the avarice of our foes shall be destitute of temptation, perhaps they will cease to disturb the tranquillity of a warlike people"[572].

Dihya began her campaign by burning productive fields and melting down precious metals, before going on to tear down cities and towns and destroy all fortifications. Sadly, although this may have made the Berber lands less attractive to invaders, it also meant that the livelihood of her own people was seriously compromised. With no hope of

[572] Edward Gibbon, The History of the Decline and Fall of the Roman Empire, Volume 2, pp.241.

growing food in their charred fields and blackened orchards and with no roof over their heads, many town and city residents became nomadic and wandered through the barren wasteland left after years of war. Inevitably, this damaged her reputation and popularity considerably... if it was true, that is.

Gibbon is pretty scathing in his treatment of the Amazigh queen, saying that her policy of "universal ruin" probably terrified those city inhabitants who shared neither her beliefs nor her nomadic upbringing. According to Gibbon, she was an unworthy leader who based her powers on "blind and rude idolatry" and the "baseless fabric of her superstition". Others, however, are suspicious of claims that Dihya was responsible for the scorched-earth policy, pointing out that it was a technique the Arabs had used previously in both Libya and Egypt. The Arabs found this was an effective way of subduing the enemy population and as they were more concerned with recruiting people for religious conversion than winning great territories and riches, this was a successful approach.

If the Arabs did instigate the scorched-earth policy, it proved effective even if many historians have attributed the blame to the Berber Queen. Regardless of who decided on the tactic, it certainly had the effect of demoralising the people and all but destroying their faith in their sorcerer queen. For many, a Muslim victory seemed inevitable, and perhaps even Dihya herself doubted her capacity to continue

resisting the Arabs. Some even suggest that she later
surrendered one of her own sons to Hasan[573].

Unlike the morally pure Joan of Arc, Dihya was a
passionate woman who was "addicted to the lusts of the
flesh with all her youthful flaming temper". She had two
sons by two different men and apparently had three
husbands on hand to satisfy her carnal needs[574].

Rumour has it that just as she surrendered one of her
own sons to Islam, she subsequently adopted one young
man from amongst the Arabic prisoners she captured during
her conflicts with Hassan. In a strangely generous act, Dihya
was known to favour releasing any prisoners she took, but
this one enemy soldier named Haled ben Yazid she took as
her own son. Little is said of Yazid after this event, but
another son seems to have played an instrumental role in her
eventual defeat.

According to some sources, when the invading Arabs
returned amongst them was one of Dihya's own sons who
had turned away from Judaism and converted to Islam.
Although it is unclear as to whether the returning Muslim

---

573 https://www.ozy.com/flashback/meet-the-warrior-queen-who-
battled-the-arabs/88537
574 https://www.bh.org.il/blog-items/queen-desert-amazing-story-
jewish-khaleesi/

army was lead by Hassan or his successor Musa, their defeat of Dihya is not in dispute.

Assuming that Hassan was leading the Arab army with Dihya's son by his side, the Berber queen he found waiting for him in the Aures mountains was a very different woman to the one who had defeated him some years before. Either as a consequence of the scorched-earth policy or through bribery and corruption, many of those who had stood behind the Dihya had defected to Hassan's army, leaving her heavily outnumbered. To further her disadvantage, her traitorous offspring knew her usual methods and was able to inform Hassan on her probable tactics.

With so much against her, it's hard to believe Dihya even bothered to engage with the opposition at all, but she did, and her small army fought so bravely and with such ferocity even their enemies couldn't fail to admire them. As any true warrior should, it is believed that Dihya was killed sword in hand fighting for her beliefs and her country. She was decapitated, and her head was given to Hassan as a prize of war. Reportedly out of respect for his former opponent, he went on to take good care of her sons, bringing them up as his own and giving them the tools to follow in their mother's footsteps, leading their own armies into battle.

Things weren't so good for the Berber people after Dihya's defeat and death; thousands were sold into slavery by the victorious Arab oppressors. Those few that stayed free ended up in isolated communities, holding out as long as they could against the formidable Arab onslaught. Some are said to have taken their own lives rather than convert to Islam, but by around 750, North Africa was almost exclusively Islamic, with little of Dihya's Jewish legacy remaining.

Despite this, Dihya has proved an important figure for a variety of people and cultures. Noted author and historian Abdelmajid Hannoum stated that "[N]o legend has articulated or promoted as many myths, nor served as many ideologies as this one". Dihya has been reborn and reinvented numerous times, serving as a figurehead for the Berbers and ironically, even the Muslims. According to some Muslim believers, Dihya didn't die on the battlefield but was rather defeated, after which she converted to Islam and became a model Muslim. This seems a highly unlikely outcome.

Nevertheless, over the past 10 centuries or so Dihya has been adopted by a wide range of different political and social groups with diverse agendas covering everything from Berber cultural and ethnic rights to feminism and Arab nationalism. The Arabs often present her as a woman in possession of supernatural powers but who eventually, recognised the legitimacy of Islam, went on to encourage her

sons to adopt the religion and create unity between the
Berbers and their former enemies[575].

Part of Dihya's chameleon capacity appears to have
come from the Berbers' own fluidity when it came to
religious beliefs. According to Ibn Khaldun, the Berbers
adopted the beliefs of pretty much every group of people
that ruled over them, first adopting Judaism while under the
influence of the Yemen kings before swiftly switching to
Christian beliefs following the Roman invasion. Such
changeability has meant the legend of Dihya could be
claimed by virtually anyone, although it is as an example of
the Berbers' religious, gender, and ethnic tolerance that she is
most remembered.

Dihya has been so celebrated by the Berber people
that a statue of her was erected in Algeria as recently as 2003.
Built by Amazigh activists, the 9-foot monument was
constructed as part of a movement to preserve the remains
of what they believe to have been a fortress erected by Dihya
during the Muslim invasion. Far from uncontroversial,
however, the unveiling of the statue was ignored by the
national press, even though the Algerian president Abdelaziz
Bouteflika attended the ceremony. Cynthia Becker suggests
that Bouteflika's presence was designed to appease the
activists while the lack of press coverage was at the

---

[575] Ed. Abdelwahab Meddeb, Benjamin Stora, 2013. *A History of Jewish-Muslim Relations: From the Origins to the Present Day*. Princeton University Press, pp.995.

instigation of the government, suggesting a conflict of interest[576].

For some, the defiant woman warrior immortalised in the effigy represents a period of history and religious activism they would rather forget. Given that the Amazigh are now Muslims, some see the statue as an act of blasphemy, celebrating a woman who strongly resisted their own religion. Indeed, Dihya has been celebrated as a "prototypical antihero, representing everything counter to Islamic values".[577]

Although in more recent times, Dihya has been taken to symbolise feminism amongst the Amazigh people, she also embodies the ethnic rights of this small populace. Certainly during her lifetime, the Amazigh enjoyed relative freedom and women were allowed leadership status – a relatively unusual aspect of any culture at the time. Not only was ancestry traced using the female line, but property was also passed down from daughter to daughter. This would come to an abrupt end with the introduction of Islam to the region, but Dihya's dramatic attempts at protecting her people have never been forgotten.

---

[576] http://www.mizanproject.org/the-kahina-the-female-face-of-berber-history/

[577] Bruce Maddy-Weitzman, *The Berber Identity Movement and the Challenge to North African States*. University of Texas Press, pp.23.

It is notable that many powerful women have been associated with having some kind of supernatural powers, and Dihya is no exception. Not only is she described as being unusually tall and "great of hair", but legend also suggests that she lived for over 100 years and when she was inspired would let out her hair and beat her breast, suggesting a state of religious ecstasy[578]. In addition to her prophetic capabilities, it has also been suggested that the Kahina's revolt against the Arabs was foretold by the appearance of a comet[579]. Legends and rumours have also swirled around Dihya's private life, suggesting that she married twice, once to a Greek and once to a fellow Amazigh.

In another story of Dihya or, on this occasion, Dahi-Yah, the beautiful young woman is ordered by the leader of another tribe to become his wife. Initially, she refused, but when the chieftain went on to intimidate and massacre her tribe, she relented and married him. The tribal chief was an unpleasant man who forced himself on her and beat her prior to their wedding. On their first night of wedded misery, however, Dihya took her revenge "smashing his skull with a nail" and ending his tyranny.

Whatever Dihya was, in terms of religion and power she has firmly established herself as an icon and symbol of

[578] https://www.geni.com/people/Dahiyya-al-Kahina-bint-D%CC%B2j%CC%B2ar%C4%81wa-al-Zan%C4%81t/6000000017423931416

[579] https://journals.openedition.org/remmm/247?lang=fr

the Amazigh people's refusal to be subordinated or converted into this or that set of religious beliefs. To this day, Dihya remains an important and popular figurehead for Berber activists who feel her power and position not only emphasises the gender equality of their culture but also their liberal beliefs and willingness to accept people of all ethnic and religious origins.

The Amazigh people continue to fight for recognition as a distinct political, ethnic and linguistic group. In certain places like Libya, even speaking the Amasizgh language can lead to arrest and charges of espionage. Meanwhile, in Morocco, the Amazigh continue to fight against both economic deprivations and to have their native tongue Tamazight recognised as an official language alongside Arabic.

It is little wonder then that a woman who was prepared to put her life on the line to secure independence and freedom for her people should continue to be celebrated among the Amazigh. Many girls are named for the Berber Queen, and her image appears regularly in the crude graffiti of Amazigh activities, serving as a visible symbol of self-determination, resistance, and freedom.

SUN TZU

"The Master of War"

When it comes to literary works on military strategy, few books have enjoyed the success and longevity of *The Art of War* by Sun Tzu. In essence, *The Art of War* is not dissimilar to Miyamoto Mushashi's *A Book of Five Rings* with both books providing fundamental insights into military strategy and some of key principles of Zen Buddhism. The warrior code is strongly emphasised in both texts and gives us an opportunity to view our other warriors in the light of Chinese beliefs and principles. When we consider the importance of self-discipline and awareness in both these military how-to books, as well as the emphasis placed on moral law and adherence to method and discipline, we can begin to see and understand the failings of other historical warrior figures, such as Basil the Bulgar Slayer who spent 20 years trying to re-establish himself as a military expert after an embarrassing first defeat at the hands of the Bulgars. Similarly, Vlad the Impaler may have successfully defended Wallachia against the invading Ottoman Empire, but rarely did his actions reveal any higher principles of self-awareness or discipline. In these respects, the Chinese warriors stand out from the rest, putting aside selfish concerns to achieve a higher state of being and therefore a greater chance of victory.

The exact place and date of Sun Tzu's birth has been the subject of some controversy, with the ancient historian Ssu-Ma Ch'ien claiming he was born in the Qi region of ancient China, in the northern section of the Shangdong peninsula[580]. Other sources dispute this claim made by the author of *The Records of the Grand Historian* and suggest that Sun Tzu was born on the other side of the country in the province of Wu[581]. Similarly, Sun Tzu's date of birth is rather imprecise, although it is acknowledged that the warrior was active during the Spring and Autumn Period of Chinese history which spanned the years 771 to 476 BC[582]. Beyond that, there is very little historical reference made to Sun Tzu's childhood and upbringing with most texts referring to the man only after he had already written his famous treatise on military strategy - *The Art of War*.

History would probably have more to offer regarding Sun Tzu's biography, but his very name complicates things considerably. Although generally referred to Sun Tzu, this wasn't his birth name but instead was an honorific title bestowed on him in recognition of his military

---

[580] Mark McNeilly, 2001, *Sun Tzu and the Art of Modern Warfare*. Oxford University Press, pp.3.

[581] Unknown, *Sun Tzu Biography*, https://www.thefamouspeople.com/profiles/sun-tzu-261.php

[582] https://en.wikipedia.org/wiki/Spring_and_Autumn_period

accomplishments. Born into the Sun family, our warrior was initially known as Sun Wu, Sunzi or Sunwuzi, with his courtesy name being Changqing[583]. Some suggest that Wu may even have been a nickname as it can mean 'military' and therefore "would have been a fitting name for one so skilled in military reasoning"[584]. Nevertheless, author Meghan Cooper and The Editorial Committee of Chinese Civilization have been able to shed some light on Sun Tzu's early life. Cooper suggests that as he was clearly literate, he was most probably descended from an aristocratic family "or the *shi*, the non-landowning aristocracy since the shi were frequently scholars and often well-educated"[585]. The Editorial Committee of Chinese Civilization seem confident in their assertions that Sun Tzu was born somewhere between 550 and 540 BC as a descendant of King Li of Chen. His father Sun Ping originally lived in the State of Qi, but civil unrest forced him and his family to relocate to Wu. Unfortunately, they have little further to add except that at the time of their move to Wu, Sun Tzu had already "accomplished much in his studies of warfare"[586].

The most probable explanation for Sun Tzu's comprehensive military training is that his grandfather Tian Shu who had "made himself notable as a mercenary

[583] Ed. The Editorial Committee of Chinese Civilization, 2007, *China: Five Thousand Years of History and Civilization*, pp.280.

[584] Meghan Cooper, 2018, *Sun Tzu*. Cavendish Square Publishing, New York. pp.32.

[585] Meghan Cooper, 2018, *Sun Tzu*, pp.33.

[586] Ed. The Editorial Committee of Chinese Civilization, 2007, *China: Five Thousand Years of History and Civilization*, pp.280.

warrior", took him under his wing and imparted the benefits of his own training and experience. According to Cooper, it was Tian Shu's accomplishments on the battlefield that first won the family the honorific surname of Sun. After going "into battle several times, proving himself to be a wise military strategist and valiant warrior... the king gave him a new surname; Sun, which roughly translates into 'power'"[587]. Certainly, Sun Tzu wasn't the last of the Suns to prove themselves as superior military men, and the family continued to pass "their military expertise from generation to generation, directly influencing the military affairs of China for hundreds of years"[588]. Indeed one Sun Bin, an alleged descendant of Sun Tzu also wrote a treatise on military strategy, rather unimaginatively entitled *The Art of War*.

Prior to his initial introduction to the King of Wu, Sun Tzu befriended Helü's loyal advisor, Wu Zixü, who recommended him to the king on numerous occasions. It is possible as a result of these commendations that the king first gave Sun Tzu an audience. The first story that gives us an insight into who Sun Tzu really was, occurred when he was first summoned by the King of Wu, King Helü. While this meeting between the ruler and his future general and advisor has been depicted by some as an interview to ascertain his suitability as a general[589], Ssu-ma Ch'ien maintains that the King called for Sun Tzu after reading his book. Either way the story pans out in the same fashion,

[587] Meghan Cooper, 2018, *Sun Tzu*, pp.34.

[588] Meghan Cooper, 2018, *Sun Tzu*, pp.34.

[589] Kiril Anastasov, 2015, *The art of war: Part 1 History*, https://www.linkedin.com/pulse/art-war-part-1-history-kiril-anastasov

with the King requesting that Sun Tzu demonstrate the theories laid out in *The Art of War* by training 180 royal concubines. This would a test of his abilities, training women to fight instead of soldiers.

Sun Tzu agreed to the test and divided the women into two companies, with one of the king's favourite ladies placed at the head of each regiment. Handing them spears, he explained the rules of command and then proceeded to have the women practice with the weapons in organised drills. Upon his first instruction, the concubines started to giggle and chatter to which Sun Tzu responded "If words of command are not clear and distinct if orders are not thoroughly understood, the general is to blame. But if his orders are clear, and the soldiers nevertheless disobey, then it is the fault of their officers"[590]. Having reiterated these instructions detailing the flow of command, Sun Tzu tried again only to have the girls collapse into laughing fits, unable to take the training seriously. Without hesitation, the military theorist "ordered the leaders of the two companies to be beheaded"[591]. Understandably, the king was less than happy about seeing two of his favourite concubines beheaded and pleaded with Sun Tzu to rethink how he was going to proceed. Sun Tzu remained steadfast, however, and said "Having once received His Majesty's commission to be the general of his forces, there are certain commands of His Majesty which, acting in that capacity, I am unable to

[590] Ssu-ma Ch'ien, *The Records of the Grand Historian* cited in *Sun Wu and his Book*, http://www.online-literature.com/suntzu/artofwar/0/

[591] Ssu-ma Ch'ien, *The Records of the Grand Historian* cited in *Sun Wu and his Book*

accept"[592]. With their leaders dead, the remaining girls suddenly had a change of heart and "went through all the evolutions... with perfect accuracy and precision"[593].

Sun Tzu passed this test, and the progress he made with training the palace girls to be soldiers was clearly successful. Now acclaimed, he could now serve the King of Wu in the capacity of an advisor and military leader. At the time, King Helü was intent on establishing Wu as an independent state and defeating their powerful neighbours, the Chu. In 506 BC, Wu managed to strengthen their military resources by entering into an alliance with the powerful Jin, situated to the north of Chu[594]. Imitating their allies, the Chu employed "self-strengthening measures to build larger armies and raise higher revenues"[595]. It would appear that this first Wu victory occurred prior to Sun Tzu's appointment within the army as it took place nearly 80 years before the Battle of Baiju, one of the few military campaigns where Sun Tzu's participation has been documented[596]. Prior to 584 BC, the Wu nation was considered "a barbarian state"[597] that shirked custom, wearing short hair when long

[592] Ssu-ma Ch'ien, *The Records of the Grand Historian* cited in *Sun Wu and his Book*

[593] Ssu-ma Ch'ien, *The Records of the Grand Historian* cited in *Sun Wu and his Book*

[594] Victoria Tin-bor Hui, 2005, *War and State Formation in Ancient China and Early Modern Europe*. Cambridge University Press, pp.58.

[595] Victoria Tin-bor Hui, 2005, *War and State Formation in Ancient China and Early Modern Europe*, pp.58 – 59.

[596] https://en.wikipedia.org/wiki/Sun_Tzu

[597] Victoria Tin-bor Hui, 2005, *War and State Formation in Ancient China and Early Modern Europe*, pp.53.

hair was the fashion and sporting tattoos which at the time were "considered to be uncivilised by the other kingdoms in the dynasty"[598]. Although we can never be sure what real authority or influence Sun Tzu had over the Wu army, it's clear they had "new weapons and training"[599] that enabled to defeat the previously powerful state of Chu.

In accordance with one of the principles posited by Sun Tzu in *The Art of War*, the Wu army bided their time and waited for the perfect opportunity to engage their enemy. With the Chu engaged in battles all along their borders, King Helü "realised that with their armies stretched thin, they would not be able to offer much resistance"[600]. As Sun Tzu asserted, "When your weapons are dulled, your ardour damped, your strength exhausted and your treasure spent, other chieftains will spring up to take advantage of your extremity"[601]. This is precisely what King Helü did, waiting until he could see his enemy was weakening, then postponing the moment of attack until he knew victory was within reach. Just as Sun Tzu predicted, "He will win who knows when to fight and when not to fight"[602]. King Helü's timing was perfect, and he struck when he knew he would

[598] Victoria Tin-bor Hui, 2005, *War and State Formation in Ancient China and Early Modern Europe*, pp.53.

[599] Victoria Tin-bor Hui, 2005, *War and State Formation in Ancient China and Early Modern Europe*, pp.53.

[600] Victoria Tin-bor Hui, 2005, *War and State Formation in Ancient China and Early Modern Europe*, pp.70.

[601] Sun Tzu, 1910, *The Art of War*. Translated by Lionel Giles, Chapter two, paragraph 2. www.suntzusaid.com

[602] Sun Tzu, 1910, *The Art of War*, Chapter three, paragraph 17.

have the greatest success. Knowing when to fight, gave the Wu the advantage they'd been looking for, and Sun Tzu's discipline of critical timing left the Chu blindsided and unprepared.

It is recorded that Sun Tzu made a last-minute decision during this campaign which even his king was ignorant of. While King Helü "travelled westward on the Huai River", Sun Tzu altered his course and landed his forces at a small cove on the east bank of the Huai River. This unexpected landing at an unlikely place surprised the Chu forces, who were not able to adjust their fighting positions quickly enough, giving the Wu a critical advantage. As Sun Tzu asserted in his book, "He who can modify his tactics in relation to his opponent and thereby succeed in winning, may be called a heaven-born captain". Certainly achieving the element of surprise worked in favour of the Wu and they soon had the Chu army broken up, routed and running for their lives. The Wu forces were persistent in their pursuit, chasing down their enemy and engaging them in a further five battles before going on to seize the Chu capital, the city of Ying[603]. This series of impressive victories was achieved by an army of just 30,000 Wu warriors against a much larger force of approximately 200,000 enemy Chu, and "has gone down in history as a famous example of a small army trouncing a much bigger force"[604].

---

[603] Ed. The Editorial Committee of Chinese Civilization, 2007, *China: Five Thousand Years of History and Civilization*. City University of Hong Kong Press, pp.283

[604] Ed. The Editorial Committee of Chinese Civilization, 2007, *China: Five Thousand Years of History and Civilization*, pp.283

Although conclusive, the Wu victory was short-lived, and the Chu army were quick to retaliate. Certain sources suggest that a rather patriotic Chu by the name of Shen Baoxu fled his homeland to implore the powerful Qin to assist them in "re-establishing the Chu kingdom to its former glory"[605]. Although initially reluctant the Qin finally agreed, and in 505 BC, the Wu were ousted from the Chu capital, and the Chu king reinstated in his capital again. The Wu ascendancy to regional power and supremacy ended less than a year after it began and while the Chu never again achieved the same dominance as it had prior to King Helü's invasion, the Wu fared worse in the aftermath. Their fledgeling empire began to collapse, and eventually, it was subsumed into the Yue state in 473 BC.[606]

As with Sun Tzu's birth, so his death is shrouded in mystery. Many maintain that he died alongside his king in the battle against the Yue[607] while some argue that his death was simply a ruse engineered by Sun Tzu to confuse the enemy; as he himself postulates in *The Art of War* - "all warfare is based on deception"[608]. Some historians suggest that he survived King Helü's death and continued to lead the Wu forces, pointing to the fact that they continued to enjoy some military successes even after the death of their monarch. Modern historians indicate that Sun Tzu died in

[605] Meghan Cooper, 2018, *Sun Tzu*, pp.71.

[606] Meghan Cooper, 2018, *Sun Tzu*, pp.71.

[607] Meghan Cooper, 2018, *Sun Tzu*, pp.71.

[608] Sun Tzu, 1910, *The Art of War*. Chapter 1, paragraph 17.

496 BC, outliving his king by some nine years and placing him at around 54 to 64 years old when he died[609].

Despite Sun Tzu's assertion that the "MORAL LAW causes the people to be in complete accord with their ruler", this wasn't always the case for the military genius himself, and there is evidence to suggest that he retreated from the king's service on more than one occasion. According to some sources, King Helü's defeat and subsequent death at the hands of the Yue was predicted by Sun Tzu who "forbid the king to war with Yue", warning him that the people of Yue were highly patriotic and fuelled by a passion for their country, full of strength and vigour. According to his own principle, if a general is "unable to estimate the enemy's strength, and allows an inferior force to engage a larger one, or hurls a weak detachment against a powerful one... the result must be rout"[610] and defeat.

With King Helü dead, his son Fuchai succeeded his father to the throne and assumed leadership of the embattled Wu, also retaining Sun Tzu in his service and his fellow military advisor, Wu Zixü. Wu was soon eclipsed and quickly fell out of favour and the "days of battle glory under Wu Zixü, and Sun Tzu were quickly forgotten"[611]. According to one story, Fuchai received a gift of a beautiful woman known as Xi Shi. So smitten was he that he began to

---

[609] https://en.wikipedia.org/wiki/Sun_Tzu

[610] Sun Tzu, 1910, *The Art of War*. Chapter 10, paragraph 19.

[611] Meghan Cooper, 2018, *Sun Tzu*, pp.80.

"spend more and more time with the women and neglecting his duties of state". Irritated by his lack of discipline and commitment to his nation, Sun Tzu complained to the new king about his attentions to his harem of concubines, suggesting that they be taken away so he could once again concentrate on the matters of state. Enraged, Fuchai had Sun Tzu executed.[612] There is very little evidence to support this narrative and may have been invented simply to give an idea of Fuchai's lack of moral succour in comparison to the strict self-discipline imposed by military leaders like Sun Tzu.

Like many of history's greatest warriors, the legacy left behind after Sun Tzu died was greater than any of his actual lifetime victories and accomplishments on the battlefield. His teachings and doctrines still influence us today, and his book *The Art of War* has become one of the most important military texts in history, while its premises have also been applied to business, financial exchanges, sports and management. Sun Tzu's writings have inspired military leaders throughout modern history, and he has been described as possessing wisdom "as immortal a value as Confucius's, which belongs to the world"[613]. Some maintain that the defeat of the French and American forces in Vietnam was due in part to the commitment of General Vo Nguyen Giap to the teachings of Sun Tzu. It was this conflict with the Vietnamese has been purported reintroduce

[612] "The Wu-Yue conflict, what it meant to China – and the world". A discussion on SinoDefence Forum, 21 September 2017. https://www.sinodefenceforum.com/the-wu-yue-conflict-what-it-meant-to-china-and-the-world.t3480

[613] Ed. The Editorial Committee of Chinese Civilization, 2007, *China: Five Thousand Years of History and Civilization*, pp.298.

The Art of War to modern readers, and it is now listed as recommended reading for Marine Corps members[614] and has been applied by General Colin Powell in subsequent conflicts. Some military enthusiasts claim that the first Gulf War was fought and won on the back of Sun Tzu's theories, with strategies based on his teaching being "performed under an overwhelming mission, unity and focus"[615] and Powell applying his "principle of deception, speed, and attacking the enemy's weakness"[616].

Certainly the fundamental principles set out in *The Art of War* apply to both military strategy and life in general. Although a military man by profession, Sun Tzu's teachings are not far from those of the peaceful Confucius, particularly when it comes to his assertion that "supreme excellence consists in breaking the enemy's resistance without fighting"[617]. While there may be incomplete details of Sun Tzu's own lifetime military accomplishments, his teachings have influenced both East and West civilisations and their approach to combat over the past 2,500 years, making his inclusion in the list of history's greatest warriors secure and unwavering.

---

[614]Bevin Alexander, Sun Tzu at Gettysburg: Ancient Military Wisdom in the Modern World pp.xii

[615] Osama El-Kadi, 2008, "Sun Tzu & The American Election", http://www.easy-strategy.com/american-election.html

[616] http://srescorp.com/strategists/sun-tzu/

[617] Sun Tzu, 1910, *The Art of War*. Chapter 3, paragraph 2.

SCIPIO AFRICANUS

"Destroyer of Carthage"

As with many of our previous warriors, little is known of Scipio Africanus's childhood and early years growing up in ancient Rome except for one random fact documented by Pliny in his hefty historical work, *The History of Nature*. Pliny suggests that Scipio and Julius Caesar were both parted "from their mothers by means of incision", marking the first mention of a caesarean section in history and distinguishing both great military men from all others who were born in the more conventional way. Right from his infancy, it seems that Scipio was destined for a life of distinction. Born in 236 BC to an important military family, from an early age Scipio is said to have behaved with the "boundless self-confidence of a patrician who knew ... he was destined to play a prominent role in Rome's public life"[618]. Roman soldier and author Sextus Julius Frontus records that when accused of lacking aggression by a critic, Scipio reportedly responded: "My

---

[618] Adrian Goldsworthy, 2003, *In the Name of Rome,* Weidenfeld & Nicolson, chapter 2. https://erenow.com/ancient/in-the-name-of-rome-the-men-who-won-the-roman-empire/3.html

mother bore me a general, not a warrior"[619]. While few stories of Scipio's childhood have survived, a few myths and legends still flutter around giving us hints about how life began for this pivotal Roman figure. One such story suggests that his mother Pomponia "had been barren until a snake appeared in her bedroom and sired the child"[620]. This legend stayed with Scipio throughout his life, giving fuel to the notion that he was "of divine birth"[621].

Author Richard Gabriel notes that aside from the occasional coin or ring bearing his likeness, "no certain physical portrayal of Scipio has survived... [suggesting] that he was probably a typical Roman and not physically remarkable"[622]. One of the earliest surviving descriptions of the man comes from the epic poem *Punica*, written around 103AD by Silius Italicus in which he is described as having "a martial brow and flowing hair... His eyes burned bright, but their regard was mild; those who looked upon him were at once awed and pleased"[623]. Although we will likely never know how young Scipio was raised and educated, his

---

[619] Sextus Julius Frontus, *Stratagems*, Book IV, pp.310.
http://penelope.uchicago.edu/Thayer/E/Roman/Texts/Frontinus/Strategemata/4*.html

[620] Richard A. Gabriel, 2008, *Scipio Africanus: Rome's Greatest General*, Potomac Books Inc., Washington, pp.4.

[621] Richard A. Gabriel, 2008, Scipio Africanus: Rome's Greatest General, pp.4.

[622] Richard A. Gabriel, 2008, Scipio Africanus: Rome's Greatest General, pp.2.

[623] Silius Italicus, *Punica*, Loeb Classical Library. Chapter VIII, lines 561-564.
https://archive.org/stream/punicasi01siliuoft/punicasi01siliuoft_djvu.txt

upbringing was probably typical for any child of higher class social status, and he was probably afforded a fashionable Greek education given his "ability to read and write Greek; his admiration of Greek habits, virtues, and fashions".[624] As it turned out, Scipio had little time for lessons after he reached maturity and he embarked on his first military campaign with the army at the tender age of just 17 years old.

The Battle of Ticinus took place in 218 BC, during the Second Punic War fought between Rome and Carthage. Scipio's father Publius Cornelius Scipio was the commander of the Roman army, unluckily facing the legendary Hannibal Barca, commanding the Carthaginians. The fight was mainly an engagement by the two opposing army's cavalry, and the Romans were resoundingly defeated, with Scipio's father very fortunate to escape with his life. According to the Greek historian Polybius, Scipio had intentionally placed his son "in command of a picked troop of horse in order to ensure his safety", but the younger Scipio thought nothing of his own safety when he saw his father "surrounded by the enemy... and dangerously wounded"[625]. Reportedly, his soldiers were unwilling to endanger themselves in what looked like a suicidal attempt to rescue their commander, but Scipio was determined to save his father and charged into the "encircling force alone"[626]. Upon seeing his "reckless daring" the other under his command had little choice but to

---

[624] Richard A. Gabriel, 2008, Scipio Africanus: Rome's Greatest General, pp.3.

[625] Polybius, *The Histories*, Loeb Classical Library. Book X, pp.109.

[626] Polybius, *The Histories*, Loeb Classical Library. Book X, pp.109.

follow suit, attacking with such force that "the enemy were terror-struck and broke up". Publius Scipio was "the first to salute his son in the hearing of all as his preserver"[627]. According to the account by Polybius, this act of courage was sufficient to give Scipio "a universally acknowledged reputation for bravery" which in later years he refrained from demonstrating in personal combat. His admirers suggested that he had come to realise that his chances of success and victory for Rome were dependent "not of a commander who relies on luck, but on one gifted with intelligence"[628].

As The Second Punic War raged on, both Scipio's father and uncle died, and the Romans desperately needed a new proconsul to lead their army into Hispania. However, the military situation there was "desperate and hope for the state so given up that no man ventured to accept the command for Spain". Scipio let it be known that he believed that the Carthaginians could and would be beaten, and "declared that he was a candidate" to led an army there. Seeing as there were no other volunteers, Scipio received great "shouts of approval" and "every single man voted that Publius Scipio should have the command"[629]. The enthusiasm ebbed though once the vote was concluded, and the crowd began to have doubts about their choice. Detractors shouted that at age 24, Scipio was too young for

---

[627] Polybius, *The Histories*, Loeb Classical Library. Book X, pp.109.

[628] Polybius, *The Histories*, Loeb Classical Library. Book X, pp.109.

[629] Titus Livius, *The History of Rome*, Book 26, Chapter 18.
http://www.perseus.tufts.edu/hopper/text?doc=Perseus%3Atext%3A1999.02.0158%3Abook%3D26%3Achapter%3D18

such an important post with so much on the line for Roman and also carried "the name of one who was setting out from two afflicted families"[630]. Scipio quieted and then addressed the crowd, managing to convince them of his suitability for the position and filling them "with a more assured hope than belief in a man's promise ... of his success usually inspires"[631]. Despite his youth, Scipio had developed a powerful personal charisma and was an excellent and compelling orator, and his appeal won over his critics as he suggested that his military strategy would be "prompted by visions... or inspired by the gods"[632]. The argument that he was really making was that he was an instrument of the divine – channelling the will of the gods.

Undoubtedly, Scipio was a pious and religious man, but Polybius doubts that he ever really believed he had divine power, despite the legends that indicated it was so. Rather, Polybius suggests, Scipio used the notion that "his strategies were divinely inspired" to make the men in his command more willing "to face perilous enterprises"[633]. Certainly, some of the events that occurred during Scipio's siege of Carthage suggested that the gods were very much on the Roman side. When he arrived in Spain, Scipio discovered that "the Carthaginian forces were divided into three bodies", each of which were situated at least "ten days' march from New Carthage"[634]. Realising that it would be

---

[630] Titus Livius, *The History of Rome*, Book 26, Chapter 18.

[631] Titus Livius, *The History of Rome*, Book 26, Chapter 19.

[632] Titus Livius, *The History of Rome*, Book 26, Chapter 19.

[633] Polybius, *The Histories*, Loeb Classical Library. Book X, pp.117.

[634] Polybius, *The Histories*, Loeb Classical Library. Book X, pp.118.

too dangerous to engage with the enemy, Scipio decided the best course of action was to besiege the city of New Carthage which was both "favourably situated ... to make the direct sea crossing from Africa" while also being the place where "the Carthaginians kept the bulk of their money and their war material"[635]. Not only would possession of New Carthage "damage the enemy but would much advance the Roman cause"[636].

Exhibiting the kind of strategic thinking that would distinguish him from other notable Roman generals, Scipio acquired information from the local fishermen he interviewed who informed him that the water in the lagoon surrounding the city "receded every day towards evening"[637]. With this crucial nugget of local knowledge, Scipio addressed his men telling them that "it was the water god Neptune who had first suggested this plan to him".[638] He went on to proclaim that not only would there be "gold crowns to those who should be the first to mount the wall" but also that he had made an accurate assessment of the situation and had the power of the gods on his side, thus fuelling "great enthusiasm and ardour among the lads"[639]. The siege of the city surged forward according to his plan, and despite heavy fighting, the Romans failed and were thrown back after their first attempt at scaling the city walls by storm. Undaunted,

---

[635] Polybius, *The Histories*, Loeb Classical Library. Book X, pp.119.

[636] Polybius, *The Histories*, Loeb Classical Library. Book X, pp.120.

[637] Polybius, *The Histories*, Loeb Classical Library. Book X, pp.120.

[638] Polybius, *The Histories*, Loeb Classical Library. Book X, pp.127.

[639] Polybius, *The Histories*, Loeb Classical Library. Book X, pp.128.

Scipio called his men back and waited for the tide of the lagoon to change, equipping some five hundred men with new ladders as he did so. When the water began to ebb away, Scipio gave the signal to attack himself, shouting for his men to run into the water and attack the battlements that lay unguarded, their Carthaginian defenders having spread themselves thin after assuming the water barrier would protect them well enough. According to Polybius "just when the escalading attack was at its height, the tide began to recede... so that to those who were not prepared for the sight the thing appeared incredible"[640]. The receding tide appeared to fulfil Scipio's prediction that Neptune would come to their assistance, giving his men even greater courage and belief in their leader. The Romans attack was a success, and they went on to capture the city.

Commanding soldiers in ancient times generally called for a ruthless devotion to achieving one's strategic goals, but as single-minded as he was on the battlefield, Scipio was known as a compassionate man with respect for human decency in both his political and private life. After securing Carthage for the Romans, Scipio's treatment of the hostages epitomised his altruistic attitude. As his soldiers were crushing the last pockets of resistance in the city, he was approached by the wife of Mandonius, a "lady... of advanced age [who] bore herself with a certain majesty"[641] who implored Scipio to ensure the women held captive would be treated "with tenderness and consideration". Scipio listened to her concerns and assured her "that nothing which is

---

[640] Polybius, *The Histories*, Loeb Classical Library. Book X, pp.134.

[641] Polybius, *The Histories*, Loeb Classical Library. Book X, pp.147.

anywhere held sacred be violated amongst us; your virtue and nobility of soul".[642] He was true to his word.

The Romans were triumphant, and his celebrating men decided to present him with a trophy by bringing him "a girl of surpassing bloom and beauty" to do with as he saw fit. While Livy and Polybius both record the story, the two narratives differ; Livy refers to the woman as one of the Carthaginian hostages and Polybius claims she was simply a woman they passed on the street and captured. In Polybius' version, Scipio turns down the young Romans' "present of the damsel" saying that if he were not their leader he would have been delighted with the gift but, as their commander "it would be the least welcome of any", indicating that while "such things afford young men most delightful enjoyment... in times of activity they are most prejudicial to the body and the mind alike"[643]. In this version, Polybius paints Scipio as a paragon of Roman virtue, willing to sacrifice his own pleasures in the interests of serving the state. Livy, on the other hand, narrates the story somewhat differently, suggesting that after the beautiful young hostage was brought before him, Scipio questioned her and discovered that she had been promised in marriage to another young man. Hearing this, Scipio promptly sent for both her parents and her betrothed and had them brought before him. Speaking to the young woman's fiancée, Scipio reportedly said "Were I allowed the pleasures suitable to my age... instead of being preoccupied with affairs of state, I should wish that I might be forgiven for loving too ardently. Now I

---

[642] Titus Livius, *The History of Rome*, Book 26, Chapter 49.

[643] Polybius, *The Histories*, Loeb Classical Library. Book X, pp.150.

have the power to indulge another's love, namely yours"[644]. Although the inference is similar, in Livy's version the emphasis is Scipio's generosity rather than his abstemiousness and ends with him presenting the groom to be with the gold given to him by the parents of the young woman as a sign of their gratitude.

For Livy, the importance of this event was to indicate Scipio's "generosity and goodness of heart" and show how these virtues enabled him to secure the loyalty of many followers, noting that a few days later he had amassed a "force of 1400 mounted men"[645]. In both versions of the of these events, Scipio is proved on the battlefield, a confirmed strategist and an inspiration to his troops as a virtuous leader of men and the best example of the noble Roman elite. Brave, honourable, courtesy and brave he seems to represent all the best of Roman virtues and therefore must have been destined to win his next challenge – the Battle of Zama, facing Hannibal and his formidable war elephants again. This is how the Roman historians depict him, anyway.

Scipio had everything to gain in his next confrontation with Hannibal, likely to be the decisive clash that would end the war once and for all. The rumours abounded that after a Roman victory "Africa was to form a new province and be allotted to Scipio without having recourse to a ballot"[646].

[644] Titus Livius, *The History of Rome*, Book 26, Chapter 50.

[645] Titus Livius, *The History of Rome*, Book 26, Chapter 50.

[646] Titus Livius, *The History of Rome*, Book 28, Chapter 40.

Riding this wave of popularity, Scipio was eager for the glory of finally crushing the Carthaginians while he could still score a final blow and convinced the Senate that the time to act was at hand. When his army finally lined up against the forces of Hannibal in Africa, Scipio assembled his men to make a speech that he hoped would inspire them. Urging them to fight with bravery, he reminded them of their past victories and called on them "to meet the foe with two objectives - victory or death"[647]. On the other side, Hannibal waited while he lined up all his war elephants, "of which he had over eighty" to form the first line of the attack. Behind them, he placed 12,000 mercenaries ready to absorb the worst of the Roman counterattack when it came. Scipio was watching and knew only too well what rampaging elephants might do to his tightly packed columns of infantry if they smashed forward. Assessing the threat, he ordered his formations to rearrange themselves in columns, thereby creating corridors through which the elephants could pass[648]. The battle started, and the two masses of soldiers started to move toward each other.

Scipio's plan worked, although even he couldn't have anticipated the level of panic that would break out "when the trumpets and bugles sounded"[649]. Some of the elephants, alarmed by the sudden crash of noise turned around and rushed back into the Carthaginian ranks, while others continued forward into the Roman light infantry causing

---

[647] Polybius, *The Histories*, Loeb Classical Library. Book XV, pp.489.

[648] Brian Todd Carey, 2007, *Hannibal's Last Battle: Zama and the Fall of Carthage*. Pen and Sword Military, UK, pp.115.

[649] Polybius, *The Histories*, Loeb Classical Library. Book XV, pp.493.

much loss "until finally in their terror some escaped through the gaps in the Roman line" that Scipio had prepared for just such an occasion[650]. With the elephants no longer an effective weapon Gaius Laelius, Scipio's close friend and Master of Horse "charged the Carthaginian cavalry and forced them to headlong flight"[651]. This disposed of Hannibal's cavalry, leaving the rest of the battle to be fought by brutal and close-range hand-to-hand combat. The Carthaginians, who had sent their experienced and war-hardened mercenaries to face the Romans in the middle of their line initially gained the upper hand, but with superior training, weapons and fighting discipline Scipio's men continued to advance. According to Polybius, the "Carthaginians behaved like cowards, never coming near their mercenaries nor attempting to back them up", and the mercenaries began to give ground until they were in full retreat from the Romans. Realising that the native Carthaginians were not reinforcing them, they started attacking them instead of Scipio's soldiers and "mercilessly slaughtered as they fled[652].

It was a complete victory for Roman arms and Scipio, and it signalled the end of the Second Punic War as he had hoped. So decisive victory was achieved at the Battle of Zama that he was awarded the title of "Africanus" in the process and became "the first Roman general to be addressed by a name derived from the location of his

---

[650] Polybius, *The Histories*, Loeb Classical Library. Book XV, pp.493.

[651] Polybius, *The Histories*, Loeb Classical Library. Book XV, pp.494.

[652] Polybius, *The Histories*, Loeb Classical Library. Book XV, pp.495.

greatest campaign"[653]. Unfortunately, Scipio's achievements earned him great acclaim amongst the people of Rome but also fuelled the jealously of his political rivals back home, and they were determined to bring him down. Returning to the capital city, Scipio found himself facing charges concocted by his long-time critic Cato, who accused him of misappropriating public funds and "not respecting the *mos maiorum* (a custom of the ancestors)".[654] His enemies pointed to Scipio's fondness of all things Greek instead of Roman, and spread vicious rumours that he was secretly betraying Rome by his willingness to embrace "Greek customs, literature and art"[655]. They equated this to a direct threat to Roman civilisation, and he was forced to defend himself publically. When formally confronted by his rivals and called upon to plead, Scipio ignored the charges they levelled at him. Instead, he pointed out "the services he had rendered for Rome in such a lofty tone that it was universally felt that no man had ever deserved higher or truer praise"[656]. In the end, his detractors had done significant damage to his public reputation and Scipio was humiliated and embarrassed; the ingratitude of the populace he had devoted his career to serving was sufficient to have destroyed his love for Rome forever.

---

[653] Brian Todd Carey, 2007, *Hannibal's Last Battle: Zama and the Fall of Carthage*, pp.141.

[654] Brian Todd Carey, 2007, *Hannibal's Last Battle: Zama and the Fall of Carthage*, pp.141.

[655] D. Kent Fonner, 1996, "Scipio Africanus", *Military History Magazine*, March 1996. http://history-world.org/scipio_Scipio.htm

[656] Titus Livius, *The History of Rome*, Book 38, Chapter 50.

Rather than spend his public life in an ungrateful city that had forced him "to stand beneath the Rostra as a defendant and have to listen to the insults of young men", a disgusted Scipio left the capital for the coastal town of Liternum where he lived out the rest of his life. So disillusioned was he with Rome that "it is said that on his death-bed he gave orders that he should be buried [in Liternum] ... so that there might be no funeral rites performed for him by his ungrateful country"[657]. It was a surprisingly ironic turn of events for the man that had so distinguished himself on the battlefield for the glory and security of his beloved Rome, cast off as disloyal by the nation for which he had fought so valiantly. Faced with the impossible choice of "standing his trial or of absenting himself from his native city", it is little wonder that a man of such pride chose the latter. As Livy states, after the Battle of Zama "the two greatest cities in the world... proved themselves, almost at the same time, ungrateful to their foremost men. Rome was the more ungrateful of the two, for whilst Carthage after her defeat drove defeated Hannibal into exile, Rome would banish the victorious Scipio in the hour of her victory"[658]. It was an unexpectedly sad end for Scipio Africanus, a great warrior for the Roman people who ultimately didn't deserve his devotion.

---

[657] Titus Livius, *The History of Rome*, Book 38, Chapter 52.

[658] Titus Livius, *The History of Rome*, Book 38, Chapter 50.

GENGHIS KHAN

"The Scourge of God"

Life in modern Mongolia today is much easier than it was in ancient times, but for a young boy born in 1162 with a life-threatening blood clot in his hand, it was certainly a challenge just to stay alive. The child would not only survive, but would grow up to become known as the Scourge of God, and was arguably one of the greatest military leaders of all time. According to Mongolian folklore, he was "descended from Börte Chino, whose name means 'greyish white wolf' and his wife Qo'ai-maral, whose name means beautiful doe"[659]. While these romantic origins are wonderful, the harsher reality is that Temüjin - or better known in the West as Genghis Khan was born to a young woman of "of unique colour and complexion"[660] who had been kidnapped by his father, Yisügei, the head of Mongol's ruling clan[661]. While his mother was heavily pregnant with

---

[659] Anon, *The Secret History of the Mongols*. Trans. Urgunge Onon. Routledge Curzon, London & New York, pp. 39.
https://jigjids.files.wordpress.com/2011/05/the_secret_history_of_t he_mongols_the_life_and_times_of_chinggis_khan1.pdf

[660] Anon, *The Secret History of the Mongols*, pp.54.

[661] https://www.biography.com/people/genghis-khan-9308634

Temüjin, his father was engaged in battle with a rival tribe known as the Tatars during which he captured their chieftain, who became Temüjin's namesake[662], whose name means "blacksmith". According to legend at the time of his birth, the infant Temüjin "held in his right hand a clot of blood as big as a knucklebone" which *The Secret History of the Mongols* tells us that foretold to his people that the infant was destined either for great things or a bloodthirsty destiny[663]. As his life unfolded, it would become apparent that he achieved both.

Having survived infancy, Temüjin's childhood was marked by a hard-living, hand-to-mouth nomadic existence in the harsh conditions of Dulüün-Boldog at the foot of the Khentii Mountains located in northern Mongolia. The natural environment was cold and challenging, and his life amongst his people was fraught with "excessive tribal violence, including murder, kidnapping, and enslavement"[664]. When he was nine years old, his father decided to find a wife for him among the Olqunu'ut relatives of his mother Hö'elün"[665]. Casting around for suitable candidates, he soon noticed a remarkably beautiful girl only 10 years old who impressed him with the "light in her face and fire in her

---

[662] https://www.biography.com/people/genghis-khan-9308634

[663] https://mythology.stackexchange.com/questions/1328/what-is-signified-by-genghis-khan-being-born-with-a-blood-clot-in-his-hand

[664] Jack Weatherford, 2004. *Genghis Kahn and the Making of the Modern World*. Crown Publishers, New York, pp.xvi.

[665] Anon, *The Secret History of the Mongols*. pp. 58.

eyes"[666]. This was a political marriage designed to cement an alliance between the two tribes; the young bride was named Börte Ujin, and she would be the future Khan's most stable, lifelong relationship that survived Temüjin's many secret affairs as well as his plural marriages to other women[667]. After the marriage celebrations were completed, it was agreed that Temüjin would remain with his new extended family as a son-in-law while his father Yisügei returned to the family home and tribe.

Unfortunately on his return journey home Yisügei was intercepted by enemy Tartar tribesmen and offered poisoned food, soon dying in agony. Upon receiving this news, Temüjin set out to return home to assume the leadership of his clan as next in the line of succession. However, when he arrived, the other members of his tribe were reluctant to follow him as leader and soon broke camp and left, abandoning Temüjin and his family to survive on their own leaving only mothers and children behind. Forced into poverty and near-starvation[668] the family survived off the land for the next several years living off fruits, ox carcasses and wild onions and garlic while Temüjin and his brothers "caught maimed and misshapen fishes"[669]. During one such fishing trip, the brothers fought over the catch as the eldest half-brother Bekhter tried to assert his authority as eldest

---

[666] Anon, *The Secret History of the Mongols.* pp. 60.

[667] Ariel Rodriguez, *The Mongol Empress Who Held Genghis Khan's Empire Together.* https://culturacolectiva.com/history/borte-ujin-mongol-empress

[668] https://www.biography.com/people/genghis-khan-9308634

[669] Anon, *The Secret History of the Mongols.* pp. 66-7.

family male. Resentful, Temüjin and his brother Qasar decided to kill him, and the two boys hunted Bekhter down with bows and arrows, "shot at him from in front and from behind"[670]; the wounds proved fatal, and thereafter Temüjin became the uncontested head of the family clan.

Although this account of his youth seems in keeping with the perspective that Genghis Khan would grow up to be dreaded as a blood-thirsty, power-hungry tyrant, it is far from representative of his childhood character. According to Jack Weatherford in his book *Genghis Kahn and the Making of Modern World* the young Mongol was not so savage, as he writes "as a child, he feared dogs, and he cried easily. His younger brother was stronger than he was and a better archer and wrestler"[671]. His capacity for ruthless fratricide can be counterbalanced with what we know of his ability to demonstrate great loyalty and personal, enduring friendships such as the loyal bond he developed with his childhood friend Jamukha, a member of a rival clan who became his declared blood brother to whom he swore eternal faithfulness – later to become his most hated enemy. It is this dual capacity for friendship and enmity that "became the defining trait of his character"[672]. The struggles of his youth also taught him the importance of family, strong alliances and "showed an instinct for survival and self-

---

[670] Anon, *The Secret History of the Mongols*. pp. 68.

[671] Jack Weatherford, 2004. *Genghis Kahn and the Making of the Modern World*, pp. xvii.

[672] Jack Weatherford, 2004. *Genghis Kahn and the Making of the Modern World*, pp. xvii.

preservation"[673]. These were vital life lessons he would never forget.

As well as being strong-willed, Temüjin was strong in body and although "good to look upon", was "remarkable more for the strength of his body and a downright manner than for any beauty of features"[674]. Tall for a Mongolian, he had long reddish-brown hair that fell in braids down his back and blue or green eyes and "his skin a white-tan"[675]. This description of the great Mongol leader is about all we have from his early life as he "never allowed anyone to paint his portrait, sculpt his image, or engrave his name or likeness on a coin".[676] Lacking any contemporary sources that demonstrate his appearance, after Genghis's death in 1227 "the world was left to imagine him as it wished"[677].

When he turned 16, Temüjin returned to claim his wife and through the marriage, cemented an allegiance between his own tribe and that of the Kereyit. Shortly after he and his bride returned home, a group of enemy Merkit warriors decided to take revenge for Hö'elün's abduction years earlier, saying "To avenge [the abduction of] Hö'elün,

---

[673] Jack Weatherford, 2004. *Genghis Kahn and the Making of the Modern World*, pp.xvi-xvii.

[674] Harold Lamb, 1936, *Genghis Khan the Emperor of All Men*. Thornton Butterworth Ltd., London, pp.23.

[675] Harold Lamb, 1936, *Genghis Khan the Emperor of All Men*, pp.23.

[676] Jack Weatherford, 2004. *Genghis Kahn and the Making of the Modern World*, pp. xxiv.

[677] Jack Weatherford, 2004. *Genghis Kahn and the Making of the Modern World*, pp. xxiv.

we will carry off their women"[678]. They successfully kidnapped Börte and reportedly gave her away to another warrior as a wife, and although Temüjin and his brothers set off in hot pursuit they lost the trail, and the Merkits were able to elude them. Desperate, he turned to Börte's father and his loyal friend Jamukha for assistance. Together they forged an alliance and along with Toghrul of the Keraite tribe could effectively field more than 20,000 soldiers against the Merkit camp. Temüjin had taken his first steps at unifying the Mongol tribes on the road to power, and months later as he led this combined force against his wife's abductors they "fled at night in panic down the Selengge" allowing him to reclaim his bride and save his unborn son[679]. Nine months later, Börte would give birth to a son they named Jochi. Although treated well as his first son, there was some lingering doubt as to whether Temüjin was really the father and as a result, Jochi was never really considered in the succession for eventual leadership of what would become the Mongol empire.

The path to ultimate glory for Temüjin didn't start out particularly well, and during a raid to capture loot, he was captured in around 1177 by warriors that had previously been his father's allies. His humiliating enslavement was short-lived, however, and he soon persuaded one of his captors to help him escape. This event earned him fame and a reputation as a clever leader, and soon a growing number of followers began to flock to his camp to join him. He began to proclaim his intention to unite all the disparate

---

[678] Anon, *The Secret History of the Mongols*. pp. 83.

[679] Anon, *The Secret History of the Mongols*. pp. 93.

tribes and end the constant regional conflicts, which appealed to a broad range of lower-class people that wanted a change from the traditional Mongolian aristocracy. This brought Temüjin into an escalating rift and conflict with his old friend Jamukha, who had risen to become Khan or leader of his own tribe and favoured the old ways, fearing the growing influence and fame of his former blood brother. When a shaman declared that the Eternal Blue Sky had destined Temüjin would rule the world, he became so popular and celebrated a leader that he was elected as Khan of the Mongol tribes in 1186 and large numbers of soldiers began to swear loyalty to him. This was all too much for Jamukha, and in 1187 he decided that something had to be done so he assembled an army of 30,000 warriors and attacked, badly beating Temüjin and routing his forces. Jamukha could have gone on to become a great figure, but he lost much of his support following the battle by ordering that some 70 prisoners be boiled alive in large cauldrons. Temüjin managed to escape capture and disappear for almost 10 years as he licked his wounds and bided his time, making new alliances and friends amongst the Mongol people.

In the year 1197 he showed up again, commanding part of an allied army of Mongols, Keraites and Jin against his old enemy the Tatars, the same people that had murdered his father. It was during this campaign that he forged his reputation as a ruthless and genocidal leader; rather than allow defeated Tatar soldiers to surrender, Temüjin declared "From early days the Tatars have destroyed our ancestors and fathers. [We must] gain vengeance on behalf of our fathers, we must seek revenge for our ancestors. Let them be killed. We will measure them against a linchpin and kill off [those who are taller than the linchpin] until all have died"[680]. The ensuing slaughter of captured prisoners left no doubt that he intended to destroy the Tatars once and for all, but for other defeated enemies he could be forgiving and build coalitions. Breaking with tradition, he would usually take conquered tribes under his protection, integrating their members with his own people and even adopting their orphaned children into his family. This benevolent assimilation inspired great loyalty amongst his followers, and as a result, he was able to forge an ordered and disciplined army[681]. After defeating the Tatars, Temüjin led his growing army against the Targuts, and soon was victorious over that tribe as well. The only Mongolian tribe left that did not recognise him as Khan were the Naimans, who had been sheltering his former friend turned rival Jamukha and his followers. In 1201, a council of the Naiman leaders and their allies elected Jamukha as their "universal ruler", which put him on a collision course with Temüjin for final supremacy of the Mongols. The two former childhood friends fought a series of battles, culminating in the Battle of Chakirmont for the final victory. Jamukha and his allies were beaten, making Temüjin the effective ruler of all Mongolia and sovereign over more than 2,000,000 people. Five years later while in hiding, Jamukha was betrayed by some of his closest followers and presented to the new Khan as a prisoner in 1206. While he executed Jamukha's betrayers for their disloyalty, he was magnanimous to his defeated rival, offering a renewal of their friendship.

---

[680] Anon, *The Secret History of the Mongols*. pp. 133.

[681] Defense Technical Information Center, 2000, *DTIC ADA378208: Genghis Khan and Maneuver Warfare*, pp.2.
https://archive.org/details/DTIC_ADA378208/page/n7

Insisting that there was only room for one Mongol lord, Jamukha asked to be executed instead and was duly granted a noble death by having his back broken by Temüjin's soldiers and was buried with the golden belt that he had been given by the Khan when they first declared themselves blood brothers.

Temüjin's victories over his tribal rivals meant the end of all the prominent confederations of other Mongols to oppose his rule, and he was quick to absorb them as allies. In particular he was pleased to align and join forces with the defeated Naimans, as they were a fairly civilised tribe with their own written language; he cemented the relationship both through arranged political marriages and by moving his capital to the city of Naiman city of Karakorum where he ruled as "the unchallenged ruler of the land from Siberia to China"[682]. In 1206, Temüjin was proclaimed "supreme Khan of all Turkish and Mongol tribes"[683]and was honoured with the name Genghis Khan, meaning "Universal Ruler" or "Oceanic Ruler"[684].

Genghis Khan spent most of his life on the battlefield or in the saddle, but he proved to as effective a political operator as he was a military strategist and commander. As

---

[682] Defense Technical Information Center, 2000, *DTIC ADA378208: Genghis Khan and Maneuver Warfare*, pp.3.

[683] Defense Technical Information Center, 2000, *DTIC ADA378208: Genghis Khan and Maneuver Warfare*, pp.3.

[684] Defense Technical Information Center, 2000, *DTIC ADA378208: Genghis Khan and Maneuver Warfare*, pp.3.

part of his doctrine of turning his former enemies into friends and loyal supports, he destroyed the old and traditional Mongolian feudal system with its foundation on family nobility and replaced it with one "based on individual merit, loyalty, and achievement"[685]. He formalised this with the introduction of the *Yassa*, the governing civilian and military code that dictated advancement on merit rather than ethnicity or race as well as promoted complete religious tolerance throughout his empire. Economically, he ushered in a period of astonishing prosperity, turning the Silk Road into "history's largest free-trade zone", while lowering taxes and making doctors, teachers and priests exempt from paying tax altogether[686]. Understanding the importance of communications across his diverse population, he also created the world's first postal system known as the Yam, which connected nearly half the world with relay stations every 20 – 60 km. At one point, there were over 50,000 horses operating along the route and approximately 1,400 relay stations in operation, suggesting the Yam covered somewhere in the region of 50-60,000km[687]. Despite his modern tyrannical reputation, Genghis Khan granted religious freedom throughout his empire and introduced an international law known as the "Eternal Blue Sky" that required that his governors and officers were as accountable to the rule of law as was the lowest citizen[688]. Although he

---

[685] Jack Weatherford, 2004. *Genghis Kahn and the Making of the Modern World*, pp. xix.

[686] Jack Weatherford, 2004. *Genghis Kahn and the Making of the Modern World*, pp. xix.

[687] IP Factly, 2015, *Link #90: The Mongol Empire Used 50,000 Horses for Their Postal System!* http://ipfactly.com/mongol-empire-yam-route/

[688] Jack Weatherford, 2004. *Genghis Kahn and the Making of the Modern World*, pp. xix.

had no formal education, he was clearly an intelligent, forward-thinking leader that understood how to rule a vast and diverse empire by relying on capable and able administrators and succeeded in building an effective governing apparatus that was stable enough to both survive and continue growing for some 150 years after his death.

On the battlefield, Genghis Khan was equally creative, never using the same tactics twice and learning new techniques while adapting his strategies accordingly. Horses then and still are an integral aspect of Mongolian life and his army was just as dependent on them as every other citizen. Each and every one of his soldiers was an experienced horseman, who could "manoeuvre a galloping horse using only their legs, [leaving] their hands ... free to shoot arrows"[689]. In order to increase their speed and mobility, Genghis ordered that his armies travel with an extra two horses for each man so that should it be needed they could change horses two or three times a day, enabling them to cover long distances without wearing out their mounts. In fact, the incredible mobility achieved by his forces was such that it has never been matched by any other form of ground soldiery[690].

With multiple marriages, an important part of Mongolian culture, the advances he made in consolidating his empire soon resulted in a fast-growing population that

[689] https://www.biography.com/people/genghis-khan-9308634

[690] Defense Technical Information Center, 2000, *DTIC ADA378208: Genghis Khan and Maneuver Warfare*, pp.5.

needed resources in order to maintain itself. Genghis Khan
was also fearful that should his men not have an enemy to
conquer, they would begin to fight amongst themselves, and
old tribal rivalries might emerge to undermine the Mongolian
nation that he had so carefully built. With the rationale of
preserving the unity of his empire, he dedicated his energies
to a lifetime of conflict, and when he sent his forces to attack
and invade China "his aim was conquest rather than simple
plunder"[691]. The neighbouring Chinese had long been the
target of raiding Mongols, and the construction of the Great
Wall of China was seen as the ultimate answer to keeping out
the nomadic warriors, but no physical barrier was enough to
keep out the hordes of Genghis Khan. As the Mongols grew
in numbers they sought to embrace their tribal unity by
living together peacefully while presenting "a united front to
external enemies"[692], and piercing the defences of the
Chinese became a national goal that led to the
unprecedented breaching of the Great Wall of China – an act
that only Genghis Khan achieved during the long history of
the Great Wall[693].

The Mongol invasion of China began in 1211 and
continued for nearly 20 years during which Genghis
perfected the art of siege warfare, while at the same time
leveraging his extensive field experience of fighting a highly

---

[691] J.J. Saunders, 1971, *The History of the Mongol Conquests*. University of
Pennsylvania Press, Philadelphia, pp.53.

[692] Anon, *The Secret History of the Mongols*. pp. 83.

[692] Anon, *The Secret History of the Mongols*. pp.12.

[693] https://www.travelchinaguide.com/china_great_wall/military-
defense/genghis-khan.htm

mobile strategy of attack. The speed at which his troops could move enabled him to "mount flank attacks with flying horse columns, to encircle the enemy and block his escape, and to synchronise distant forces by signalling with smoke, lanterns, and coloured flags"[694]. His men seemed unstoppable as Genghis directed them through the northern borders of China, storming and starving cities as he went and forcing the armies of the opposing Chin Dynasty deeper into the south.

At the same time his forces were fighting in China, Genghis decided to attack the Khwararmian Dynasty – a Turkish empire that spanned Afghanistan, Turkestan, and Persia[695]. Although he had initially taken a diplomatic route in his dealings with the Turks, relations between the two empires fell apart when his diplomatic mission was attacked in Otrar. Outraged, he spent a year building his army and planning his strategy before launching his attack. After carefully gathering intelligence on the enemy forces, he learned that the Shah of Khwarazmia had separated his army into smaller units, the better to garrison various cities and guard against internal feuding by his warlords. He wasted no time in launching his warrior hordes against the fragmented enemy, even though his men were exhausted from the long and arduous journey. Using superior tactics and strategy, he was able to overwhelm the Shah's smaller units piecemeal, not allowing them to combine into a larger and unified defensive force that might have had better success in opposing his invasion. Genghis started his revenge against

---

[694] Anon, *The Secret History of the Mongols*. pp.12.

[695] https://www.biography.com/people/genghis-khan-9308634

the Khwarazmia where the conflict really started – the city of Otrar. His soldiers seized it easily, and were able to capture the same governor that had ordered the attack on his diplomats the year before. The Mongol leader was ruthless, and ordered the wholesale massacre of most of the city's civilian population, while the survivors were sold into slavery. For the enemy governor, he reserved a special punishment, executing him by having molten silver into his ears and eyes in retribution for the attacks on his diplomatic mission.

The rest of the Mongol conquest of Khwarazmia was equally brutal. The capital of Samarkand was taken after Genghis sent his soldiers forward to attack, using captured enemies as human shields. Promising to spare any Khwarazmians that surrendered, he reneged after taking the city and executed any soldiers that had been fighting against his troops. He ordered that all the survivors be evacuated, assembled outside the walls and systematically killed. The Mongols then built pyramids of severed human heads as a warning to the rest of the population that resistance would not be tolerated.

Meanwhile, Genghis moved on to attack the city of Bukhara while ordering two of his generals to set about completely destroying all remnants of the Khwarazian Empire by destroying buildings, entire towns, slaughtering populations and burning large swaths of farmland. When Bukhara fell to his men, Genghis had the survivors brought out so he could address them. It was here that the Mongol leader made one of his most famous pronouncements, declaring to the people gathered that they "know that you have committed great sins and that the great ones among you have committed these sins. If you ask me what proof I have for these words, I say it is because I am the punishment of God. If you had not committed great sins, God would not have sent a punishment like me upon you"[696]. As he was speaking a fire broke out in the city, burning it to the ground before his men could loot it completely. Before he left to attack another settlement, he ordered that all captured craftsmen and artisans be sent back to Mongolia, all able-bodied males be drafted into his army, and the young women and children be sold into slavery. The wealthy trading city of Urgench was next, where the same pattern was repeated after his men took the city in bloody street fighting. This time the captured population was the largest yet, and to kill all the "useless mouths" each Mongolian soldier was assigned a number of civilians to kill personally in order to get rid of them all. After the slaughter was complete, the capture and destruction of Urgench could be counted as one of the bloodiest massacres in all human history. Genghis Khan would go on to annihilate the Khwarazians and then return east to continue his invasion of China with the same brutality and success as he defeated every force raised against him.

Genghis Khan's military ability is unquestionable, and he is possibly the most talented military strategist and leader the world has ever seen[697]. A lifetime of commitment to

[696] Ala-ad-Din 'Ata-Malik Juvaini, The History of the World Conqueror. Trans. Mirza Muhammad Qazvini. Harvard University Press, Massachusetts, 1958, pp.104

[697] Defense Technical Information Center, 2000, *DTIC ADA378208:*

warfare saw him conquer "more than twice as much [land] as

any other man in history"[698] , but despite all the blood he shed of others he was destined to die peacefully at the ripe old age of seventy. As the historian and author Jack Weatherford asserted that while "[h]history has condemned most conquerors to miserable, untimely deaths... Genghis Khan ... passed away in his camp bed, surrounded by a loving family, faithful friends, and loyal soldiers"[699]. More than any other warrior we've encountered in these pages Genghis Khan's legacy is the most far-reaching and long-lasting. Not only is he lauded as being the father of globalisation[700], he is also credited with being "the most important man of the last thousand years"[701]. While this may be a sweeping statement, when you consider that the greatest "story of the past thousand years is that a single species fully exerted its will upon the earth"[702] it begins to make sense. So far-reaching were Khan's conquests - both military and sexual that not only was he responsible for laying the foundations of great nations like Russia, China, Afghanistan, Hungary, Poland and Syria, but he also spread his genes so far and wide that the biological evidence suggested by DNA research is that one in every 200 men is descended from

Genghis Khan and Maneuver Warfare, pp.8.

[698] Jack Weatherford, 2004. *Genghis Kahn and the Making of the Modern World*, pp. xviii.

[699] Jack Weatherford, 2004. *Genghis Kahn and the Making of the Modern World*, pp. xx.

[700] Jeffrey E. Garten, 2016. *From Silk to Silicon: The Story of Globalization Through Ten Extraordinary Lives*. HarperCollins, UK.

[701] Jack Weatherford, 2004. *Genghis Kahn and the Making of the Modern World*, pp. xx.

[702] John Man, 2004. *Genghis Khan: Life, Death and Resurrection*. Bantam Books, London, pp.19.

Genghis Khan[703].

The extent of Genghis Khan's legacy that echoes down through the ages puts our other warriors to shame. Not only was he victorious in most of his battles, but he also "established a century of peace" by ensuring people had a better life under his rule and allowing them the freedom to "follow their traditional culture and religion without fear of persecution"[704]. His beginnings may have been humble, but the empire he built was based on from clear thinking, planning, and ruthless implementation; according to Weatherford the Mongol's "confidence, clarity, choices and consequences, and consistency were his most effective weapons", weapons that even modern leaders seem to be seriously lacking[705]. As Chaucer said, Khan was a king in all aspects of his life, both public and private, and "there was nowhere in no region/ So excellent a lord in all things/ He lacked nothing that belonged to a king"[706].

The Mongolians believed that even after his death, Genghis Khan's spirit lived on in his *sulde* or Spirit Banner. During his lifetime he had two banners made, woven from the tails of his finest stallions. The Mongol leader "had one banner made from white horses to use in peacetime and one

---

[703] John Man, 2004. *Genghis Khan: Life, Death and Resurrection*, pp.16.

[704] Jack Weatherford, 2016, "What Genghis Khan Could Teach Trump", *The Daily Beast*. https://www.thedailybeast.com/what-genghis-khan-could-teach-trump

[705] Jack Weatherford, 2016, "What Genghis Khan Could Teach Trump", *The Daily Beast*.

[706] Geoffrey Chaucer, The Canterbury Tales, The Squire's Tale, http://www.mongolinternet.com/history/canterbury_tales.htm

made from black horses for guidance in war". His white Spirit Banner disappeared and was lost but the black one "survived as the repository of his soul"[707]. A great warrior and leader during his lifetime, Genghis Khan was "the founder of the world's most extensive land empire" and has proved himself truly immortal, living on today in the genes of his descendants[708].

[707] Jack Weatherford, 2004. *Genghis Kahn and the Making of the Modern World*, pp.xvi.

[708] John Man, 2004. *Genghis Khan: Life, Death and Resurrection*, pp.19.

ALEXANDER THE GREAT

"Ruler of the World"

Even today the name Alexander the Great lives on as one of the most famous men that ever lived, even if there is some debate over who and what he was; while some have called him a Greek, to others he was a barbarian raider, depending what side you were on. History has judged him a great military leader, an inspired and brave warrior and at one-time ruler over much of the known ancient world. Even as an infant he was something of a miracle, with his birth preceded by strange visions and even stranger events. Born in 356 BC, Alexander was the son of Philip II, King of Macedonia and victor of the famous Battle of Thermopylae. Although Alexander would spend much of his life fighting for the Greek people as a whole, he was not technically Greek. His people were from the kingdom of Macedonia, which while situated in northern Greece today was at the time linked to both Anatolia and Greece. The debate regarding Alexander's actual cultural identity continues to rage even today, so it's with some temerity that we identify him as a Greek-Macedonian and leave his cultural origins to historical scholars.

According to Plutarch, Alexander was conceived on the night Philip II consummated his marriage to his fourth wife, Olympias. During her first night of wedded bliss Olympias reportedly had a dream that "a thunder-bolt fell upon her womb"[709], causing a fire that spread out from her body before being extinguished. During her pregnancy, King Philip supposedly had his own vision in a dream, in which he placed a seal bearing the figure of a lion on her womb, a vision which one seer interpreted as being a sign that the child in her womb was a "son whose nature would be bold and lion-like"[710]. Even before he was born, great things were expected of the baby boy whose mother had been seen lying with a serpent[711] and according to legend when Alexander took his first breath the Temple of Artemis at Ephesus burnt to the ground, causing the Magi priests of the temple to lament "that woe and great calamity for Asia had that day been born"[712]. For his father Philip, however, there were other signs that his new child was born to achieve greatness and fame. The king's own military victory over the Parmenio, his general's victory over the Illyrians and his racehorse's win at the Olympic Games all seemed momentous portents that Alexander was going to be special. For Philip, a "son whose birth coincided with three victories would always be victorious"[713].

---

[709] Plutarch, *The Parallel Lives*, "The Life of Alexander: Part 1". Loeb Classical Library, 1919, pp.227.
http://penelope.uchicago.edu/Thayer/E/Roman/Texts/Plutarch/Lives/Alexander*/3.html

[710] Plutarch, *The Parallel Lives*, "The Life of Alexander: Part 1", pp.228.

[711] Plutarch, *The Parallel Lives*, "The Life of Alexander: Part 1", pp.228.

[712] Plutarch, *The Parallel Lives*, "The Life of Alexander: Part 1", pp.232.

[713] Plutarch, *The Parallel Lives*, "The Life of Alexander: Part 1", pp.232.

Certainly, the young Alexander was no ordinary boy. He was described as being both "impetuous and violent", with a haughty disposition and a painful sense of entitlement. When he was only seven or eight years old, while his father was away he was introduced to a visiting group of Persian ambassadors, who were impressed by his maturity and searching mind and remarked that "the much-talked-of ability of Philip is nothing compared with his son's eager disposition to do great things"[714]. So great was Alexander's ambition that he cursed each announcement of his father's successful conquests and military campaigns, complaining to his friends that "my father is beating me to everything! He is leaving me no worlds to conquer"[715].

Despite his precocious nature, Alexander was clearly an intelligent and capable boy – a fact that he proved at the age of 12 when he managed to tame a horse than no one else in the crowd could manage. The horse had been offered to Philip for thirteen talents, the equivalent of around $15,000 today but as the animal seemed both "wild and unbroken" King Philip was prepared to send it away and be done with it. Alexander spoke up and proclaimed that he could train it, declaring "This horse... I could manage better than others have"[716]. Much as Philip adored his son, he laughed at his bravado and decided that he could teach Alexander a lesson in humility. He bargained with the young prince, and they made an agreement that if Alexander couldn't tame the horse

---

[714] Plutarch, *The Parallel Lives*, "The Life of Alexander: Part 1", pp.236.

[715] Philip Freeman, 2011, *Alexander the Great*. Simon and Schuster, New York, pp.19.

[716] Plutarch, *The Parallel Lives*, "The Life of Alexander: Part 1", pp.239.

he would forfeit its purchase price from his own pocket. The wager was made, and Alexander made his way into the training area and approached the animal cautiously. He was a keen observer and had noticed that "the horse was greatly disturbed by the sight of his own shadow falling in front of him and dancing about" so placing his hand on the bridle, he turned it toward the sun so that the shadow was no longer a distraction. Once "he had calmed the horse a little in this way... he quietly cast aside his mantle and with a light spring safely bestrode him"[717]. The assembled group of onlookers were amazed, and young Alexander's strategy and success so impressed his father that he reportedly cried tears of joy and admiration. According to the story, when Alexander finally dismounted, his father embraced him and said "My son, seek thee out a kingdom equal to thyself; Macedonia has not room for thee"[718]. Prophetic words indeed, and Alexander intended to do just that.

Growing up, the prince benefited from a formal education from a young age, but as Alexander matured his father felt his "spirit and intellect had moved beyond his boyhood tutors" and called upon the philosopher Aristotle, "the greatest mind of the age" to further his studies[719]. Not only did Aristotle teach his young student the foundations of ethics, logic, poetry and politics, he also taught him about the natural world and inspired in Alexander the "love of the art of healing"[720]. As his knowledge grew, so did his ego and

---

[717] Plutarch, *The Parallel Lives*, "The Life of Alexander: Part 1", pp.239.

[718] Plutarch, *The Parallel Lives*, "The Life of Alexander: Part 1", pp.240.

[719] Philip Freeman, 2011, *Alexander the Great*, pp.24.

[720] Plutarch, *The Parallel Lives*, "The Life of Alexander: Part 1", pp.244.

arrogance, and he began to tell his father that he intended to surpass the achievements of the classic Greek heroes Agamemnon and Achilles. In fact, the young man went so far as to promise that he "could never submit to any mortal whatsoever being king over me". Amused, his father pointed out that "I am king, and you are subject to me, Alexander". Alexander shook off Philip's point and retorted "I hearken to you, not as king, but as father"[721]. Other than his father, the young Macedonian would never acknowledge another master over him for the rest of his life.

By the age of 16, Alexander was granted what he undoubtedly saw as his natural position, becoming Regent in his father's absence from the kingdom. According to some historians, when Philip presented his son with the royal seal ring "it was meant as a test. If Alexander could successfully resist the temptations of such power for a few months, his position as heir would be secured"[722]. However, no sooner had his father left on military campaign Alexander went right to work, leading an attack on the rebellious Thracian Maedi people on the borders of his kingdom, crushing the beginnings of a revolt and subsequently proclaiming that their land now belonged to Macedon[723]. When he returned him, Philip was proud of his son's actions, but father and son frequently quarrelled as their ambitions clashed. Circumstances became particularly tense at the wedding between King Philip and his bride named Cleopatra. At the celebration dinner, well-wishers toasted the couple and the

---

[721] Dio Chrysostum, *Discourses*. Loeb Classical Library, 1936, pp.60-61.

[722] Philip Freeman, 2011, *Alexander the Great*, pp.28.

[723] Philip Freeman, 2011, *Alexander the Great*, pp.28.

new queen's uncle Attalus pleaded aloud to the gods to give the couple a legitimate heir to the kingdom. Enraged, Alexander demanded "But what of me, base wretch? Dost thou take me for a bastard?" an outburst that provoked King Philip into drawing his sword on his own son. Fortunately, according to Plutarch "his anger and his wine made him trip and fall" at which point Alexander mocked him saying, "Look now, men! Here is one who was preparing to cross from Europe into Asia; and he is upset in trying to cross from couch to couch"[724]. The moment of crisis had passed, and tempers calmed down so that the rest of the evening celebrations did not end with any bloodshed.

Despite their differences, father and son were close, and when Philip decided to teach the Athenians a lesson with a sharp military campaign, Alexander was at his side and strategically placed in the ranks of the Macedonian troops at Battle of Chaeronea. Full of high spirits following their victory at the Battle of Marathon, the Athenian generals were certain they would "crush this upstart barbarian on the field of battle"[725]. Along with their veteran warriors and elite troops such as the Sacred Band of Thebes on their side, the Athenians were supremely confident of victory as they marched into the fight. However, they were no match for the highly disciplined and trained force that Phillips had put in the field and combined with Alexander's brilliance, quick thinking and personal leadership the Athenian army were soon annihilated and the warriors of the Sacred Band of

---

[724] Plutarch, *The Parallel Lives*, "The Life of Alexander: Part 1", pp.248.

[725] Philip Freeman, 2011, *Alexander the Great*, pp.29.

Thebes with them[726]. Although gracious in his victory, Philip "was reluctant to give Alexander the credit he deserved for his decisive role in the battle"[727].

In 336 BC, Alexander's world changed and his chance to build his own legacy finally arrived. While attending the wedding of his daughter, his father King Philip was brutally murdered by one of his own bodyguards, a man named Pausinas. While there have been many theories as to the motive for the killing and whether Olympias or Alexander were directly involved in any plot, it is certain that there was a great deal of political and personal conflicts surrounding Alexander's succession to power, and he took the throne amidst "great jealousies, dire hatreds, and dangers on every hand"[728]. The moment news of Philip's death reached the neighbouring kingdoms and states they assumed that Macedonia's influence was going to evaporate on the world stage and they "prepared to forget Macedonia and recommence their usual intrigues and wars"[729]. Bullied and threatened by Phillip's army for years, they declared war and began to mobilise their armies against what they thought was a young and inexperienced new ruler. Completely misjudged, Alexander determined to stamp out any ambitions his neighbours were harbouring and assembled his own forces and planned an aggressive series of attacks.

---

[726] Philip Freeman, 2011, *Alexander the Great*, pp.29-30.

[727] Philip Freeman, 2011, *Alexander the Great*, pp.30.

[728] Plutarch, *The Parallel Lives*, "The Life of Alexander: Part 1", pp.252.

[729] Sir Charles William Chadwick Oman, 1898. *A history of Greece from the earliest times to the death of Alexander the Great*. Longmans, Green, and co., New York, pp.523.

Ignoring the advice of his senior counsellors who felt they should make peace with their neighbours and focus on consolidating his power within Macedonia, Alexander instead gathered an army of 3,000 men and marched toward Thessaly[730]. A "heaven-born general" with his father's "great military machine"[731] under him, "[i]n six months Alexander accomplished almost as much against his wild northern neighbours as Philip had done in ten years"[732]. Securing territories "as far as to the river Danube", Alexander continued through the famous pass of Thermopylae, determined that "since Demosthenes had called him a boy while he was among the Illyrians and Triballians, and a stripling when he had reached Thessaly, he wished to show him that before the walls of Athens he was a man"[733].

Alexander spent the next two years smashing rebellions both north and south as he secured his territory and power until only Thebes and Athens were the only real threats to him. Subsequently arriving with his army at Thebes, Alexander not only destroyed the opposing army but then went on to destroy the city, razing it to the ground to send any who would oppose him a clear message. Plutarch speculates that Alexander did this to put fear into the hearts of the Greeks and to please the Phocians and

---

[730] Patha Bose, 2003. *Alexander the Great's Art of Strategy*. Penguin Books, India, pp.95.

[731] Sir Charles William Chadwick Oman, 1898. *A history of Greece from the earliest times to the death of Alexander the Great*, pp.522.

[732] Sir Charles William Chadwick Oman, 1898. *A history of Greece from the earliest times to the death of Alexander the Great*, pp.523.

[733] Plutarch, *The Parallel Lives*, "The Life of Alexander: Part 1", pp.254.

Plataeans who had both denounced the Thebans. Although he completely achieved his goal of defeating Thebes, "the terrible act of destroying an entire culture and society... hungover Alexander all his life" and he often expressed remorse over his actions in this campaign. The complete destruction of Thebes convinced Athens that accommodation was the best policy, and with her surrender all of Greece was temporarily at peace, allowing Alexander to pursue his ultimate goal – the conquest of the Persian Empire. He assembled an allied army of over 50,000 men and crossed the Hellespont to begin the conquest of Asia. According to contemporary sources, he declared his intent to conquer the entirety of the Persian Empire as soon as he arrived, dramatically throwing his spear into Asian soil and proclaiming that he duly accepted Asia as a gift bestowed by the gods. Supremely confident, he understood the momentous challenge ahead for his troops, but he was determined and knew that "if he was to seriously pursue the mantle of the 'Ruler of the World'"[734] he would have to attack, beat and conquer Persia, the superpower of the ancient world at the time.

Alexander may have had tremendous ambitions, but they almost all came to an end as he fought his first muddy and chaotic battle in Asia after a "barbarian battle-axe... touched the topmost hair of his head", his helmet barely resisting the great blow[735]. Although the Battle of Granicus was hard-fought, Alexander demonstrated his tactical brilliance and used his cavalry "as a 'disruptive' technology"

---

[734] Patha Bose, 2003. *Alexander the Great's Art of Strategy*, pp.111.

[735] Plutarch, *The Parallel Lives*, "The Life of Alexander: Part 1", pp.267-8.

marking one of the greatest turning points in military history[736]. Leading his cavalry in a wedge formation, he charged straight into the centre of the Persian army and punched a hole through which his infantry could rush in and attack the poor quality enemy troops in the rear. The enemy army shuddered, broke and then ran for their lives as the Macedonians and their allies cut them down. The victory was total, with Plutarch claiming that although the Persians lost 20,000 infantry and 2,500 cavalry only 34 of Alexander's men were killed[737]. This crushing and decisive victory was the first of many triumphs, with the young Macedonian leading his men "across the Persian territories of Asia Minor, Syria and Egypt without suffering a single defeat"[738].

Alexander marched on, taking the provincial capital of Sardis on his way along the Ionian coast, capturing all the cities he encountered on the way, seemingly unstoppable. Arriving at Gordium, he was shown the famous Gordian Knot and again demonstrated his single-mindedness and dedication to achieving any goal. According to legend, the Knot was actually a large but intricate tangle of bark, woven into a thick cord and comprised of several smaller knots so tangled and tightly tied together that it was impossible to see how they were fastened or how they could be pulled apart. An oracle had proclaimed that any man who could unravel the elaborate bundle of knots was destined to become the ruler of all Asia, so Alexander reasoned that the end justified

---

[736] Patha Bose, 2003. *Alexander the Great's Art of Strategy*, pp.119.

[737] Plutarch, *The Parallel Lives*, "The Life of Alexander: Part 1", pp.269.

[738] http://www.bbc.co.uk/history/historic_figures/alexander_the_g reat.shtml

the means and wasting no time simply sliced the knot apart with his sword in one stroke. The young Macedonian was a man that could get things *done*.

In the spring of 333 BC, Alexander crossed the Taurus and was seeking a decisive battle against the Persians, arriving in Syria near Cilicia. The Persian army was much larger and led by Darius in person, but he was crushed by the Macedonians at Issus. Darius fled for his life after his formations collapsed, leaving behind his wife, mother, daughters and an immense collection of treasure chests that were all captured by the Greeks. The Persian ruler was desperate and offered Alexander a peace treaty, ceding lands and making a large cash bribe for the return of his family. Unimpressed, Alexander rejected the offer, sending Darius a message that since he was now king of Asia everything belonged to him anyway. To drive home his point, he occupied all of Syria and most of the coastal land of modern-day Lebanon, Joran and Israel and proceeded to take the city of Tyre by siege by the end of 332 BC. All the men he captured alive were executed, and their women and children marched off into slavery.

Unstoppable, Alexander continued to move southward along the coast, intent on capturing Egypt next. Word travelled fast that he was coming, so all the towns along his route quickly surrendered, hoping to avoid the fate of the citizens of Tyre. The stronghold at of Gaza was different, and the Persian commander there was determined to hold out against the Greeks as long as he could to allow Darius to raise another army and come to his rescue. His position was a strong one with tall, formidable walls, and with all the advance warnings he had received there was ample time to gather a large inventory of supplies to withstand a long siege. As Alexander's army surrounded the city, his generals and engineers surveyed the defences and pronounced them impregnable, arguing that the place simply could not be taken. This was exactly the wrong thing to tell the Macedonian conqueror, who was then more determined than ever to take it and ordered that mounds of earth be built up near the city walls from which to attack. The Gazans could see the threat taking shape and decided to do something about it; when they thought the moment was right they sent out a raiding party to attack and destroy the Greek siege equipment. Alexander himself led the savage counterattack, killing many of the enemy and driving the rest scurrying back into Gaza. He then launched his soldiers at the walls, and after the first two attempts were beaten back his men succeeded in penetrating the defences and forcing the surrender of the stronghold. As he did at Tyre, he ordered the men to be executed, and the rest became slaves. For the defeated commander, Alexander reserved a special punishment after the Persian refused to kneel before him; he was tied to the back of a chariot and dragged alive around the city walls by his heels. Free to continue his invasion into Egypt, Alexander and his men were hailed as liberators by an adoring population and founded the city of Alexandria in his own honour.

He turned north again in 331 BC and headed into Mesopotamia, determined to finish off the Persians once and for all. Darius was waiting for him with a new and larger army, but he was out-generalled by Alexander again and was crushed. The Persian ruler fled the field but was murdered by his own supporters as the Greek army captured Babylon, then the city of Susa, then marched on victorious into Media and Parthia as Alexander took his men on a grand tour of central Asia, sweeping any opposition away and founding new cities as he went – all called Alexandria. Soon he was master of all of Persia, and after consolidating his position turned his ambitions further east.

Next came his invasion of India where he fought and won more battles, each time thrusting deeper and deeper into the Indian subcontinent, personally leading a campaign in 327/326 in which he continued his pattern of reducing captured cities to rubble and slaughtering their inhabitants as he subjugated the countryside. He got as far east as the Beas River in northern India and was determined to keep going until the mutiny of his army forced him to change plans. His men were exhausted and homesick after so many years of non-stop fighting, and the veteran Greeks troops refused to keep marching east away from their families. Finally persuaded to turn around, they marched back into Persia conquering a few more cities and tribes along the way. In the end, it was his army that wore out, not Alexander and they journeyed back unconquered and undefeated.

Led by Alexander in person, his effective and efficient military machine was simply unstoppable. As disciplined as his troops were on the battlefield Plutarch claims that Alexander himself set the example for his men to follow in his private life, refusing to lay hands on imprisoned noblewomen and showing "also the most complete mastery over his appetite". Plutarch goes on to assert that "to the use of wine also he was less addicted than was generally believed", despite most historians accepting the legacy of Alexander as a heavy drinker whose "daytime intoxication, drew critical attention and disparagement from his contemporaries"[739]. It is true that Alexander was such a lover of liquor that later in his reign during his invasion of India, he organised a wine-drinking competition involving 41 contestants. The locals were unused to such an event, but it took a decidedly fatal toll on his own men. His companion Promachus won the contest after downing around four gallons of wine but died three days later of alcohol poisoning, "and of the rest, according to Chares, forty-one died of what they drank, a violent chill having set in after their debauch"[740].

Despite his predilection for drinking, Alexander was a great military leader and politician, if something of a megalomaniac, which given his unbeaten military record is easy to understand. One example of this occurred during his campaign in Syria when he visited the shrine of Ammon. When greeted by one of the priests, he "misinterpreted (perhaps intentionally) the priest's greeting *ô paidion* ('o boy') for *ô pai dios* ('o son of Zeus')" an incident that left a profound impression Alexander, and thereafter "openly called himself son of Zeus"[741]. In his personal life,

---

[739] John Maxell O'Brien, "Alexander the Great", ALCOHOL AND ALCOHOLISM, Volume 16, Issue 1, 1 March 1981, Pages 1–4,

[740] Plutarch, *The Parallel Lives*, "The Life of Alexander: Part 7", pp.420.

[741] Ed. Joseph Roisman and Ian Worthington, 2010. *A Companion to Ancient Macedonia*. Wiley Blackwell, pp.195.

Alexander was as astute as he was on the battlefield and his first marriage to Roxane was one of strategical and political manoeuvring. By marrying this daughter of a Sogdian nobleman named Oxyartes, Alexander "would effectively link his base of power (Macedonia and Greece) to his newly conquered territory (Asia)"[742]. A wife also meant an heir to the throne, although Alexander would not live to see his namesake born.

At the age of 32, Alexander had paused and was enjoying a life of luxury and excess while staying in the ancient Babylonian palace of Nebuchadnezzar II. He was planning on launching another series of military campaigns, beginning with an invasion of Arabia but he would not live long enough to realise them. The recent death of his closest friend Hephaestion had devastated him, and Alexander perceived many portentous omens that made him "distrustful now of the favour of Heaven and suspicious of his friends"[743] and began to spend more time alone. According to Plutarch, he was encouraged to socialise when his admiral Nearchus and Medius of Larissa came to the palace to call on him, and together they spent the night and all the next day drinking heavily. Rising to the occasion, Plutarch reports that Alexander "gave a splendid entertainment" even returning to his guests after his customary bedtime bath "to hold high revel" and drink from the "Bowl of Hercules" – a large bowl of unmixed wine in honour of the Greek demigod hero. It was shortly after this

---

[742] Ed. Joseph Roisman and Ian Worthington, 2010. *A Companion to Ancient Macedonia*, pp.196.

[743] Plutarch, *The Parallel Lives*, "The Life of Alexander: Part 7", pp.430.

that he developed a high fever and lost his ability to speak. He attempted to "flush the fever" by taking even more wine, but the fever soon became delirium, and the great Macedonian king "died on the thirtieth day of the month Daesius"[744].

There will always be great debate about how this unstoppable war leader died; some suggest that Alexander died from malaria following his foray into India[745], while other researchers from the University of Maryland blame typhoid, neither of which are consistent with the symptoms described by both Plutarch and Diodorus[746]. The most obvious cause of death appears to be alcohol poisoning, especially since "in the rage of his fever and a violent thirst, he took a draught of wine"[747]. However, neither of the contemporary reports indicate that Alexander was vomiting, while the "major effect of alcohol poisoning is continual vomiting"[748]. He may have been poisoned; as "rival and descendant of Heracles"[749] when the cup or Bowl of Heracles was passed around Alexander could be relied on to drink from it first. However, the time between the onset of

---

[744] Plutarch, *The Parallel Lives*, "The Life of Alexander: Part 7", pp.434.

[745] Graham Philips, 2012. Alexander the Great: Murder in Babylon. Virgin Books, pp.13

[746] Graham Philips, 2012. Alexander the Great: Murder in Babylon, pp 14-15.

[747] Plutarch, cited in Graham Philips, 2012. Alexander the Great: Murder in Babylon, pp 10.

[748] Graham Philips, 2012. Alexander the Great: Murder in Babylon, pp 16.

[749] Robin Lane Fox, 2006. Alexander the Great. Penguin Books, UK, chapter 32.

Alexander's illness and his eventual death makes this theory unlikely.

The death of their great hero-king threw the Greek nation into immediate turmoil, as there was no obvious or legitimate heir; his son Alexander IV was only born after he was gone. According to Diodorus, when Alexander was on his deathbed he was asked to whom he wanted to leave his kingdom, to which he responded "to the strongest"[750]. Predictably, the empire he had forged would not survive him long, and by 321 BC his officers and generals soon carved out their own power bases amid rivalry and dissension, beginning 40 years of war until things settled down.

History calls Alexander of Macedonia "the Great" due to his incredible military record, having never been defeated in battle despite almost always fighting against superior numbers. He was a master of bold strategy, an expert at using terrain to his advantage and inspired fierce devotion and loyalty in his troops by fighting personally alongside them – usually leading his cavalry on daring charges into the thick of the enemy. The legacy he left behind was not just one of unparalleled military success; his campaigns greatly increased the contacts and trade between the East and West, and the influence of the Greek civilization that he spread had long-lasting impacts on the lands of Asia, while back at home his own countrymen achieved a sense of the wider

[750] Diodorus Siculus, *The Library of History*. Loeb Classical Library, 1963. Book XVII, pp. 468.
http://penelope.uchicago.edu/Thayer/E/Roman/Texts/Diodorus_Siculus/17F*.html

world that they had never known existed before. Some of the more than 20 cities he founded still survive today, notably Alexandria in Egypt which evolved to become an important centre of commercial trade and commerce. Wherever his soldiers went, so too went the seeds of Greek culture, art and ideals that would shape the peoples of Asia for generations. It would have surely pleased Alexander to know that he achieved this lasting impact, as he had long aspired to bring together the cultures of Europe and Persia, blending the best elements of both to produce a civilisation that was better than either and would endure. Although mainly remembered for his triumphs as a military leader, Alexander was also an intelligent, educated and passionate man who knew that "whatever possession we gain by our sword cannot be sure or lasting, but the love gained by kindness and moderation is certain and durable"[751], much like the legacy the man left behind him.

---

[751]

https://www.brainyquote.com/quotes/alexander_the_great_802533

THE END

ABOUT THE AUTHOR

A Mr Kingsbury worked as a committed educator in the fields of History and Social Studies within the public school system for 15 years. He is now happily retired and living in the Laurentian mountain range of Quebec, Canada with his black Labrador named Scipio. An amateur historian and military enthusiast, his passion is writing and the ceramic arts.

Other works by the Author:

History's Greatest Warriors Volume 1
http://www.rodgerlaz.com/historys-greatest-warriors.html

History's Bloodiest Revolutions
http://www.rodgerlaz.com/historys-bloodiest-revolutions.html

Made in the USA
Monee, IL
31 March 2022